D1211802

REPRINTS OF ECONOMIC CLASSICS

The Nature and Origin of Public Wealth

Also published in

REPRINTS OF ECONOMIC CLASSICS

By JAMES MAITLAND, 8TH EARL OF LAUDERDALE

THREE LETTERS TO THE DUKE OF WELLINGTON [1829]

An Inquiry Into
THE NATURE AND ORIGIN
OF PUBLIC WEALTH

And Into The Means And Causes
Of Its Increase
(1804)

By James Maitland, 8th Earl of Lauderdale

Edited With An Introduction And Revisions
Appearing In The 2nd Edition (1819)

By Morton Paglin

REPRINTS OF ECONOMIC CLASSICS

AUGUSTUS M. KELLEY · PUBLISHERS
NEW YORK · 1966

FIRST EDITION 1804

(Edinburgh: Archibald Constable & Company, 1804)

Second Edition 1819

This Reprint of the first edition with the changes from the second published 1962

Reprinted 1967

LIBRARY OF CONGRESS CATALOGUE CARD NUMBER

66 - 24414

PRINTED IN THE UNITED STATES OF AMERICA
by SENTRY PRESS, NEW YORK, N. Y. 10019

CONTENTS

INTRODUCTION

James Maitland Lauderdale is one of the secondary figures in the history of economic thought whose major contribution, *The Inquiry into the Nature and Origin of Public Wealth*, is a work of marked originality and insight, deserving a perusal by anyone interested in the development of economic ideas. Lauderdale's bellicose attack on Adam Smith and the defenders of the Smith tradition provoked an acidulous review by Henry Brougham in the *Edinburgh Review* (July, 1804). Brougham exposed some faults in Lauderdale's reasoning and thereby felt it necessary to reject his work in toto. By so doing, he and other contemporaries missed the drift of some highly significant arguments on consumer choice, utility, and demand, and on the effects of saving, spending, taxes, and debt retirement on national output. Malthus, in contrast, picked up a number of Lauderdale's basic ideas, but he failed to acknowledge his intellectual indebtedness.

The *Inquiry* was first published in 1804; a second "enlarged and revised" edition appeared in 1819, but a comparison of the two editions shows no significant change, merely slight stylistic alterations and a few added comments. The basic illustrative statistics are the same in both editions except for a table, appended to the second edition, containing figures on the annual changes of the National Debt from 1786 to 1818. Lauderdale excuses himself for not bringing in more recent data throughout the book; his explanation is given in a long footnote which is reprinted below together with the table.

Lauderdale may have been prompted to issue a second edition of the *Inquiry* because by 1818 there was a distinct possibility that a large scale debt retirement policy, employing the sinking fund, would be effectively pursued. A glance at the figures which Lauderdale inserts in the new appendix points up what was happening. In 1816 there was deficit financing to the extent of fifty million pounds; it was the year which marked the culmination of a period of large and persistent deficits brought on by the Napoleonic conflict. In 1817 there was a pronounced fiscal policy shift: a tax surplus of over sixteen million pounds was used to retire debt, and in 1818 a budget surplus was again employed to retire debt of the value of eighteen million pounds. This undoubtedly was an important contributory factor in the movement of the English economy from prosperity to stagnation in the post-Napoleonic period. To Ricardo the stagnation of trade was something of a puzzle; his explanation of the depression was largely in terms of a flight of capital from England suffering under "a great load of taxation." He recommended the annihilation of the debt by means of a capital levy or other such device which would afford relief "from the army of tax gatherers, revenue officers, and smugglers who are now supported out of the industry of the country, and which aggravates the evil of taxes."[1] But to Malthus and Lauderdale the explanation lay in a fiscal policy which reduced aggregate demand below the level necessary for full employment. Although Malthus gave no credit to Lauderdale, the last section of Chapter VII in his *Principles* (1820) clearly derives from Lauderdale's *Inquiry* of 1804, 1819 which he had cited previously in an uncomplimentary fashion.[2] Both men recognized the deflationary effects produced by tax surpluses, and it is to Lauderdale's credit that he developed at an early date a train of analysis which led to significant conclusions on debt and fiscal policy while keener minds were groping in the dark.

The basic text used in this reprint is a photographic copy of the 1804 edition which enables the reader to assess the extent of Lauderdale's theoretical innovations. Historically, this is the significant

---

[1] *Notes on Malthus: Works*, Sraffa edition, vol. II, p. 452.
[2] *Principles*, 1st ed., p. 352; 2nd ed., p. 314.

edition. Lauderdale's ideas on saving, taxation and debt policy were refreshingly original in 1804. By 1819 when the second edition appeared, these ideas no longer had the quality of bold originality; ideas launched by Lauderdale in 1804 were by 1819 in the air — in the pamphlet literature, and in the following year, as noted above, presented with the authority of Malthus in the first edition of his *Principles* of *Political Economy*.[1] By 1821 this unconventional approach to saving, spending, debt and taxes had filtered down to the newspaper reader as can be seen from a series of four letters to the *London Times* under the heading "On the Revenue and Taxation." It is of interest that we have Ricardo's reaction to these ideas and especially his identification of their intellectual lineage:

> "A writer in the Times of this morning appears to have adopted some of Malthus' principles, and the conclusions he draws from them are so wild and extravagant, that if we had no other reason for suspecting their fallacy, these would afford them. This writer recommends that we should raise loans now instead of the taxes with which we are burthened, and for this sagacious reason, because it will promote expenditure and take off the superfluity of our productions."[2]

To this may be added the observation that Lauderdale, perhaps more than Malthus, can be held responsible for this "wild and extravagant" approach to fiscal problems and employment.

Lauderdale's reputation as an innovator in economics rests mainly on (1) his perceptive treatment of consumer choice and demand, and the role they play in value theory, (2) a perhaps somewhat inflated estimate made by Böhm-Bawerk of Lauder-

---

[1] For a more extensive treatment of this topic see my *Malthus and Lauderdale: the Anti-Ricardian Tradition*. (New York: Augustus M. Kelley, 1961.)

[2] Letter of Ricardo to Trower, 2 March 1821, *Works*, vol. VIII, p. 349.

dale's treatment of the return to capital, (3) an analysis of the effects of consumption and saving on aggregate demand with particular application to taxation and debt management problems.

It is not necessary in an introduction to restate in detail arguments printed in the text which follows it, but it may be useful to indicate some other works of Lauderdale which contain an elaboration and development of themes presented in the *Inquiry*. Lauderdale was not an economic analyst who developed much in the way of new ideas and new techniques after his one major contribution, the *Inquiry*. But if there is an exception to this statement, it is to be found in his tract entitled *Three Letters to the Duke of Wellington*.[1] Here we see the application of an idea which showed a high level of insight into the process of income creation and the role of public finance in the determination of the national output. Although Lauderdale has nowhere near the analytical powers of Ricardo, it is profitable to compare the limited and restricted conclusions reached by Ricardo in his 1820 essay on the *Funding System* with Lauderdale's searching and revealing analysis exhibited in the *Three Letters to the Duke of Wellington*. Ricardo, bound by the preconceptions of Say's Law, confined himself to the redistributive income effects of carrying a public debt and to exposing (as Robert Hamilton[2] had done before him) the illusions of debt retirement in the sinking fund schemes extant at the time. Lauderdale was not concerned with the fraudulent appearance of debt retirement that was occasionally pursued by the

---

[1] Will soon be reissued in the Augustus M. Kelley series of reprints of economic classics. Originally published, London, 1829.

[2] *Inquiry Concerning . . . the National Debt of Great Britain*, 3rd edition, Edinburgh, 1818. Ricardo considered the effects of taxation and debt retirement on national output to be nil, and he repeated Say's Law to quiet "the doubts of those who speak of the mischievous effects of the sinking fund" on aggregate demand. (*Funding System, Works*, vol. IV, p. 178.)

ministers of government. He was concerned with the drastic effects on total demand that would result from a sinking fund policy diligently and honestly pursued. Taxation would reduce consumption by almost an equivalent amount among taxpayers, while the proceeds of the tax used to buy consols on the open market would force up the price of bonds but would not lead to an offsetting increase of consumption by stockholders. By virtue then of a superior original insight Lauderdale was able to focus on a central issue of consequence while authors such as Hamilton and Ricardo were giving detailed analyses of all issues except the basic fiscal policy issue.

While Lauderdale's analysis of aggregate demand led to views on debt policy well in advance of his time, his analysis of trade policy presents a curious and intellectually confused picture. The reader of the *Inquiry* who goes no further than this source would conclude that Lauderdale was an ardent supporter of free trade (cf. pp. 359-65, below). Yet in the great Corn Law debates of 1814-1815, and in subsequent debates through 1828, Lauderdale in both pamphlets and speeches to the House of Lords appeared as a champion of agricultural protectionism. Free trade as a general principle he formally accepted, but there were always mitigating circumstances which required departure from the general principle: taxes on the British farmer, national security which called for a large domestic supply of grain, and finally, income and price stability which protection from the vicissitudes of foreign supply supposedly made possible. Hence in the *Letter on the Corn Laws* (1814), Lauderdale concludes that ". . . the reasoning of the Author of the Wealth of Nations which has unfortunately long misled the public on the subject of our Corn Laws, is in itself as unfounded as the opinions he has stated are untenable . . ." (p. 21). The reader of the *Inquiry* should be aware of these opinions when he reads in the conclusion of the *Inquiry* (both editions) "that

xi

all impediments thrown in the way of commercial communication, obstruct the increase of wealth . . ." (p. 365, below). Malthus's pamphlets on the Corn Laws are in the same tradition, namely, a denial that the benefits of free trade in terms of maximizing total product, would outweigh the considerations cited by Lauderdale above. Malthus in fact had been reading the Lauderdale pamphlet about the time he was preparing his own, and the Malthus-Ricardo correspondence indicates that Ricardo, on this issue, placed them in the same intellectual camp.[1]

What place does Lauderdale occupy in the development of economic thought? While rigid and precise categorizing is not likely to be very fruitful or defensible, it is here suggested that Lauderdale's work assumes greater meaning and significance when it is considered as antecedent to and part of the Malthus tradition. Sixteen years before the appearance of Malthus's *Principles*, Lauderdale focused attention on the highly variable nature of aggregate demand and showed that it was fundamentally tied to individual decisions to spend or save, and to government fiscal decisions to create budgetary surpluses or deficits. Malthus continued this line of thought but without Lauderdale's strategic emphasis on debt policy and taxation.

In the area of value theory Lauderdale and Malthus sought to put meaning into the supply and demand analysis of value by going behind the usual expressions and relating supply price to costs, and consumer choice and utility to demand and price. They both developed and applied the concept of a demand schedule and differentiated commodities according to their elasticity of demand — although they lacked the precise formulation of the notion. In general it may be said that Malthus paid more attention to costs and supply while Lauderdale emphasized consumer choice and demand. Finally,

---

[1] Ricardo, *Works*, vol. VI, pp. 169-70.

xii

with regard to economic policy and social outlook, both men refused to adopt a simple maximum output criterion of welfare when the policy issues under consideration involved agriculture and the Corn Laws. They shared the belief that a society committed to a large agricultural sector, supplemented by industry, was a more stable and desirable society than one engulfed by the onrushing industrial revolution. Hence they were given to traditionalism and conservatism while Ricardo and the utilitarians were committed to political and economic reforms which would remove all restrictions on the progress of a free market industrial society.[1]

Second Edition Changes

As was noted above, the changes in the 1819 edition of the *Inquiry* (published by Archibald Constable, Edinburgh) are mainly minor stylistic ones. A second and longer advertisement replaced the original one, and a long footnote at the end of Chapter IV supplemented by an additional table inserted after Appendix VIII constitute the significant additions. These are reprinted below.

For those unfamiliar with British debt practices, the table requires a brief explanation. The first column "total debt" is a sort of fictitious concept which includes debt actually outstanding plus debt which has been redeemed by the sinking fund commissioners but which is technically carried on the

---

[1]Lauderdale's public life shows a marked division. In his early years he was an associate of the liberal Whig, Charles Fox, and was sympathetic to the ideals of the French Revolution. He later swung over to an ultra-Tory position and consistently opposed political and economic reforms. His speeches in the House of Lords show that he fought against liberalization of trade, against protective social legislation of all kinds, and against the reform bill of 1832. His legislative record on the important issues can conveniently be followed in William Smart, *Economic Annals of the Nineteenth Century*, 2 vols., 1910-17.

books. The difference between columns two and three represents the net annual surplus or deficit while column 4 indicates the net total debt which is significant for fiscal analysis.

I wish to express my thanks to Father Richard E. Mulcahy of the Department of Economics, University of San Francisco, who kindly arranged with the Gleeson Library, U.S.F., to provide the copy of Lauderdale's *Inquiry* which was used in preparing this reissue.

MORTON PAGLIN

Portland State College
Oregon, February, 1962

MAJOR CHANGES IN 2nd EDITION

AN

INQUIRY

INTO THE

NATURE AND ORIGIN

OF

Public Wealth,

AND INTO THE

MEANS AND CAUSES OF ITS INCREASE.

BY

THE EARL OF LAUDERDALE.

———

SECOND EDITION, GREATLY ENLARGED.

———

EDINBURGH:

PRINTED FOR ARCHIBALD CONSTABLE & CO. EDINBURGH;

LONGMAN, HURST, REES, ORME, AND BROWN,

AND HURST, ROBINSON, AND COMPANY, LONDON.

———

1819.

ADVERTISEMENT.

It is now nearly fourteen years since the publication of the First Edition of this Inquiry; and, though the author is perfectly aware, that some of his speculations were then unfavourably received, he has, after a careful review of the opinions it contains, seen nothing essential he could wish to alter.

In the rectitude of most of his doctrines, he is indeed confirmed,—not only by the approbation with which they have been distinguished in France, in Germany, in Italy, and America,—but, because he perceives, that many of the opinions which,

in this country, at first excited doubt and
hesitation, have gradually gained ground to
such a degree, that, in most recent publications, they are assumed as indisputed and
incontrovertible.

Labour is now no longer regarded as a
measure of value ;—it is, on the contrary,
admitted, that nothing can possess the character of forming, at all times, and in all
places, an accurate measure of value.

The distinction betwixt productive and
unproductive labour,—as founded on the
produce of labour being immediately consumed, or reserved for future use,—is ex-
ploded.

The origin and nature of the profit of
capital is now universally understood : it
is, by all, admitted, that capital derives its
profits, either from supplanting a portion
of labour which would otherwise be performed by the hand of man ;—or, from its
performing a portion of labour which is be-

yond the reach of the personal exertion of man to accomplish.

Parsimony has ceased to be regarded as the most active means of increasing public wealth ;—and, though the author's opinions on this subject were formerly stated to be the most unmeasured and prejudiced of all his speculations, the greatest advocates for the system of forcing parsimony by legislative authority, in the shape of a sinking fund, now agree to the necessity of limiting the extent to which it ought to be carried. Hitherto, indeed, we have had no experience of the effects of the Sinking Fund, when not counteracted by borrowing to a greater extent :—yet there are many who admit the consequences, as stated in the Inquiry, of withdrawing such a portion of revenue from expenditure in consumable commodities, and forcibly converting it into capital.

The reader will, therefore, find, in this Edition of the Inquiry, no change in the

doctrines it contained. The Author certainly has made great alterations; but these
are confined to the objects of giving a more
distinct view of the effects of parsimony on
public wealth, and of extending the illus-
trations of the various opinions he has sub-
mitted to the public on the Science of Political Economy.

July 1818.

progress of public wealth. *

    * Since the publication of the first edition, the arrangement

268   OF PARSIMONY, AS A MEANS, &c.

of the sinking fund has been, on two different occasions, inter-
fered with, but the same principle has, throughout, been perse-
vered in; and, as the subject is here introduced, not for the
purpose of giving a history of that establishment, but to illus-
trate the mistake that writers on political economy have
fallen into, in considering parsimony to be a source of public
wealth, it is therefore unnecessary to enter into minute details of the plans that have been adopted; more particularly
as the effects of this accumulating fund have hitherto been uniformly counteracted, even since the peace, by the money government has been under the necessity of borrowing, to defray
the national expenditure, as will distinctly appear from the account contained in the Appendix, No. IX. which shows the
amount of debt contracted, and the amount of debt redeemed,
in each year, from the 1st of February 1786, when the sinking fund was established, to the 1st of January 1818; and
also, the total amount of unredeemed debt in each of these
years.

AN

INQUIRY

INTO THE

NATURE AND ORIGIN

OF

PUBLIC WEALTH,

AND INTO THE

MEANS AND CAUSES OF ITS INCREASE.

BY

THE EARL OF LAUDERDALE.

EDINBURGH:

PRINTED FOR ARCH. CONSTABLE & CO., EDINBURGH :
AND
T. N. LONGMAN & O. REES, LONDON.

1804.

TO

HIS ROYAL HIGHNESS

THE PRINCE OF WALES.

SIR,

Iꜰ gratitude for kindnefs uniformly fhown me, did not point out Your Roʏᴀʟ Hɪɢʜɴᴇss, as the Perfon to whom I ought to infcribe any little effort of my induftry; the anxious zeal, which conftantly animates Your Roʏᴀʟ Hɪɢʜɴᴇss's breaft, for the welfare of a People amongft whom, fortunately for the Britifh Empire,

You

(*xxvii*)

You hold a ſtation ſo illuſtrious and pre-eminent, would naturally ſuggeſt Your ROYAL HIGHNESS, as the Perſon under whoſe protection a Work ought to be placed, the object of which is to elucidate the elementary principles of a ſcience, on which the Happineſs as well as the Wealth of mankind depends.

I am, with the higheſt ſenſe of duty, and moſt profound feeling of reſpect,

> SIR,
>> Your ROYAL HIGHNESS's
>> Much obliged,
>>> And moſt humble Servant,
>>>> *LAUDERDALE.*

ADVERTISEMENT.

I<small>T</small> was the intention of the Author to have printed, along with this, a fecond volume, on the Legiſlation of Commerce and Finance, and on the Effects of Commercial Treaties. But as his ideas on thefe fubjects form only inferences from the general principles here ſtated, many of which, he is aware, are not only new, but even repugnant to received opinions, he has thought it more prudent to paufe, and delay the execution of the remaining part of his plan, till he difcovers how far the opinions he has advanced in the prefent publication ſhall ſtand the teſt of public criticifm.

The Author's fole object is the inveſtigation of truth; and if he indulges himfelf in further fpeculations on this important fubject, he will be as ready, on being convinced of his error, to retract any opinions he has delivered, as he will be obſtinate in defending them, if aſſailed by prejudice.

CONTENTS.

INTRODUCTION.

THOUGH language, from which proceeds the power of both recording
and communicating our ideas, muſt be
deemed the principal ſource of improvement in man; yet it has been ſuggeſted *,
that he " who conſiders the errors and ob-
" ſcurity, the miſtakes and confuſion, that
" are ſpread in the world by an ill uſe of
" words, will find ſome reaſon to doubt
" whether language, as it has been employ-
" ed, has contributed more to the improve-
" ment or hinderance of knowledge :" and
in truth, notwithſtanding all the benefits
we derive from it, it is certain that the
careleſs and improper uſe of language often produces much miſconception, even in
the ordinary occurrences of life.

In

* LOCKE on the Human Underſtanding, B. III.
Ch. xi. § 4.

In all difcuffions, therefore, where accuracy is required, we cannot be too cautious in adopting terms of art, or technical terms of expreffion, without inquiring into the juftnefs of that mode of reafoning from which they have derived their origin.

Words have been reprefented, and indeed are ufually confidered, as the tranfcript of thofe ideas which are in the minds of men.

Thus, when we find a phrafe in general ufe, we are apt to regard it as conveying the common teftimony of mankind in favour of that fpecies of reafoning which at firft fight appears to have fuggefted it; and adopt, from a fuppofed idea of authority, opinions, which a little examination would make us reject. By fuch careleffnefs, men often become habituated to the common ufe of phrafes and expreffions, without having even called in queftion their propriety; and thefe, forming the bafis of further reafoning, give birth to ideas founded on a feries of mifconceptions,

mifconceptions, and confequently to new phrafes and turns of expreffion that tend to perpetuate fallacies. It is by thefe means that language has, in all fciences, been often found a moft powerful fupporter of prejudice, and a moft active promoter of error.

Speculation in Political Oeconomy unavoidably leads to this train of reflection; for there is no fcience fo much expofed to this fource of error. The fubjects of many of the fciences originating in the conceptions of the learned, are never treated of but by men of fuperior education and improved minds, whofe language muft of courfe partake of the accuracy of their ideas. But Public Oeconomy, which profeffes to teach the means of increafing the wealth of a State, and of applying it to the moft ufeful purpofes, is of neceffity, in all ftages of fociety, a fubject of difcuffion, even amongft the moft vulgar and illiterate, whofe rude and erroneous conceptions muft
naturally

naturally lead to expreſſions founded on inaccuracy, and pregnant with error.

A ſtrong illuſtration of the effect which language has upon the tenor of œconomical reaſoning, may be derived from conſidering the mercantile ſyſtem of political œconomy, ſo long prevalent, which taught us to eſtimate the progreſs of our wealth by the Balance of our Trade.

If the balance of trade was to have been reſted upon as a means of aſcertaining the increaſe of opulence, one would have naturally thought, that the manner in which the merchant makes up his account of profit and loſs, would have ſuggeſted itſelf as the method of eſtimating the national gain by foreign trade.

Thus, as DAVENANT obſerves, we would have been led to examine how much the returns imported are worth more than the commodities exported; and attributed to the
nation

nation fo much gain as the value of the
Imports exceeded that of the Exports.

But Money being, in its capacity of an
inftrument of commerce, the immediate
means of procuring all the conveniencies
of life ; whilft, as the practical meafure of
value, we are accuftomed to eftimate commodities by the quantity of money they will
exchange for ; *Money* and *Wealth* came to
be ufed, not only in common language, as
fynonymous ; but, in the ideas of men, *to
get money* became expreffive of the only
means of growing rich.

Habituated to this mifapplication of language, and to the ideas they derive from
it, the fupporters of the mercantile fyftem,
making up the accounts of the public in a
manner directly the reverfe of that they
would have followed in making up their
own, rejoiced at the excefs of the Exports
over the Imports ; concluding, that the difference muft be received in Money, and conceiving

ceiving that the commodities exported, were merely valuable as inftruments to procure Money, which they alone regarded as wealth.

Though the prevalence of the mercantile fyftem, for above a century, and many confequent errors in the reafonings of our œconomical writers, as well as in the fyftem of European legiflation, all arifing out of the habit of conceiving Wealth and Money to be fynonymous, form powerful illuftrations of the effects of language in producing erroneous ideas in œconomical reafonings; it is perhaps not the moft fatal error introduced into the fcience of political œconomy by the fame means.

The terms we ufe, in talking of the wealth of a nation, or of the riches of individuals, are in all languages exactly the fame. They denote, that private riches are univerfally confidered in no other light than as a portion of national wealth. The fum-
total

total of the riches of thofe who form the community, is thus regarded as neceffarily conveying an accurate ftatement of the wealth of a nation; and this idea has become fo univerfally prevalent, that, even by philofophers, exchangeable value has been announced as the bafis of wealth *. An increafe of the fortune of any member of the fociety, if not at the expence of any individual belonging to the fame community, is uniformly deemed an augmentation of national wealth; and a diminution of any man's property, if not producing an increafe of the riches of fome of his fellow-fubjects, has been confidered as of neceffity occafioning a concomitant diminution of national wealth : "For," fays an eminent philofopher, " the capital of a " fociety, which is the fame thing with that " of all the individuals who compofe it,

" can

---

* See PHYSIOCRATIE, *Philofophie Rurale*, and the works of all the Oeconomifts.

" can be increafed only in the fame man-
" ner *."

That public wealth, however, ought not
to be confidered as merely reprefenting the
fum of individual riches, is undoubted † ;
and that much of obfcurity, and even of
error, has exifted in œconomical reafoning
from confounding them, will be made apparent.

As

* Smith's Wealth of Nations, vol. I. p. 4to. edit. in
4to.—To the fame purpofe fays Hecato the Rhodian, as
reprefented by Cicero : " Sapientis effe, nihil contra mores,
" leges, inftituta facientem, habere rationem rei familiaris :
" neque enim folum nobis divites effe volumus, fed liberis,
" propinquis, amicis, maximeque reipublicæ : fingulorum
" enim facultates et copiæ, divitiæ funt civitatis." De Off.
L. iii. c. 15.

† The words *Wealth* and *Riches* are, in common language, ufed as fynonymous. There is no term by which we
can defign the Wealth of a Nation, which is not equally
applicable to the Riches of Individuals. In treating of
private fortune, however, the word *riches* will be uniformly
ufed ; and in expreffing public opulence, the word *wealth.*
To be more diftinct, Private or Individual will be generally
prefixed to Riches, and Public or National to Wealth.

As a clear underftanding of the relation which Public Wealth and Individual Riches bear to each other, appears of the higheft importance, in fecuring accuracy in every fubject that relates to the fcience of Political Oeconomy; the firft and fecond chapters of this Inquiry, are therefore devoted to the confideration of the nature of *Value*, the poffeffion of which alone qualifies any thing to form a portion of individual riches;—to an explanation of what Public Wealth is, and of what conftitutes Individual Riches;—and to an examination of the relation in which they ftand to each other.

The meaning annexed in this work to the phrafe Public Wealth being thus explained, the third chapter contains an inveftigation of the Sources of Wealth, in which Land, Labour and Capital, are feparately treated of as the fources of wealth;—an opinion which, though it has been announced by fome,

fome, and hinted at by others, does not feem to have made on any author fo ftrong an impreffion as to be uniformly adhered to in the courfe of his reafonings.

An idea which has generally prevailed, (though it feems in itfelf a paradox), that wealth may be increafed by means by which it is not produced, in particular by parfimony, or deprivation of expenditure, has made it neceffary to inveftigate this fubject in the fourth chapter, as a preliminary to an Inquiry into the Means and Caufes of the Increafe of Wealth; which is the object of the fifth chapter.

CHAP.

CHAP. I.

OF VALUE,

AND THE POSSIBILITY OF AN ACCURATE MEASURE OF VALUE.

BEFORE proceeding to confider what conftitutes public wealth and private riches, or
to inveftigate the circumftances which lead
to the increafe of either, it is neceffary to
underftand diftinctly the nature of Value ;
and, by that means, to poffefs a clear idea
of what it is which alone can give to any
commodity the character it muft acquire,
in order to form a part of individual
riches.

The

The term *Value*, whatever might have
been its original fenfe, as it is ufed in common language, does not exprefs a quality
inherent in any commodity. There is nothing which poffeffes a real, intrinfic, or
invariable value. The poffeffion of no quality, however important to the welfare of
man, can confer value; for water, the
moft neceffary of all things, feldom poffeffes it.

Experience fhews us, that every thing is
uniformly confidered as valuable, which,
to the poffeffion of qualities, that make it
the object of the defire of man, adds the
circumftance of exifting in fcarcity. To
confer value, therefore, two things appear
requifite: 1. That the commodity, as being
ufeful or delightful to man, fhould be an
object of his defire : 2. That it fhould exift in a degree of fcarcity.

With refpect to the variations in value,
of which every thing valuable is fufceptible,

tible, if we could for a moment fuppofe
that any fubftance poffeffed intrinfic and
fixed value, fo as to render an affumed
quantity of it conftantly, under all circumftances, of equal value ; then the degree of
value of all things, afcertained by fuch a
fixed ftandard, would vary according to the
proportion betwixt the quantity of them
and the demand for them, and every commodity would of courfe be fubject to a variation in its value from four different circumftances.

1. It would be fubject to an increafe of
its value, from a diminution of its quantity.

2. To a diminution of its value, from an
augmentation of its quantity.

3. It might fuffer an augmentation in
its value, from the circumftance of an increafed demand.

4. Its

4. Its value might be diminifhed, by a failure of demand.

As it will, however, clearly appear, that no commodity can poffefs fixed and intrinfic value, fo as to qualify it for a meafure of the value of other commodities, mankind are reduced to felect, as a practical meafure of value, that which appears the leaft liable to any of thefe four fources of variation, which are the fole caufes of alteration of value.

When in common language, therefore, we exprefs the *value* of any commodity, it may vary at one period from what it is at another, in confequence of eight different contingencies.

1. From the four circumftances above ftated, in relation to the commodity of which we mean to exprefs the value. And,

2. From

2. From the fame four circumftances, in relation to the commodity we have adopted as a meafure of value.

As the value, therefore, of all commodities depends upon the poffeffion of a quality that makes them the object of man's defire, and the circumftance of their exifting in a certain degree of fcarcity; it follows that the variation of all value muft depend upon the alteration of the proportion betwixt the demand for, and the quantity of, the commodity, occafioned by the occurrence of one of the four circumftances above ftated; and that a variation in the expreffion of value, may be occafioned by the occurrence of any of the eight circumftances we have alluded to. The truth of thefe propofitions may be varioufly illuftrated.

Water, it has been obferved, is one of the things moft ufeful to man, yet it feldom poffeffes any value; and the reafon of

this

this is evident : it rarely occurs, that to its quality of utility, is added the circumftance of exifting in fcarcity : but if, in the courfe of a fiege, or a fea-voyage, it becomes fcarce, it inftantly acquires value ; and its value is fubject to the fame rule of variation as that of other commodities.

Gold is no where to be found in abundance; but fcarcity alone cannot give it value, any more than utility alone can confer value on water. We are accordingly told, that the poor inhabitants of Cuba and St Domingo, when firft difcovered by the Spaniards, not knowing the ufe of gold, confidered it as little bits of pebble, juft worth the picking up, but not worth the refufing to any body that afked it; and that they in reality gave it to their new guefts at the firft requeft *. But the knowledge of its utility by the Spaniards, and its poffeffing therefore qualities, that to them made it an object

ject

* Wealth of Nations, vol. I. p. 219. 4to edit.

ject of defire, added to the circumftance of
its fcarcity, foon gave it value; and the degree of its value came fpeedily to be fixed
even in the minds of the natives, on the
fame principle as that of food, and of all
other commodities.

Though the fcarcity of gold and filver,
and the demand for them, have made them
what is called *moft precious*, that is, under
the general circumftances of mankind,
commodities of the greateft value; yet particular circumftances may occafion fuch a
fcarcity of, and demand for, things of a very
ordinary nature, as to make them, for a
time, of a value fuperior even to thofe metals. Thus, as Mr LOCKE well obferves, in
a man of war, filver may not be of equal
value to gunpowder, and a famine may certainly occafion gold's not being worth its
weight in bran.

The value of every thing is fo completely dependent upon the proportion betwixt
the

the demand for it and the quantity of it,
that the poffeffion of no quality, whatever
excellence it might add to a commodity,
could produce any material alteration in
its value, if it did not affect either the demand for it, or the quantity of it. Suppofing there could be conferred on Corn the
important attribute, that one grain, when
given to an infant on the day of its birth,
fhould fecure a century of robuft health ;
(though it is certain there could not be added to it a qualification more to the general
tafte of mankind), yet, as this would produce no alteration in the quantity of grain,
and, from the fmall quantity that would be
thus confumed, hardly any perceptible increafe in the demand for it, we fhould not be
able to difcern any variation in its value.

So little has the quality of things to do
with their value, that it very often happens, when a commodity poffeffes, in the
higheft degree of perfection, all the qualities which make it defirable, its value is
                                    the

the loweft; and when, on the contrary it
poffeffes them in a very inferior degree, its
value is the higheft. This is almoft conftantly the cafe with Grain. In a fine feafon it is always of a fuperior, in a bad feafon of an inferior quality; yet, as the fine
feafon generally produces an increafed, and
a bad feafon a diminifhed quantity; with a
thorough contempt of the quality, the value of the corn is always regulated on the
principle here ftated; and the greatnefs of
the quantity, though of fuperior quality,
reduces its value; whilft the diminution of
its quantity, though of very inferior quality, increafes the value in the market.

The value of Cattle, though the recom-
mendations with regard to breed, fatnefs,
and every other quality that renders them
defirable, and even the number of them
fhould remain unaltered, is always found to
vary in proportion to the fcarcity or abundance of the food on which they are nourifhed. The value o certain inferior fpecies

of

of grain is alfo often increafed, without
any alteration either of the quantity or
quality of it, but merely in confequence of
an augmentation of demand, arifing from a
fcarcity of the better forts of grain, which
ufually form the bread of the community.

We have often occafion to obferve that,
whilft a web of cloth or a piece of filk have
fold at very confiderable prices, if there remains a fmall quantity of them, this Rem-
nant, as it is called, brings a very inferior
price to what was given for the greater part
of the fame cloth, and of the fame piece of
filk. On the other hand, a fmall quantity of
ftock, in the 3 or 4 *per cents*, is uniformly fold
in the Alley above the market-price of the
commodity ; and yet the fmall pieces of filk
and cloth are of the fame quality with the
whole of the refpective webs, and the ftock
is exactly productive of the fame advantages with any other portion of ftock ; the variations depending, in thefe cafes, totally
upon alterations in the degree of demand ;
there

there being few people who wifh for fo fmall a piece of cloth, and many who, in confequence of wills and trufts, are obliged to purchafe fmaller portions of ftock for ac- cumulation than are ufually expofed in the market.

Thus we may perceive, that the exiftence of value is perfectly independent of any in- herent characteriftic in the commodity it- felf; that there is no fuch thing as intrinfic value; and that alterations in the degrees of value are not dependent upon any change of quality, but always on fome change of proportion betwixt the quantity and the demand for a commodity;—a fure proof of which is, that we cannot exprefs value, or a variation of value, without a comparifon of two commodities; and every variation in the expreffion of value, muft depend upon fome alteration in the proportion betwixt the quantity of, and demand for, one or other of the commodities compared.

For

For example, if the price of grain is to
be expreſſed in ſilver, it might vary, in conſequence of the circumſtance of the alteration of the proportion betwixt the quantity
of the grain and the demand for it; it might
alſo alter, in conſequence of the variation
betwixt the proportion of ſilver and the demand for it. It may happen, too, that alterations might take place in both thoſe
proportions; which muſt likewiſe generally
produce a variation in the expreſſion of value. For, though it is poſſible that there
ſhould exiſt alterations in both, and that
the relative proportion betwixt the quantity and demand for each ſhould ſtill be
preſerved, yet it is highly improbable, that,
under ſuch circumſtances, this equilibrium
ſhould be maintained.

The opinions, that are here ſtated, concerning the nature and the cauſes of the variation of value, are nowiſe new. They have
been hinted at by many; and by ſome they
have been long ago explained with tolerable
accuracy.

accuracy *. They do not, however, appear
to have been fo clearly underftood as to
deftroy the idea of any thing poffeffing
a real and fixed value, fo as to qualify it to
form a meafure of value. After this philofopher's ftone many have been in fearch;
and not a few, diftinguifhed for their knowledge and their talents, have imagined that
in *Labour* they had difcovered what conftituted a real meafure of value. Of this fancy
Sir WILLIAM PETTY's mind feems to have
been fully poffeffed, when he compofed the
following

* The following extract, from Mr LAW's Treatife on
Money, publifhed in Scotland in 1705, feems to convey an
accurate idea of the nature of value. " Mr LOCKE fays,
" the value of goods is according to their quantity, in pro-
" portion to their vent. The vent of goods cannot be
" greater than the quantity, but the demand may be
" greater. If the quantity of wine brought from France
" be 100 ton, and the demand be for 500 ton, the de-
" mand is greater than the vent, and the 100 ton will fell
" at a higher price than if the demand were only equal to
" the vent; fo the prices of goods are not according to
" the quantity in proportion to the vent, but in proportion
" to the demand."

following paſſage * : " Suppoſe a man could,
" with his own hands, plant a certain ſcope
" of land with corn; that is, could dig or
" plough, harrow, reap, carry home, threſh,
" and winnow, ſo much as the huſbandry of
" this land requires, and had withal feed
" wherewith to ſow the ſame. I ſay, that
" when this man hath ſubducted his ſeed
" out of the proceed of his harveſt, and al-
" ſo what himſelf hath both eaten and gi-
" ven to others in exchange for clothes, and
" other natural neceſſaries, that the re-
" mainder of corn is the natural and true
" rent of the land for that year ; and the
" medium of ſeven years, or rather of ſo
" many years as make up the cycle, with-
" in which dearths and plenties make their
" revolution, doth give the ordinary rent of
" the land in corn.

    " But a further, though collateral que-
" ſtion may be, How much Engliſh money
                         " this

* Treatiſe of Taxes and Conſtitutions, p. 23. 4to edit.
1667.

" this corn or rent is worth? I anfwer, fo
" much as the money which another fingle
" man can fave within the fame time, over
" and above his expence, if he employed
" himfelf wholly to produce and make it;
" viz. Let another man go travel into a coun-
" try where is filver, there dig it, refine it,
" bring it to the fame place where the
" other man planted his corn, coin it, &c.;
" the fame perfon, all the while of his
" working for filver, gathering alfo food
" for his neceffary livelihood, and procu-
" ring himfelf covering, &c. I fay the fil-
" ver of the one muft be efteemed of equal
" value with the corn of the other."

The fame idea is ftated by Mr HARRIS,
in his ingenious Effay on Money and Coins:
" The values of land and labour do, as it
" were of themfelves, mutually fettle or ad-
" juft one another; and as all things or
" commodities are the products of thofe
" two, fo their feveral values are naturally
" adjufted by them. But, as in moft pro-
                                    " ductions,

" ductions, *labour* hath the greateſt ſhare,
" the value of labour is to be reckoned the
" chief ſtandard that regulates the value of
" all commodities ; and more eſpecially, as
" the value of land is, as it were, already
" allowed for in the value of labour itſelf."

The Author of the Inquiry into the
Wealth of Nations, is, however, the perſon
who has ſtruggled moſt to eſtabliſh the opinion, that labour may be conſidered as an
accurate meaſure of value ; and Baron
HERTZBERG, who, in his Diſcourſe on the
Wealth of Nations, has declared that it is
admirably proved in the profound and
claſſical work of Dr SMITH, that labour is
the true, univerſal and exact meaſure of
the value of all goods and merchandiſe, is
not the only diſtinguiſhed diſciple who has
maintained this doctrine.

After all, it is the effect that this opinion has, in deſtroying all juſt idea of the
nature of value, and the authority of thoſe
who

who have held it, rather than the ingenuity or even plaufibility of the manner in
which it is fupported, that makes it worthy of confideration.

To thofe who underftand any thing of
the nature of value, or on what its variations depend, the exiftence of a perfect
meafure of value muft at once appear impoffible: for as nothing can be a real meafure of length and quantity, which is fubject to variations in its own dimenfions, fo
nothing can be a real meafure of the value
of other commodities, which is conftantly
varying in its own value. But as there
is nothing which is not fubject to variations, both in its quantity and in the demand for it, there can be nothing which is
not fubject to alteration in value.

In the learned work, however, alluded
to, the author, without defcending to any
reafoning, qualifies labour for fuftaining the
character of a meafure of value, by decla-
ring,

ring, that "labour alone never varies in its
" own value *." And this appears more extraordinary, becaufe labour is the thing
moft fubject to variation in its value, and
is of courfe, of all others that could have
been felected, the worft calculated to perform that duty.

As, however, nothing elfe has ever been
held out as conftituting an accurate meafure
of value; and as the opinion ftill has its advocates, that labour is fuch, though completely deftructive of every correct view
of the nature of value, it is perhaps worth
while, in order to extinguifh the idea of
the poffibility of its forming an accurate
meafure of value, fhortly to prove that, of
all things, it is the leaft qualified for this
tafk, by references to what feems the leaft
fufpicious authority,—opinions delivered in
that very work, which declares labour to
poffefs fixed and invariable value; and
which has been affirmed to contain fub-
stantial

* Wealth of Nations, vol. 1. p. 38. 4to edit.

ſtantial proof that labour is a real meaſure
of value.

Things may alter in their value :

1. At periods not remote ; as for example,
of the ſame year.

2. At remote periods of time.

3. In different countries.

4. In different parts of the ſame country.

Theſe may be generally conſidered as
the four caſes which give riſe to alterations
in the value of all commodities ; for, generally ſpeaking, there is nothing ſubject to
variation of value at the ſame time, and in
the ſame place. Labour, however, it will appear, in the opinion of the learned author,
who ſtyles it the ſole thing invariable in its
value, is ſubject not only to all the uſual
ſources of variation, but poſſeſſes excluſively the characteriſtic of varying at the ſame
time and place.

1. That

1. That labour varies in its value at different periods of the fame year, every perfon muſt know, who has obferved, that " the demand for country labour is greater " at hay-time and harveſt, than during the " greater part of the year ; and *wages riſe* " *with the demand.* In time of war, when " forty or fifty thouſand failors are forced " from the merchant fervice into that of " King, the demand for failors to mer- " chant ſhips neceſſarily rifes *with their* " *ſcarcity,* and their wages, upon ſuch oc- " caſions, commonly rife from a guinea and " feven and twenty ſhillings, to forty ſhil- " lings and three pounds a month *."

2. That labour varies in its value at diſtant and remote periods of time, feems eſtabliſhed by the following facts : " The " *real* recompence of labour, *the real* quan- " tity of the neceſſaries and conveniencies " of life which it can procure to the la- " bourer.

* Wealth of Nations, vol. 1. p. 142. 4to edit.

" bourer, has, during the courfe of the
" prefent century, increafed perhaps in a
" ftill greater proportion than its *money-*
" *price* *."

And, again, " The *money-price* of labour in
" Great Britain has indeed rifen during the
" courfe of the prefent century. This, how-
" ever, feems to be the effect, not fo much
" of any diminution in the value of filver
" in the European market, as of *an in-*
" *creafe of the demand* for labour in Great
" Britain, arifing from the great, and al-
" moft univerfal, profperity of the coun-
" try †."

3. The comparifon made betwixt England and America, fhews clearly the difference that takes place in the value of
labour in diftant and remote countries :
" England

* Wealth of Nations, vol. 1. p. 95. 4to edit.

† Ibid. vol. 1. p. 251. 4to edit.

" England is certainly, in the prefent
" times, a much richer country than any
" part of North America. The wages of
" labour, however, are much higher in
" North America than in any part of Eng-
" land. In the province of New York,
" common labourers earn three fhillings
" and fixpence currency, equal to two fhil-
" lings Sterling a-day; fhip-carpenters ten
" fhillings and fixpence currency, with a
" pint of rum, worth fixpence Sterling,
" equal in all to fix fhillings and fixpence
" Sterling; houfe-carpenters and brick-
" layers eight fhillings currency, equal to
" four fhillings and fixpence Sterling; jour-
" neymen tailors five fhillings currency,
" equal to about two fhillings and tenpence
" Sterling. Thefe prices are all above the
" London price; and wages are faid to be
" as high in the other colonies as in New
" York. The price of provifions is every
" where in North America much lower
" than in England. A dearth has never
" been known there. In the worft feafons
                                    " they

" they have always had a fufficiency for
" themfelves, though lefs for exportation.
" If the *money-price* of labour, therefore,
" be higher than it is any where in the
" mother country, its *real price*, the real
" command of the neceffaries and con-
" veniencies of life which it conveys
" to the labourer, muft be higher in a
" ftill greater proportion *." Further,
" Labour in America is fo well rewarded,
" that a numerous family of children, in-
" ftead of being a burden, is a fource of
" opulence and profperity to the parents.
" The labour of each child, before it can
" leave their houfe, is computed to be
" worth L. 100 clear gain to them. A
" young widow, with four or five young
" children, who, among the middling or
" inferior ranks of people in Europe, would
" have fo little chance for a fecond huf-
                                    " band,

* Wealth of Nations, vol. I. p. 85. 4to edit.

" band, is there frequently courted as a
" fort of fortune *."

4. The following facts not only fhew the
extraordinary variations in the value of labour, that take place in different parts of
the fame country ; but the ingenious reafoning, which accompanies it, points out
why thefe variations on the value of labour
muft be more permanent than in any other
commodity. " Eighteen pence a day may
" be reckoned the common price of labour
" in London and its neighbourhood.   At a
" few miles diftance it falls to fourteen and
" fifteen pence.   Ten pence may be rec-
" koned its price in Edinburgh and its
" neighbourhood.   At a few miles diftance
" it falls to eight pence, the ufual price of
" common labour through the greater part
" of the low country of Scotland, where it
" varies a good deal lefs than in England.
" Such a difference of prices, which it
                                    " feems

* Wealth of Nations, vol. I. p. 65. 4to edit.

" feems is not always fufficient to tranf-
" port a man from one parifh to another,
" would neceffarily occafion fo great a
" tranfportation of the moft bulky commo-
" dities, not only from one parifh to ano-
" ther, but from one end of the kingdom,
" almoft from one end of the world to the
" other, as would foon reduce them more
" nearly to a level. After all that has been
" faid of the levity and inconftancy of hu-
" man nature, it appears evidently from
" experience that a man is of all forts of
" luggage the moft difficult to be tranfport-
" ed *."

Thus labour feems to partake of thofe
four fources of variation, which are the general reafons of alteration in the value of
all commodities. But this is not all : for
this pretended accurate meafure of value is
not capable even, like other commodities,
of forming a true meafure of value at the
fame

* Wealth of Nations, vol. I. p. 91. 4to edit.

fame time and place; which is evident, when we recollect, that, " at the fame time " and place, the real and the nominal price " of all commodities are exactly in propor- " tion to one another. The more or lefs " *money* you get for any commodity, in " the London market, for example, the " more or lefs labour it will at that time " or place enable you to purchafe or com- " mand. At the fame time and place, " therefore, *money* is the exact meafure of " the real exchangeable value of all com- " modities *." Whereas, on the other hand, it muft be obferved, that the value of labour " cannot be afcertained very ac- " curately any where, different prices be- " ing often paid at the fame place, and for " the fame fort of labour, not only accord- " ing to the different abilities of the work- " men, but according to the eafinefs or " hardnefs of the mafters †."

Now,

* Wealth of Nations, vol. I. p. 44. 4to edit.

† Ibid. vol. I. p. 94.

Now, the variation here pointed out muſt be in the real value of labour, and not in that of the money by which we expreſs its value; becauſe money, at the ſame time and place, forming an exact meaſure of the exchangeable value of all commodities, cannot, under ſuch circumſtances, vary in its own value.

Indeed, it appears moſt extraordinary, that the Author of the Wealth of Nations ſhould ever have conſidered labour as an accurate meaſure of value; for in Book II. Chap. III. of his work, he treats of *productive* and *unproductive* Labour, and therein announces an opinion, which forms one of the moſt ſtriking features of his theory, that a great portion or deſcription of labour is totally unproductive: and it muſt be obſerved, that a propoſition holding forth a mathematical point as a meaſure of dimenſion, would not be more abſurd than propoſing any thing unproductive as a meaſure of value.

Great,

Great, therefore, as the authorities are who have regarded labour as a meafure of value, and who by fo doing have contradicted that view of the nature of value which has been given, it does not appear that labour forms any exception to the general rule, that nothing poffeffes real, fixed or intrinfic value ; or that there is any folid reafon for doubting the two general principles we have endeavoured to eftablifh :—

1. That things are alone valuable in confequence of their uniting qualities, which make them the objects of man's defire, with the circumftance of exifting in a certain degree of fcarcity.

2. That the degree of value which every commodity poffeffes, depends upon the proportion betwixt the quantity of it and the demand for it.

CHAP.

CHAP. II.

OF PUBLIC WEALTH,

OF INDIVIDUAL RICHES,

AND OF THE RELATION THEY BEAR TO EACH OTHER.

THOUGH the advantages which all reasonings on Political Oeconomy must have derived from a clear explanation of what constitutes national or public wealth are apparent ; and though a precise understanding of what wealth is, seems a necessary preliminary to the discussing, with any degree of accuracy, the means of increasing it ; we must regret, that a definition of

Public

Public Wealth is no where to be found.
This deficiency, however, does not appear
to have proceeded fo much from any fenfe
of difficulty in defining national wealth, or
in defcribing wherein it is conceived to confift, as from a general feeling of its being
needlefs to exprefs that about which all men
are agreed. For the theories and opinions
of all fpeculative writers fufficiently fhew,
that they have entertained, on this fubject,
the fame ideas with thofe who, in the exercife of the practice of taxation, have been
obliged to exprefs their opinions more diftinctly.

National wealth has by all been confidered merely as made up of the riches
of individuals belonging to the community; the capital of a fociety has been
regarded, in every refpect, as the fame
with that of all the individuals who compofe it * ; and the fum-total of the fortunes
of individuals, has been conceived to con-

vey

* Wealth of Nations, vol. I. p. 409. 4to edit.

vey an accurate defcription of the mafs of national wealth. Parfimony, which experience teaches us, is the moft ufual means of increafing private fortune, is univerfally reprefented as the parent of public wealth. Frugality is faid to increafe, Prodigality to diminifh, the public capital *. Every prodigal is reprefented as a public enemy, and every frugal man as a public benefactor †. So much, indeed, is public wealth univerfally deemed the fame thing with the mafs of private riches, that there appears no means of increafing the fortune of an individual, when it is not done directly at the expence of another, that is not regarded as productive of national opulence.

On this principle have proceeded the various ftatements of national wealth, which have at different times been fubmitted to the public. Thus, by Sir WILLIAM PET-
TY'S

* Wealth of Nations, vol. I. p. 421. 4to edit.

† Ibid. vol. I. p. 414.

TY's computation, in the year 1664, the total wealth of the nation, confifting of lands, houfes, fhipping, gold and filver coin, wares, merchandife, plate, furniture, &c. amounted to two hundred and fifty millions. In the beginning of the eighteenth century, GREGORY KING computed the landed and perfonal property at fix hundred and fifteen millions. Mr HOOKE computed the whole value of real and perfonal property, about fifty years ago, at two thoufand one hundred millions Sterling. Sir WILLIAM PULTENEY, about thirty years after, valued the landed and perfonal property at two thoufand millions. The total amount of the wealth of Great Britain, confifting of the value of articles above enumerated, has alfo been computed by Dr BEEKE, to be nearly two thoufand five hundred millions Sterling, exclufive of one hundred millions Sterling, the value of foreign poffeffions belonging to the fubjects of Great Britain*.

It

---

* Thefe ftatements are taken from Mr ARTHUR's Financial and Political Facts; in moft inftances, however, they have been compared with the originals.

It is, however, impoffible to fubfcribe to the idea, that the fum-total of individual riches forms an accurate ftatement of public wealth.   Though the opinion has been univerfally prevalent, it muft be deemed falfe and unfounded by every man who confiders the fubject, after having formed, and familiarized himfelf to, an accurate and diftinct opinion of the nature of value.

It muft, then, appear, that a commodity being ufeful or delightful to man, cannot alone give it value ; that to obtain value, or to be qualified to conftitute a portion of private riches, it muft combine with that quality, the circumftance of exifting in a certain degree of fcarcity.   Yet the common fenfe of mankind would revolt at a propofal for augmenting the wealth of a nation, by creating a fcarcity of any commodity generally ufeful and neceffary to man.   For example, let us fuppofe a country poffeffing abundance of the neceffaries

and

and conveniencies of life, and univerfally
accommodated with the pureft ftreams of
water:—what opinion would be entertained
of the underftanding of a man, who, as the
means of increafing the wealth of fuch a
country, fhould propofe to create a fcarcity of water, the abundance of which was
defervedly confidered as one of the greateft
bleffings incident to the community? It is
certain, however, that fuch a projector
would, by this means, fucceed in increafing
the mafs of individual riches; for to the
water, which would ftill retain the quality
of being ufeful and defirable, he would add
the circumftance of exifting in fcarcity,
which of courfe muft confer upon it value;
and, when it once obtained value, the fame
circumftances that fix the value of its
produce for a certain number of years,
as the price of the poffeffion of land which
produces food, would equally fix the value
of the produce of fprings for a certain number of years, as the price of the poffeffion
of that which produced drink; and thus
the

the individual riches of the country would
be increafed, in a fum equal to the value of
the fee-fimple of all the wells.

But further to illuftrate this propofition,
that the wealth of the nation, and the mafs
of individual riches, cannot be regarded as
in every refpect the fame, let us for a moment fuppofe it poffible to create as great
an abundance of any fpecies of food as
there exifts of water: what would be
thought of the advice of a man, who fhould
cautioufly recommend, even at the moment
of the preffure of fcarcity, to beware of
creating this boafted abundance? for, however flattering it might appear as a remedy for the immediate evil, it would inevitably diminifh the wealth of the nation.
Yet ridiculous as this opinion might appear, as every thing, which partakes of the
abundance of water or air, muft at once
ceafe to poffefs value ; it follows that, by
occafioning fuch an abundance, the fum-
total

total of individual riches would moſt certainly be diminiſhed, to an extent equal to
the total value of that ſpecies of food, whoſe
value would by this means be deſtroyed.

When we reflect on the ſituation of this
country, it appears, indeed, almoſt ſelf-evi-
dent, that the ſum-total of individual riches
cannot be conſidered as affording an accurate ſtatement of public wealth.

At preſent, the capital of the national
debt amounts nearly to five hundred millions. We have ſeen, and know, that war,
even in the courſe of the firſt year, may ſink
the value of this capital twenty *per cent.* ;
that is, that it may diminiſh the maſs of individual fortunes one hundred millions; and
thus impoſe upon any man, who made up
the account of public wealth on the principle, that an accurate ſtatement of it was
to be derived from adding together the
fortunes of individuals, the neceſſity of
ſaying,

faying, that one hundred millions of our wealth had vanifhed.

But this is not all. The value of many things finks at the fame time. In the value of land, in particular, we have feen a confiderable diminution, which would create the neceffity of a further reduction in this ftatement of public wealth. Yet the furface of the national territory remains unaltered ; the landlord receives the fame rent ; the ftockholder is paid the fame intereft ; and there is no one thing, on which a man can lay his hand as an article of national wealth, which does not appear, to retain the fame qualities that rendered it either ufeful or defirable, and to be in every refpect unaltered.

It feems, therefore, apparent, that an increafe in the mafs of individual riches does not neceffarily increafe the national wealth: that it is poffible to imagine a very important increafe of national wealth, which muft diminifh the mafs of individual riches ; and

and that the practice of confidering the
fum-total of individual riches, as calculated to convey an accurate idea of national
wealth, muft be regarded as erroneous.

Indeed, a little further confideration
makes it evident, that, if we could fuppofe
Nature to beftow on any community, or Art
to procure for them, fuch an abundance,
that every individual fhould find himfelf in
poffeffion of whatever his appetites could
want, or his imagination wifh or defire,
they would poffefs the greateft poffible degree of national wealth; though, under fuch
circumftances, it is impoffible that any
commodity could obtain the attribute of
value : for, like water and air, all commodities, that partake of their abundance, muft
at once be divefted of value, or of the poffibility of conftituting any part of individual riches. The inhabitants of a country
thus abounding in all that man can defire,
would, without the poffibility of poffeffing
riches, enjoy all the wealth and comforts
which

which the largeft fortunes can fecure. Diminifh this fuppofed abundance, it is obvious you will impoverifh the community ;
but you will, by fuch diminution, infallibly confer value on the commodities ufed
or defired by man, and of courfe create individual riches. Subfequent, however, to
this diminution, which occafions the exiftence of riches, thofe who remain poffeffed,
even of the largeft fortunes, cannot enjoy
a greater quantity of the objects of their
defire, than the community at large poffeffed, in that fuppofed ftate of fociety where
abundance precluded the exiftence of value, and of courfe the poffibility of individual riches *.

Important

* Though the opinions entertained by the œconomifts
lead them uniformly to confound Wealth and Riches, it
being their principle, *que la valeur vénale eft la bafe de toute
richeffe, que fon accroiffement eft accroiffement de richeffes*, (Philofophie Rurale, p. 60.) : " That value in exchange is the ba-
" fis of wealth, and that the increafe of price is an increafe
" of wealth ;" yet there are paffages in their writings,
which evidently fhew, that the diftinction betwixt wealth
and

Important as this diftinction, which we
have endeavoured to eftablifh, between the
wealth of a nation, and the fum-total of
the riches of individuals, will afterwards
appear to be, in regulating our opinions on
every queftion relating to the fcience of
Political Oeconomy; it is perhaps ftill
more important to obferve, that in proportion as the riches of individuals are increafed by an augmentation of the value of any
commodity, the wealth of the nation is generally diminifhed; and in proportion as the
mafs of individual riches is diminifhed, by
the diminution of the value of any commodity, the national opulence is generally
increafed.

No

and riches had occurred to them ; for example : " It is ne-
" ceffary to diftinguifh wealth from riches. The former
" poffeffes value in ufe, but no value in exchange. The
" latter poffeffes a value both in ufe and in exchange. It
" is not fufficient for a nation to poffefs wealth; it is ne-
" ceffary it fhould endeavour to procure great riches, in or-
" der to adminifter, by means of commerce, to the defires
" of all the members of which it is compofed." *Phyfiocra-*
tie, p. cxviij. (For the original, fee APPENDIX, No. I.).

No man can doubt that an abundance of
grain is a moſt important article of national wealth. As little can it be doubted,
that a ſcarcity of grain is a moſt ſerious
ſymptom of national poverty ; yet we are
told, by great authority *, that a defect in
the harveſt will raiſe the price of corn in
the following proportions :

Defect.			Above the common rate
1. Tenth,			3. Tenths.
2. Tenths,	Raiſes the price		8. Tenths.
3. Tenths,			1.6 Tenths.
4. Tenths,			2.8 Tenths.
5. Tenths,			4.5 Tenths.

According to this opinion, therefore, a
deficiency of three-tenths of the common
produce of the country in grain, would increaſe the value of the grain that remained

160

* GREGORY KING's Calculation, publiſhed by DAVE-
NANT, vol. II. p. 224.

160 *per cent.*; that is, fuppofe the ufual
produce of any country to be 300 quarters
of grain, and the total value of that grain to
be L. 300; if the grain was reduced three-
tenths in quantity, viz. to 210 quarters,
then the value of thefe 210 quarters would
be L. 546. Thus the wealth of the nation
being diminifhed by the lofs of three-tenths
of the whole of its produce of grain, the
value of its grain would thereby be increafed from L. 300 to L. 546; and there
would, by that means, be added to the
mafs of individual riches, a fum nearly
equal to the value which the whole grain
of the country bore when no fuch fcarcity
exifted.

On the other hand, it is conjectured by
authority equally refpectable *, that the
production of one-tenth part more grain
than is ufually confumed, would diminifh
the value of the grain one-half; that is,
that

* See Spectator, No. 200.

that if the produce of a country was 300 quarters, and its general value L. 300, if the wealth of the nation fhould be increafed by the production of 30 more quarters of grain, then the mafs of individual riches would be diminifhed L. 135, as the value of the 330 quarters, at 10 s. a quarter, would only amount to L. 165; whereas the value of the 300 quarters, before the produce was increafed, at 20 s. a quarter, amounted to L. 300 *.

So

* That the diminution of the quantity has the effect of raifing the value for which the total of any commodity fells at the market; and the increafe, the effect of diminifh-ing it; is an obfervation made by many writers, though they difagree about the ratio in which it is increafed and di-minifhed. Thus, " Merchants obferve, that if the com-" modity in market is diminifhed one-third beneath its " mean quantity, it will be nearly doubled in value; and " that if it is augmented one-third above its mean quanti-" ty, it will fink near one-half in its value; and that by " further diminifhing or augmenting the quantity, thefe " difproportions between the quantity and prices vaftly " increafe." Confiderations on the Policy of Entails, by Sir JOHN DALRYMPLE, p. 14.

So truly is this principle underftood by
thofe whofe intereft leads them to take advantage of it, that nothing but the impoffibility of general combination protects the
public wealth againft the rapacity of private avarice; for wherever combination
has been poffible, mankind have found, in
the diminution of their wealth, the fatal
effects of this difpofition. It is on this
principle that the Dutch were faid to burn
a confiderable quantity of fpiceries, whenever mankind was favoured with a fertile
feafon; and that they gave to the natives
of the feveral iflands premiums for collect-
ing the young bloffoms and green leaves
of the nutmeg trees, by which means they
deftroyed them. It was a fimilar motive
that, in the year 1731, induced the proprietors of the old vineyards in France, to
folicit an order in Council, which they obtained, prohibiting both the planting of
new vineyards, and the renewal of thofe
old ones, of which the cultivation had been
interrupted for two years, without a particular

cular permiſſion from the King, to be
granted only in conſequence of information from the *Intendant* of the province,
certifying that he had examined the land,
and that it was incapable of any other culture. The ſame idea led the tobacco-
planters in Virginia to paſs an act of Aſ-
ſembly, by which they reſtrained the cultivation of tobacco to 6000 plants for every negro kept; and afterwards induced
them to agree, in plentiful years, to burn a
certain proportion of tobacco for every negro.

From theſe conſiderations, it ſeems evident, not only that the ſum-total of individual riches cannot be conſidered as an accurate deſcription or definition of the
wealth of a nation; but that, on the contrary, it may be generally affirmed, that
an increaſe of riches, when ariſing from
alterations in the quantity of commodities,
is always a proof of an immediate diminution of wealth; and a diminution of riches,

is

is evidence of an immediate increafe of wealth : and this propofition will be found invariably true, with the exception of a fingle cafe, which will be afterwards explained.   Thus, it becomes neceffary to adopt a definition of Public Wealth, which conveys a different idea of it from that which has been generally received ; and it is therefore fubmitted, that Wealth may be accurately defined,—*to confift of all that man defires, as ufeful or delightful to him* *.

But if National Wealth is truly and rightly defined, to confift of all that man defires as ufeful and delightful to him ; as, (from the explanation that has been already

dy

---

* In the *Projet d'une dixme Royale*, publifhed in the name of the Marechal De VAUBAN, and generally conceived to be his work, (though VOLTAIRE, in his *Doutes fur le teftament du Cardinal de RICHELIEU*, fays it was written by M. DE BOIS GUILBERT), Wealth is nearly accurately defined in the followiug terms : " *La vrai richeffe d'un Royaume confifte dans* " *l'abondance des denr. es.*" " The true wealth of a natiou " confifts in the abundance of its commodities."

dy given of the nature of value, or of the circumſtances that entitle any thing to the character which qualifies it for forming a portion of individual riches), we know, that by adding the circumſtance of ſcarcity to the qualities which make any commodity a component part of public wealth, we ſhould give it value, and thus qualify it to form a portion of individual riches, it follows, that individual riches may be defined, —*to conſiſt of all that man deſires as uſeful or delightful to him; which exiſts in a degree of ſcarcity.*

With regard to the degree in which any commodity is to be claſſed as forming a portion of individual riches, it has already been explained and made evident, that the value of every thing depends upon the proportion betwixt the demand for it, and the quantity of it. But to underſtand thoroughly the nature of individual riches, and the changes and variations of which they are ſuſceptible, it will be neceſſary to examine

examine into the alterations of value which the variation of that proportion in any one commodity, may create in the general mafs of individual riches.

The value of every commodity, it has been obferved, may be altered :

1. By a diminution in its quantity ;

2. By an increafe in its quantity ;

3. By an increafe of demand ;

4. By a diminution of demand.

And, to explain this fubject thoroughly, each of thefe cafes muft be confidered in its order, as well as the effects which they are likely to produce, not only on the commodity itfelf in relation to which they occur, but fubfequently with a view to the effects which they indirectly produce upon the value of all other commodities, which form portions of individual riches.

1. *Of*

1. *Of the Effects of the Diminution of the Quantity of any Commodity on the Value of that Commodity.*

On firſt conſideration, it naturally occurs, that if the members of a ſociety had devoted a portion of their reſpective riches for the acquiſition of any given commodity, and a ſudden ſcarcity had occaſioned the exiſtence of only half of the uſual quantity of that commodity, the ſame portion of other goods, remaining applicable to the acquiſition of the half which had antecedently been employed in acquiring the whole, the value of any quantity of it would be doubled.

For example: if one thouſand pound weight formed the ordinary conſumption of ſugar in any ſociety, and L. 50 repreſented the value of thoſe commodities which the different members of the ſociety allotted to give in exchange for ſugar, ſugar would then be at one ſhilling a pound; becauſe one pound

is

is a thoufandth part of one thoufand pound, and one fhilling a thoufandth part of L. 50.

But if the fupply of fugar was diminifh-ed to five hundred pound weight, one pound of fugar would then form the five hundredth part of the whole fupply; and therefore it would be natural to conclude, that it would be worth two fhillings a pound, as that fum is the five hundredth part of L. 50.

This reafoning, however, would be found altogether fallacious; for the alteration of value, which the diminution of the quan-tity of any commodity creates, depends upon a principle totally different.

One thoufand pound weight of fugar was the quantity the fociety defired, when fu-gar was at the price of one fhilling a pound, and the quantity they were accuftomed to enjoy. To convey an idea of the real ef-fect of diminifhing at once the fupply of

fugar

fugar to five hundred pound weight, let us
fuppofe that this fociety confifted of one
hundred families, each of whom had the
habit, at the time the fupply amounted to
one thoufand pound weight, of confuming
ten pound weight of fugar ; for the acquifition and payment of which, each family,
in the diftribution of the order of their expences, ufed to facrifice of the commodities
they poffeffed the value of ten fhillings, making of courfe the total value of commodities facrificed to the acquifition of fugar by
the hundred families amount to L. 50.

Each of thefe families being in the habit,
according to this hypothefis, of confuming
ten pounds weight of fugar ; it muft be a
wifh natural and common to them all, to
continue enjoying, as nearly as poffible, the
fame quantity of that commodity to which
they were habituated.   As the taftes of
men are, however, various, fome muft be
willing to facrifice much more of their
other enjoyments than others, though
all of them will probably be willing to deprive

prive themfelves of fome part of them for
this purpofe ; it being highly improbable
that fugar, or any other article whofe quantity is fuddenly diminifhed, fhould happen
to be the one, among all the numerous objects of their defire, the confumption of
which any of thefe families will moft in-
cline to relinquifh or abridge.

Thus, the defire for fugar, which either
tafte or habit may have created, may, in
fome of thefe families, make them willing
to deprive themfelves of a portion of their
other enjoyments, equal to the value of
twenty fhillings, rather than abridge their
confumption of fugar. The defire of others
for that article may be fo great, that, rather than forego confuming, as nearly as
poffible, the quantity to which they were
habituated, they would facrifice thirty fhillings worth of their other enjoyments.
And as there is no anfwering for the effects of tafte and habit, there might exift
in the fociety men willing to facrifice forty fhillings worth of their other enjoyments,

ments, for the purpofe of retaining, as nearly as may be, the quantity of fugar to which they were accuftomed.

The competition that would be thus created, *might*, it is evident, raife the price of fugar, in a degree far beyond what we fhould be apt, at firft fight, to expect from the diminution in its quantity. Indeed, it *muft* have this effect, were it not that fome of the confumers of fugar, preferring the enjoyment of the other things to which they were habituated, might be, on this account, willing to retrench in that article, or perhaps to renounce the ufe of it altogether. On this laft fuppofition, the five hundred pound weight of fugar, which in confequence of the fuppofed diminution in the quantity would form the whole fupply of the market, would ultimately be acquired by the remaining confumers of fugar, in fhares proportioned to the facrifices which each was willing to make for the acquifition of it. But fuppofing the demand, created by the facrifices which

which all were willing to make, to be fuch
as to raife the price of every ten fhillings worth of fugar thirty fhillings more
than formerly, then one hundred times
thirty fhillings, making L. 150, in addition to the former L. 50, in all L. 200,
would reprefent the value of commodities
facrificed for the acquifition of fugar; and
fugar would of courfe be at eight fhillings
the pound; one pound of fugar being the
five hundredth part of five hundred pounds
weight, and eight fhillings being the five
hundredth part of L. 200.

This hypothetical ftatement of the increafe in the value of fugar, which the abftracting of one-half of the fupply might occafion, without pretending to give any accurate notion of the precife extent to which
the value of the commodity would be raifed, will lead the imagination to form,
with greater facility, a juft idea of the
manner in which the diminution of the
quantity of a commodity may affect the
value of it.

It

It is obvious that the defire of mankind to
continue their ufual enjoyments, muft, with
certainty, raife the price of every commodity of which the quantity is diminifhed:
this rife of value muft undoubtedly, in fome
inftances, check the demand for it; and that
again tends to counteract the effects the diminution of the quantity of the commodity would otherwife have in raifing its
value. The rife of value, therefore, of any
one commodity, in confequence of the diminution of its quantity, muft be regulated
by the perfeverance of the confumers in
their defire to enjoy the fame quantity;
which muft univerfally depend on the nature of the commodity in which the fcarcity exifts; as the obftinacy in attempting
to acquire the fame quantity of it, muft
be proportioned to the degree of inclination which either neceffity, habit, or tafte,
has created for it. Thus, though we have
known grain, meat, and other articles of
firft neceffity, in certain fituations, and under certain circumftances, rife in value
from

from one to fifty *, articles of tafte or luxury have hardly, in any inftance, ever been found to rife to double or triple their ufual value.

The diminution of quantity, therefore, muft raife the price of different commodities in different degrees, having always a more powerful effect in proportion to the degree in which the commodity itfelf appears neceffary.

2. *Of the Effects of the Increafe of the Quantity of any Commodity on the Value of that Commodity.*

IN confidering the effects of the diminution of the quantity of any commodity on its total value, it was remarked, that it naturally occurred, that if the members of

any

* See the account of the prices of grain, &c. in the fiege of Paris, 1590. *Rapport entre l'Argent et les Denrées*, p. 44, 45.

any fociety had devoted a portion of their refpective riches for the acquifition of that commodity, and a fudden fcarcity had occafioned the exiftence of only half its ufual quantity, the fame proportion of other goods remaining applicable to the acquifition of the half which had antecedently been employed in acquiring the whole, the value of any given quantity of it would be doubled.

In like manner, in confidering the effects of the increafe of any commodity on the value of the commodity, we are alfo led, at firft fight, to conclude, that if the quantity of any commodity fhould be fuddenly doubled, the fame portion of other goods remaining applicable to the acquifition of it, which had been employed before the augmentation in acquiring what now conftitutes one-half of the commodity, the value of any given portion of it would be reduced one-half.

This reafoning, however, would be found juft as fallacious, as that which was ftated

to

to occur on firſt conſidering the diminution of the quantity of any commodity ;
for the effects of the increaſe of the quantity of a commodity, upon the value of
that commodity, depend alſo on a very
different principle.

To convey an idea of the real effects of
increaſing the quantity of any commodity
on the value of that commodity, let us
again ſuppoſe a ſociety, in which one thouſand pound weight of ſugar formed the ordinary conſumption ; and L. 50 repreſented the value of thoſe commodities which
the growers of ſugar acquired in exchange
for their ſugar, and which of courſe they
were habituated to enjoy.

If, all at once, there came into the market
two thouſand pound weight, the value of ſugar, by this alteration in the proportion betwixt the quantity and the demand for it,
would be ſuddenly reduced. The conſumers
of ſugar would find, that they could get the
quantity of that article they were habituated

ted to enjoy, by facrificing a much finaller
quantity of their property to the acquifition of it. The growers of fugar, on the
contrary, would difcover, that they could
by no means procure, in exchange for fugar, the fame quantity of the objects of
their defire ; each of them, however, naturally endeavouring to obtain the fame
things to which he was formerly habituated, would be induced, for that purpofe, to
prefs his fugars on the confumers ; and
though at firft, in fome inftances, the market might be fo managed, by not producing
too much at a time, that the reduction of
price might be comparatively trifling, yet
the avidity of each of the growers of fugar,
to obtain, in exchange for his fugar, as
nearly as poffible the fame quantity of
thofe commodities which he was formerly
accuftomed to enjoy, would ultimately
force the market, in fuch a manner as to
render the fugar, thus doubled in quantity,
incapable of acquiring any thing like the
fame quantity of goods which the growers
of

of fugar formerly obtained in exchange for
the commodity they reared.

It is true, that this reduction of price
would create new confumers of fugar,
which would, in a degree, counteract the
effects of the augmentation of the quantity of fugar upon the value of that commodity, in the fame manner as the rife of value, in confequence of the diminution of
the quantity of a commodity, has been defcribed to be checked, by fome of the confumers renouncing the ufe of it ; and the
effect of increafing the quantity, in diminifhing the value of any commodity, muft
undoubtedly be more or lefs in proportion
as the diminution of its value creates fources of demand.

The alteration, therefore, in the value of
commodities, in confequence of the increafe of the quantity of them, muft depend, in a great degree, on the nature of
the commodities themfelves.

With

With refpect to the neceffaries of life, if a peculiarly fertile feafon fhould create an extraordinary abundance of them, as every perfon muft generally enjoy nearly as much of thofe as he can confume, without which he could not exift ; there is hardly a poffibility of conceiving any fudden fource of extended demand, capable of counteracting the effects of the abundance. But, on the value of thofe ornaments and luxuries, which fcarcity has rendered precious, a proportionable increafe of quantity could never effect the fame variations : as the reduction of the price of an article, (which, after all, would be fo fcarce), muft increafe the number of candidates for it, and thus create new fources of demand, fufficient to abforb the additional quantity, long before its value was very greatly depreffed.

The increafe of quantity, therefore, muft fink the price of different commodities in different degrees, having always a more
powerful

powerful effect in proportion to the degree
in which the commodity has been confidered neceſſary, and, as ſuch, is an article
of general conſumption.

Thus, though it appears probable, as conjectured by Sir RICHARD STEELE, that an
increaſe of one-tenth more than is uſually
conſumed of grain, might diminiſh the value of the grain in the country one-half;
yet the exiſtence of a tenth more of diamonds, or a tenth more of gold, never
could have ſuch an effect.

3. *Of the Effects of an Increaſe of Demand
for any Commodity, on the Value of that
Commodity.*

As the value of every commodity depends alone on the proportion betwixt the
demand for it, and the quantity of it, and as
ſimilar alterations in the proportion betwixt
the demand and the quantity of any commodity, may be produced, either by variations

tions in the quantity of it, or by variations
in the demand for it; it follows, that fimilar effects muft enfue, whether the variation
is produced by an alteration in the quantity of the commodity, or by an alteration
in the demand for it; provided always,
that in confequence of fuch alterations, the
fame proportion is eftablifhed betwixt the
demand for, and the quantity of the commodity.

For example: let us fuppofe any two focieties poffeffed of the fame quantities of
all forts of commodities, and each enjoying a fupply of a thoufand pound weight
of fugar, for which there exifted a fteady
and fettled demand; if, in the one country,
the fupply of the market fhould be diminifhed to five hundred pound weight, it
is obvious, that the demand would be
double the quantity for which there exifted a fupply; and if, in the other country,
the fupply continuing at one thoufand
pounds weight, there fhould fuddenly arife

a demand for two thoufand pounds weight, it is equally obvious, that, in this cafe, the demand would be double the quantity for which there exifted a fupply. The new proportion, therefore, eftablifhed betwixt the demand and the quantity, would, in either cafe, be exactly the fame; and of courfe, the value of any given quantity of fugar muft, in either cafe, undergo exactly the fame alteration.

If, therefore, we could fuppofe that there was any accuracy in conjecturing, that the diminution of the fupply of fugar from one thoufand to five hundred pound weight, would raife the value of fugar from one fhilling to eight fhillings a pound, it follows, that fugar, if the demand was by any means doubled, would alfo rife to eight fhillings a pound; the whole thoufand pound weight would then be worth L. 400; and of courfe L. 350 worth of goods, antecedently allotted for the purchafe of other commodities, muft be added, in confequence of the increafed demand, to the

L. 50

L. 50 worth, previoufly applicable to the acquifition of the one thoufand pounds weight of fugar, when the fugar was at one fhilling a pound.

In ftating the effects of the diminution of one-half of the fupply of fugar, it was obferved, that the augmentation of the price might induce fome of the confumers of fugar, who preferred the full enjoyment of other things, to which they were habituated, to renounce in whole or in part the ufe of fugar ; and that the rife in its value, by the reduction in its quantity, might, in fome degree, receive a check from this circumftance. In like manner, when the value of fugar rifes in any great degree by a fudden extenfion of demand, fuch as we have here fuppofed, it is obvious, that a fimilar check to the rife of its value, will, to a certain extent, be given, by fome of thofe who were habituated to enjoy fugar at one fhilling a pound not choofing to facrifice to the acquifition of fugar fo much of
the

the other commodities they were accustom-
ed to enjoy, as becomes neceffary to obtain
fugar in confequence of the rife in its value.

The degree, however, in which this
check will operate, as in the former cafe,
muft depend upon the nature of the commodity for which the extenfion of demand
takes place. It is obvious, that no rife in
value can induce men to renounce the acquifition of the neceffaries of life, provided any facrifices they can make will procure them ; and this check will therefore
operate, juft in proportion to the degree of
inclination which either neceffity, habit or
tafte, had created for the commodity ; that
is, it will be more inconfiderable, in proportion as the inclination to obtain the
ufual quantity of it is lefs urgent.

4. *Of*

4. *Of the Effects of Diminution of Demand for any Commodity, on the Value of that Commodity.*

FROM what has been faid on the three cafes of the variation in the value of commodities, which have been already confidered, it muft be at firft fight clear, that as this fourth, and only remaining circumftance, which can caufe variation of value in any commodity, again fuppofes an alteration in the proportion betwixt the demand for, and the quantity of, the commodity in which it takes place; it muft alfo produce effects fimilar to thofe that have already been defcribed.

If, for example, we fuppofe a fociety, whofe ufual fupply of fugar amounted to one thoufand pound weight, for which there exifted a fettled and fteady demand; fhould an alteration in the ftate of this fociety,

ciety, all at once induce them to be fatisfied with five hundred pounds weight, the
demand would of courfe be reduced one-
half. Sugar muft, therefore, become cheaper; and the natural defire in the growers
of fugar, to acquire as nearly as poffible, in
exchange for their fugars, the quantity of
other commodities that they were habituated to enjoy, would lead them to force the
market in fuch a manner, as to make the
one thoufand pounds weight of fugar fell
for a fum much fmaller than the L. 50,
which formed the value of the whole
thoufand pound weight, when fugar was at
one fhilling a pound.

The reduction of the value of fugar
might, as in the cafe of diminution of value by augmentation of quantity, create
new fources of demand; but as, in that
cafe, it was obferved, that the extent of the
alteration of value depended upon the nature of the commodity, the extenfion of
the quantity having always a more powerful

ful effect in reducing the value, in proportion to the degree in which the commodity has been confidered neceffary ; fo, in the
prefent cafe, the alteration, which the reduction of demand operates, muft alfo depend upon the nature of the commodity,
and will be regulated on the fame principle.

Before concluding this fubject, it is neceffary to remark, that though variations in
value, whether produced by alteration of
the quantity of commodities, or of the demand for them, provided they occafion
fimilar alterations in the proportion, muft
produce the fame effects upon the value of
any commodity, or in the degree in which
it forms a portion of individual riches ; yet
they indicate very different effects on the
ftate of national or public wealth : for it
has already been obferved, that by the diminution of the quantity of a commodity,
its value will be increafed, though the national opulence is by that means diminifhed ;

ed ; and that an augmentation of the quantity of a commodity muft diminifh its value, though by this means the national
opulence is increafed. When, however, an
increafe of the value is produced, by an
augmentation of demand, or the value of
any commodity is reduced by a diminution
of demand, the national opulence or public
wealth of the community is, at the moment of the alteration in the demand, in
every refpect unaltered and unchanged,
notwithftanding the variation which takes
place in individual riches.

Having now explained the manner in
which the value of commodities, or the
degree in which they form a portion of
individual riches, is affected ; *firft*, By
a diminution of the quantity of a commodity ; *fecondly*, By an increafe in its
quantity ; *thirdly*, By an increafe in the
demand for it ; and, *fourthly*, By a diminution of demand for it ; I proceed to
confider, what effect the alteration in the

order

order of the expenditure, (which a diminution or augmentation in the value of any
one commodity muſt produce), will, in each
of theſe events, occaſion on the ſum-total of
individual riches.

1. Of the Effects of the Alteration in the Order of Expenditure, occaſioned by a Diminution in the Quantity of any Commodity.

IF, in any ſociety, the quantity of ſugar,
as we have already ſuppoſed, be diminiſhed
from one thouſand pounds weight to five
hundred; ſhould the conjecture that has been
made, to wit, that this might increaſe the value of ſugar from L. 50 to L. 200, be accurate ; it would be, at firſt ſight, natural
to ſuppoſe, that the additional L. 150 worth
of commodities, now applied to the purchaſe of ſugar, which uſed to be employed
in the acquiſition of other articles, would
reduce the value of thoſe articles juſt as
much as the value of ſugar was, by this
means, increaſed ; and that, therefore, the
ſum-

fum-total of individual riches would remain the fame. But a little attention muft convince any one, after perufing the remarks which have been made on the confequence of alteration in demand, as well as on the effects of alteration in quantity, that this cannot be the cafe.

As the taftes of men, as well as their attachments to different habits, are various; if by any means they were induced to facrifice L. 150 worth of their other enjoyments to the acquifition of fugar, it is probable that they would obtain this extra fum by a diminution of confumption, more or lefs, of every commodity which forms a portion of individual riches.

With a view, however, to explain the effects of this derangement of expenditure, let us fuppofe that the taftes of men fhould lead them to procure the L. 150, the advanced fum we have fuppofed to be neceffary to obtain the five hundred pounds weight

weight of fugar, by transferring to the acquifition of fugar a part of the commodities which they formerly allotted to obtain the three articles of butchers-meat,
wine, and muftard ; and let us further fuppofe, that the confumers of fugar actually
withdrew L. 50 from the ufual expenditure in each of thefe articles.

If L. 50 worth of commodities ufually
allotted to the purchafe of butchers-meat,
was withdrawn from the acquifition of
that article, the demand for butchers-meat
muft be diminifhed, and the eftablifhed
proportions betwixt the demand for it
and the quantity of it, altered in fuch a
manner as to reduce its value. But we
have already fhewn, that a diminution
of demand for any commodity reduces
the price of the whole commodity, much
more than the fum which reprefents the a-
mount of the demand that is abftracted from
it ; and it is evident, that the natural avidity in the proprietors and retailers of but-
chers-

chers-meat, to acquire and confume the ufual quantities of commodities, which they were accuftomed to receive in exchange for this article, would, (as has been remarked in the cafe of the growers of fugar), induce them to force the market to fuch a degree, as to render L. 50 a very inadequate reprefentation of the total diminution of the value of all the butchersmeat in the market, which the abftracting of L. 50 worth of demand would create; for, in reality, the value of the butchers-meat would be thus diminifhed in a much larger fum.

It is obvious, too, that fimilar effects will be produced in the diminution of the value of muftard and of wine, by the fuppofed abftraction of L. 50 worth of commodities, which ufed to be appropriated to the purchafe of thofe articles.

The eagernefs of the growers and poffeffors of each of thefe articles, to attain as nearly

nearly as poffible the fame quantity of
commodities in exchange for it, muft, as in
every cafe of diminution of demand, reduce
the value of the article much more than
the amount of the value of the demand abftracted.   The effect, however, of abftracting L. 50 worth of demand from butchers-
meat, from wine, and from muftard, muft
be very various in degree; becaufe, abftracting a demand to the extent of L. 50,
muft produce a very different effect on the
proportion betwixt the demand for, and
the quantity of, each of thefe commodities.

It is plain that, whilft it might diminifh
the demand for muftard one-half, it might
perhaps abftract only a fifth of the demand
for wine ; whereas, in the cafe of the butchers-meat, it might probably annihilate
only a twentieth or a thirtieth of the ufual
demand : and as this would have very different effects in altering the proportion betwixt the quantity and the demand of each
of

of thefe articles, fo it muſt alter, in a very
different ratio, the value of a given quantity of each ; which has already been exemplified in the calculation quoted from
DAVENANT concerning the price of corn*.

2. *Of the Effeӕs of the Alteration in the Order
of Expenditure, occaſioned by an Increaſe of
Demand for any Commodity.*

As we already know, that an augmentation of demand, if it eſtabliſhes ſimilar proportions betwixt the demand for, and the
value of, any commodity, muſt produce ſimilar effeӕs upon the value of any portion of it; let us ſuppoſe, inſtead of the
ſupply of ſugar being reduced from one
thouſand pound weight to five hundred, that
the ſupply remaining the ſame, (to wit,
one thouſand pound weight), there ſhould
ariſe a ſudden demand for two thouſand
pound weight. On this ſuppoſition, if we
were right in conjeӕuring, that ſugar, by the
diminution

* See page 51.

diminution of the one-half of its quantity, would rife to eight fhillings a pound, fugar muft then alfo rife to the fame price, in confequence of the increafed demand; and the value of the whole one thoufand pound weight of fugar would of courfe be L. 400.

In this cafe, inftead of L. 150 worth of goods being abftracted from the acquifition of other commodities, it is evident the confu ers of fugar would be under the neceffity of abftracting L. 350 worth of articles, which they antecedently devoted to the acquifition of other enjoyments; and if we fuppofe their taftes, in like manner, to lead them to procure this fum, by curtailing their confumption of butchers-meat, wine and muftard, there would be, all at once, a deficiency in the ordinary demand for each of thefe articles to the extent of the third part of this L. 350; that is, to the extent of L. 116, 13 s. 4 d., which would produce a much more formidable diminution in the value

of

of butchers-meat, wine and muftard, than was occafioned by abftracting L. 50 worth of demand from each; and of courfe impoverifh, in a much greater degree, the proprietors of thofe articles.

It is extremely important here to obferve, that though, by this means, the mafs of individual riches would be much diminifhed, yet this laft hypothefis proceeds upon the idea that fugar, butchers-meat, wine and muftard, fhould all of them exift in the fame quantities; and, indeed, that the ftate of no one commodity whatever fhould be altered: that is, that the wealth of the nation fhould remain exactly the fame; the diminution of individual riches, being, in this inftance, alone created in confequence of a fuppofed change of tafte, which produces a fudden alteration in the demand for one commodity.

Further: though the confequences of this fudden demand for an increafed quantity of

of fugar, in reducing the value of butchers-meat, wine and muftard, of which
we have attempted to give a view, muft
have a confiderable effect on the diminution of the mafs of individual riches,
by its operation on the value of thefe three
articles ; its effects will not terminate here :
for the proprietors of butchers-meat, wine
and muftard, having, from the reduction of
the value of their property, lefs to beftow
on their different enjoyments, the demand
for other commodities muft be by this
means diminifhed, and that, in every cafe,
to a greater degree than the amount of the
fum which reprefents the demand abftracted ; for it is important always to recollect,
that every abftraction of demand muft produce a diminution in the fum-total of the
value of the commodity from which it is
abftracted, greater than is expreffed by the
fum abftracted.

It is on this principle, that a great and
fudden alteration of demand for any commodity

modity or clafs of commodities, has been always found to produce a fatal diminution of individual riches, though the wealth of the nation remains unaltered and unchanged : and this is a propofition the truth of which does not depend upon any theory. The merchants of this country have feverely felt it, both at the commencement of the laft, and of the prefent war *. It is the knowledge mercantile men derive from experience of the calamitous effects of a fudden alteration of demand, that leads them often to declare, (what, to thofe who have not ftudied the fubject, appears ridiculous), that they prefer even the calamities of continued warfare, with all its attendants, fuch

as

* The following ftatement of bankruptcies, taken from the London Gazette, feems to fhew, that the effects of this derangement of expenditure, is felt, more or lefs, at the commencement of every war.

	Bankruptcies.		Bankruptcies.		Bankruptcies.
In	1752, - 158	In	1774, - 360	In	1784, - 517
	1753, - 214		1778, - 675		1791, - 604
	1754, - 244		1779, - 544		1792, - 628
	1756, - 278		1780, - 449		1793, - 1304
	1757, - 274				

as advanced wages, increafed freights, and
infurances, to a fluctuation betwixt war
and peace ; and the theory here advanced
explains the grounds of the affertion.

Indeed, nothing can more forcibly illuftrate the truth of this doctrine, than the
events which happened at the commencement of the laft war. The fudden demand
for all thofe articles which warfare makes
neceffary abftracting a large portion of
the demand from the commodities prepared and preparing for the market, on the
fuppofition it was* to remain in the ufual
ftate, diminifhed thereby the value of the
commodities on hand to fuch a degree, that
the merchants and manufacturers were incapable of making good their engage-
ments.

In this fituation, Government aided the
mercantile intereft with loans of money, in
two hundred and thirty-eight different cafes,

fes, amounting in all nearly to two million two hundred thoufand pounds *. This empowered the merchants to retain their goods for a time; and as the quantity imported and manufactured was foon curtailed, in confequence of the effects of the war, the proportion came within a fhort time to be reftored betwixt the demand and the quantity, in fuch a manner, that the commodities refuming their former value, thofe who received affiftance were enabled to repay Government without any lofs : which was to be expected, becaufe, though the value of the commodities was diminifhed in confequence of the fudden alteration of demand, they remained in fubftance : the wealth of the nation was in fact nowife affected by it ; and the goods in hand were fure to refume their value, whenever, by the diminution of fupply, the proportion came to be reftored betwixt the

* The exact fum was L. 2,202,200.

the quantity of them and the demand for them *.

3. Of the Effects of the Alteration in the Order of Expenditure, occasioned by an Increase in the Quantity of any Commodity.

THE variation likely to be effected in the value of a commodity, by an increase of its quantity, has been already traced out and exemplified, by supposing the usual supply of sugar in any society to be at once increased from one to two thousand pound weight. The reduction of the value

---

* It is perhaps unfortunate, that the cause of this evil, as well as the mode in which the relief operated, never was sufficiently explained ; otherwise it would have been impossible that similar relief should have been refused at the commencement of the present war : because, as the evil originates with measures which Ministers think it necessary to take for the public safety, it is not alone views of expedience which ought to induce Government to aid the mercantile interest, for the merchants must appear to have in equity a right to such assistance.

lue of that article, which muſt naturally
enſue from the manner the growers of ſugar will be induced to preſs it on the market, in conſequence of their avidity to obtain the uſual quantity of the objects of
their deſire, has been pointed out; and it
appears obvious, that the conſequence of
thus reducing the ſum-total of commodities applicable to the acquiſition of ſugar, muſt be, that a part of what was formerly applied to the purchaſe of this article, becoming unappropriated, will remain
in the hands of the conſumers of ſugar, to
be uſed for the acquiſition of ſuch other
commodities as are moſt ſuitable to their
taſte.

For theſe articles, therefore, whatever
they may be, there muſt of courſe be an
additional demand; and the value of each
of them muſt riſe juſt in proportion, as more
or leſs of the goods formerly applied to the
acquiſition of ſugar, is now appropriated to
acquire that particular article.

Though

Though reafon teaches us that this muft be the cafe, it is not alone to be inferred from theory and fpeculation. In practice, the effect of a great increafe of the quantity of a commodity, in raifing the price of other commodities, has been long a matter of notoriety. It has been long a common and conftant remark of thofe who habitually attend to the value of public fecurities, that the price of ftock, in a fertile feafon, will ftand perceptibly higher, by two or three *per cent.*, than in a year of fcarcity.

Grain is, indeed, the article moft neceffary to man; and as mankind muft generally enjoy nearly a fufficiency of that on which their exiftence depends, a fudden increafe in the quantity of fuch an article, muft, as has been fhewn, produce a greater diminution in its value, than a proportionable increafe of quantity would produce in the value of articles of tafte; becaufe there is hardly a poffibility of conceiving a fudden fource of extended demand, and of

means

means of fatisfying that demand, for a
thing of which every man muft have nearly enough ; whereas, the reduction of value produced in articles of tafte, by a fimilar increafe of quantity, (which, after this
increafe, will ftill remain comparatively
fcarce), muft create new fources of demand
for them, long before their value can be
materially reduced.

The effect, therefore, of an increafe in
the quantity of grain, in raifing the price
of other commodities, muft be more eafily
perceived; but there is no commodity whatever, of which the quantity can be increafed fo as to diminifh its value, without occafioning an augmentation of the value of
fome other article.

4. *Of the Effects of the Alteration in the Order
    of Expenditure, occafioned by a Diminution
    of Demand for any Commodity.*

As there never exifts a defire, and confequently a demand, for any commodity,
but

but from the circumftance of its power to fatisfy either the appetite or tafte of mankind; fo there never exifts a diminution in the demand for any commodity, but— either in confequence of a rife in the value of fome other commodity, the full enjoyment of which man prefers, making it neceffary to abftract fome part of the commodities ufually appropriated to the acquifition of it, that by their means he may obtain, as nearly as poffible, his ufual quantity of the commodity he prefers;—or in confequence of fomething being difcovered better adapted to fatisfy the fame defires.

It appears, therefore, that the effects in the alteration of the order of expenditure occafioned by a *diminution* in the demand for any commodity, have been already confidered, and treated of under the head of the effects in the alteration of the order of expenditure occafioned by the *increafe* in the demand for any commodity.

This

This part of the fubject was there illuftrated, by pointing out the confequences of diminution of demand for the articles of butchers-meat, wine and muftard :
it is, therefore, here only neceffary to
repeat, that the effects in the diminution of
demand for any article, never terminate
by diminifhing the value of the commodity
in relation to which they take place ; becaufe, as the proprietor of that commodity
muft, by the diminution of its value, have
lefs to beftow on the acquifition of the various objects of defire he was accuftomed
to enjoy, fo a diminution in demand muft
alfo take place with regard to them ; and
the fame confequences muft, indirectly
through them, enfue with relation to other
commodities, which the poffeffor of this
laft clafs of goods was habituated to enjoy.

Though it feems eftablifhed by the fore-
going reafoning, that an augmentation in
the riches of individuals may be attended
with a diminution of the national wealth,
that

that the riches of individuals may be diminifhed by a nation's becoming more weal-
thy, and that, while the national wealth
remains unaltered in every particular, there
may be, from the circumftance of variation in demand, a diminution or augmentation in the fum-total of individual riches ;
(though, indeed, it can feldom happen that
an increafe of the one fhould produce a
fimilar increafe in the other) ; yet there
is a poffibility that the mafs of individual
riches may be fo increafed under fuch circumftances, that the increafe will indicate
a proportional augmentation of national
wealth.

Let us fuppofe, for inftance, that the fupply
of fugar fhould fuddenly increafe in any fociety ; for example, from one thoufand to
fifteen hundred pound weight ; and that the
demand fhould increafe in the fame proportion : let us further fuppofe, that every perfon who grew or fabricated any commodity with which fugar was purchafed, fhould
have,

have, in like manner, produced an extra quantity of various articles, for which the growers of fugar fhould have alfo a proportionably increafed demand. Then, as the hypothefis implies, that in every inftance there would be maintained the fame proportion which exifted antecedent to the increafe of production, both betwixt the quantity and demand for each of the commodities ufually facrificed to the acquifition of fugar, and betwixt the demand for, and quantity of, fugar itfelf; the increafe of value muft be, in fuch a cafe, exactly proportioned to the increafe of quantity: that is, the mafs of individual riches, and the wealth of the nation, will increafe in the fame proportion.

It follows then, that, when we come to examine whether the wealth of the nation will really be augmented by any propofed regulations, (as men are only interefted in foliciting legiflative arrangements in confequence

fequence of their effect in increafing individual riches), we muft confider :—

1. Whether that augmentation of individual riches is produced folely by the diminution of the quantity of any commodity.

2. Whether it is produced folely by an augmentation of demand for any commodity.

For, in the firft of thefe cafes, there muft of neceffity be a diminution of national wealth;—in the fecond, national wealth will neither be increafed nor diminifhed; and, in both cafes, though there will be an immediate increafe of individual riches, as far as the value of one commodity contributes; yet, in confequence of the derangement of expenditure, there will be a much greater diminution in the value of other commodities, and, of courfe, a great fall-
ing

ing off in the general mafs of individual riches.

If, however, we find, that the means propofed tend to increafe proportionably both the quantity of and the demand for any commodity, and at the fame time to create funds for the acquifition of this additional quantity, without diminifhing the demand for any other commodity, it may be then confidered as a propofition which will undoubtedly augment, in the fame proportion, both the riches of individuals and the wealth of the nation.

For example: if the fupply of fugar is increafed from one thoufand to fifteen hundred pound weight, and there fhould, that year, be produced by the confumers of fugar an extra quantity of grain, (for which the growers of fugar fhould have a demand), juft fufficient to pay for the increafed quantity of fugar, then, as the proportion betwixt the demand for and the quan

tity

tity of fugar would be preferved, notwithftanding the increafed fupply; and as the
proportion would be in like manner preferved in relation to grain, and nowife altered in any other commodity; the increafe of
individual riches would be in direct proportion to the increafe of the quantity of
grain and fugar : that is, public wealth and
individual riches would increafe in fimilar
proportions.

But if it fhould appear, that the means
propofed tend only to create a rife in the
demand and the quantity of one commodity,—of fugar for example; and that this
additional quantity of fugar is to be paid
for, by abftracting a portion of commodities from the acquifition of other objects of
defire; then the national wealth may indeed be increafed in the fame proportion
with individual riches in the fingle article
of fugar : that is, the quantity of fugar and
the value of it will increafe in the fame
proportion. But the diminution of demand
for

for other commodities, from the purchafe
of which there was abftracted that which is
now applied to the acquifition of the additional quantity of fugar, muft reduce the
price of them fo as to diminifh the mafs of
individual riches; becaufe, as has been already explained, the abftraction of demand to a
given amount always finks the value of the
commodity from whence the demand is
abftracted, to a much greater amount than
the value abftracted.

For inftance : if the growers of grain,
whom we fuppofe to have had a demand
for, and to have purchafed the increafed
quantity of, fugar, inftead of having an increafed quantity of grain to pay for it, had
paid for it by abftracting from the acquifition of butchers-meat, wine and muftard, a
quantity of grain which they formerly facrificed to the purchafe of thefe commodities; then the reduction of the price of thefe
articles, in confequence of the diminution
of demand for them, muft (notwithftanding

ing the national wealth and the mafs of riches are proportionably increafed in as far as fugar is concerned), occafion a diminution in the mafs of individual riches ; becaufe the diminution upon thofe articles muft be much greater than the increafe in the value of fugar.

The conclufion is therefore inevitable, that there exifts only one cafe, and that a very improbable one,—(to wit, when the quantity and the demand for any commodity are proportionally increafed, and funds at the fame time are created for the acquifition of the increafed quantity, as well as the fatisfaction of the increafed demand),—in which an increafe in the mafs of individual riches produces a fimilar effect on the wealth of the nation.

It is further neceffary to remark, that when variations in value, or in the mafs of individual riches, are created by alterations in the quantity of any commodity, the oppo-

fite

fite effect in all cafes immediately takes
place in public wealth. A diminution of
the value of a commodity, in confequence
of an alteration of its quantity, is an invariable fymptom of an immediate increafe
of its quantity ; and of courfe of an increafe
of public wealth : an augmentation of the
value of a commodity, in confequence of
an alteration of its quantity, is an invariable fymptom of an immediate diminution
of its quantity, and confequently of a diminution of public wealth.

But if there is a diminution in the value
of a commodity, in confequence of a variation in the demand for it, this is no fymptom of an immediate alteration in the
quantity of the commodity ; but it is a fure
prefage of future diminution of its quantity, and of courfe a diminution of public
wealth ; and if there is an augmentation in
the value of a commodity, in confequence
of an alteration in the demand for it, this
in like manner is no fymptom of an alteration

tion in the quantity of a commodity; though it is always followed by a reduction of its quantity, and of courfe by a reduction of public wealth.

A confirmation of the opinion, that private riches and public wealth can hardly ever increafe in fimilar proportions, is not, therefore, the only valuable information we derive from contemplating the variations which changes of quantity and of demand create, not only in the value of the commodities in which they take place, but alfo indirectly in that of all other commodities; and of courfe in the value of the mafs of what is annually produced by nature and art.

For, as exchangeable value (the poffeffion of which conftitutes any commodity a portion of individual riches), is, when accurately confidered, merely the practical means of expreffing the degree of defire for any particular article of wealth, it is alfo moft

material

material to obferve the forcible manner in
which, from this analyfis of the caufes of
variation in the value of commodities, it
appears, that demand muft at all times regulate both the quantity and quality of
what is produced.

Thus, when variations in value are created by an increafe of demand for any commodity, the induftry of the community is
not alone directed to increafe the production of that article, by the extraordi.ary
encouragement derived from its a ent-
ed value ; for a part of the induftry is at
the fame time called off from the for ation
and production of other articles, by the
difcouragement which a diminution in
their value creates ; a was exemplified in
the effects of an increafed demand for fugar in raifing the price of that article, and
in depreffing the value of wine, butchers-
meat and muftard, and confequently that
of various other articles.

                                    In

In like manner, when variation in value is occafioned by a diminution of demand, it difcourages the production of the commodity for which the demand is diminifhed, not alone by the great reduction of its value ; for, at the fame time, new and highly advantageous channels of induftry are pointed out for thofe who were employed in producing it, by the extenfion of demand for, and confequent rife in, the value of other commodities, which it has been made apparent muft take place.

It follows alfo from what has been ftated, that when variation of value is occafioned by alterations in the quantity of commodities, demand muft act with the fame compounded energy ; for, when the quantity of a commodity is increafed, the production of it is not alone difcouraged by the great diminution of its value, but the induftry of the community is at the fame time directed towards the formation of articles, to the acquifition of which thofe

goods

goods are applied, which have become unappropriated in confequence of the cheapnefs of the abundant commodity, whofe
value is now increafed by this additional
demand.

In like manner, when the quantity of
any commodity is diminifhed, demand operates in reftoring the ufual fupply, not only
from the encouragement it gives to thofe
who are concerned in producing that article, by the great rife in its value; but,
with augmented energy, from the circumftance, that the neceffary fall in the price
of other commodities calls off a portion of
induftry from the formation of them, whilft
it points it to the production of the article
whofe quantity is reduced.

CHAP.

CHAP. III.

OF THE SOURCES OF WEALTH.

THOUGH it may appear extraordinary, that the fources of wealth, which have been the object of much fpeculation, fhould not have been long ago accurately inveftigated and defined; it is neverthelefs certain, that there is no fubject on which there has exifted, and does exift, more marked variety of opinion.

Land, Labour and Capital are indeed the only fources to which the origin of any part of our wealth has ever been afcribed.

afcribed.   But while fome have eagerly
contended, that Land is the fole fource of
opulence, and that whatever is acquired
by Labour or Capital is derived from the
landholder, others have difcovered equal
anxiety to attribute the origin and increafe
of our wealth to Commerce and Manufactures ; that is, to the operation of Labour
and Capital.

That fyftem which reprefents the produce of land as the fole fource of the revenue, and the wealth of a nation *, has long
had its difciples in this country, who have
confidered the earth as the fountain of all
the riches and abundance of the world,
partly proceeding from its mines and its
fifheries ;

---

* This opinion is of very ancient date. It is faid to have
been a faying of ARTAXERXES, King of Perfia, That " the
" authority of the Prince muft be defended by a mili-
" tary force ; which force can only be maintained by
" taxes ; and all taxes muft, at laft, fall upon agriculture."
GIBBON's Hiftory, vol. 1. p. 256. 4to edit.

fifheries ; principally from what is nourifhed on its furface *.

“ What we call commodities," (fays an
ingenious author of the 17th century †), " is
" nothing but land fevered from the foil.
" Man deals in nothing but earth. The
" merchants are the factors of the world, to
" exchange one part of the earth for ano-
" ther. The King himfelf is fed by the
" labour of the ox ; and the clothing of the
" army, and victualling of the navy, muft all
" be paid for to the owner of the foil as the
" ultimate receiver. All things in the world
" are originally the produce of the ground,
" and there muft all things be raifed."

The

---

* See the Treafure of Traffic by LEWIS ROBERTS, 1641.
VANDERLINT's Effay to make Money plenty. Alfo, LOCKE
on lowering the Intereft, and raifing the Value of Money.

† Several Affertions proved, in order to create another
fpecies of Money than Gold, 1696.

The fyftem, on the other hand, which gives to commerce the pre-eminence as a fource of wealth, was for years the favourite, if not the eftablifhed doctrine, in this country *. Its followers held, that thofe nations who have no mines of gold and filver, have no means to get them but by foreign trade : that in proportion to the quantity of thofe metals which a nation can thus obtain, the prices of its commodities, the numbers of the people, and therewith the value of its land, rife and fall : that if the exports of a nation exceed the imports, foreigners muft pay the balance in treafure, and that the nation muft of courfe grow rich : that if, on the other hand, the imports exceed the exports, the balance muft be paid to foreigners in treafure, and the nation grow poor.

This laft opinion, though early oppofed by men of eminent talents, has long formed

the

* See Appendix, No. II.

the groundwork on which European legiflation has proceeded,—if we may judge
from the rules and regulations that it has
been the object of the Legiflature of this
country, as well as the laws of others, to
eftablifh.

Of late years, thefe opinions have been
reprobated by the Oeconomifts in France,
and by the Author of the Wealth of Nations in this country ; and the fallacious, as
well as the dangerous confequences of
them, have been expofed.   But though we
are indebted to Dr SMITH, and to that
fect of philofophers, for fetting afide a fyftem replete with error, we, unfortunately,
derive neither from the one nor the other
a fatisfactory folution of that moft important queftion in Political Oeconomy, What
are the fources of Wealth ?

The prejudices of mankind, with reafon,
(as we fhall have ample opportunity of
fhewing), revolt at the opinions maintained,

ed, with so much perseverance and ingenuity, by the followers of QUESNAY, which totally set aside labour and capital as sources
of wealth; and which regard that part of
the produce of the earth remaining after
payment of the total expences of culture,
as alone contributing to the wealth of a
nation: and we derive from Dr SMITH
no assistance in forming our opinions on
this important subject; for he seems to
have had no fixed ideas in relation to
it. Indeed, there is no opinion that has
been any where maintained on the subject
of the sources of national wealth, which
does not appear to have been adopted in
different parts of the Inquiry into the
Wealth of Nations.

1. " The annual labour of every nation
" is" at one time stated to be " the fund
" which originally supplies it with all the
" necessaries and conveniencies of life
" which it annually consumes, and which
" consists always either in the immediate
                                    " produce

" produce of that labour, or in what is pur-
" chafed with that produce from other na-
" tions *.

2. Lands, mines and fifheries, elfewhere,
are regarded as replacing " with a profit,
" not only the capitals employed on them,
" but all the other capitals employed in the
" community †." That, however, which,
replaces all the capitals employed in the
community, and is the fource from whence
they derive their profit, muft be the fole
fource of wealth. Mankind are, therefore,
here confidered as deriving the whole of
their wealth from land.

3. Again: plain reafon is ftated to dictate, that the real wealth of a country confifts in the annual produce of its land and
labour ‡; and this opinion, which coin-
cides

* Wealth of Nations, vol. 1. p. 1. 4to edit. This opinion
is maintained by Mr HUME. See his Difcourfe of Commerce, p. 12. edit. 1752.

† Wealth of Nations, vol. 1. p. 338. 4to edit.

‡ Ibid. vol. 1. p. 414.

cides with that of the Bifhop of Cloyne *,
and the learned Author † of the Effay on
Money and Coins, is moſt generally adhered to by Dr SMITH.

4. In another part of the work, however, we find it afferted, that " land
" and capital ſtock are the two original
" fources of all revenue, both private and
" public : capital ſtock pays the wages
" of productive labour, whether employ-
" ed in agriculture, manufactures or com-
" merce ‡." Land and capital are therefore here deemed the fole fources of wealth;
and labour is confidered as deriving from
them

* Queriſt. Quer. 4. " Whether the four elements, and
" man's labour therein, be not the true fource of wealth."

† " Land and labour together are the fources of all
" wealth. Without a competency of land, there would be
" no fubfiftence ; and but a very poor and uncomfortable
" one without labour. So that *wealth* or *riches* confiſt either
" in a property in land, or in the products of land and la-
" bour."

‡ Wealth of Nations, vol. II. p. 560. 4to edit.

them its wages, without adding to the opulence of the community.

5. Lastly, We are taught to consider land, labour and capital, as being, all three, sources of wealth; for we are told, that " whoever derives his revenue from a fund that " is his own, must draw it either from his " labour, his stock, or his land. The revenue " derived from labour is called Wages; that " from stock Profit; and from land Rent *;" an opinion which seems to have been hinted at by Sir WILLIAM PETTY †, when he stated it as an impediment to the wealth of England, that taxes were not levied upon lands, stock and labour, but chiefly upon land alone; though land and labour are generally considered by that ingenious writer as the sole sources of wealth ‡.

In

---

* Wealth of Nations, vol. 1. p. 63. 4to edit.

† Tracts, Edit. 1768, p. 268.

‡ " Labour is the father and active principle of wealth, " as lands are the mother." Treatise on Taxes and Contributions, 1667, 4to edit. p. 47.

In treating of Political Oeconomy, the ſcience which profeſſes to diſplay and to teach the means of increaſing the wealth of a ſtate, it would ſeem that the firſt and moſt anxious object of inquiry ought to have been, What wealth is, and from what ſources mankind derive it? for it appears impoſſible to diſcuſs with preciſion the means of increaſing any thing, without an accurate notion of its nature and of its origin. Yet, if we reject the doctrine of the Oeconomiſts, it is in vain we look for a decided and preciſe opinion upon the origin of wealth, in any modern work on public œconomy; and it is impoſſible not to think, that the anxiety of the œconomiſts to overthrow that ſyſtem, which regards commerce as the ſole ſource of opulence, has led them, in rejecting labour and capital as original ſources of wealth, beyond the bounds that reaſon authoriſes.

The liberal doctrines to which this theory led, by inculcating the impropriety of all

all legiflative reftraints, or interference in commercial tranfaction, muft command approbation; but they are nowife inconfiftent with the opinion we fhall endeavour to eftablifh, that land, labour and capital are, all three, original fources of wealth; that each has its diftinct and feparate fhare, (which it is moft neceffary fhould be defined and underftood), in the formation of thofe objects which are defirable to man, and which have been fhewn to conftitute his wealth.

Though thefe three original fources of wealth, in the various ftates of exiftence in which hiftory difplays man, contribute to his wealth in very different proportions, yet in every ftate of fociety in which he is known to exift, each, more or lefs, affords its fhare.

Confumption, moft undoubtedly, muft always precede production; but, long before man cultivated the earth as a means of procuring

procuring his fubfiftence, he muft have derived his wealth from all of thefe fources. To
appropriate the fruit of a tree or an animal
for food, he muft have, in a certain degree,
laboured; and it will be fhewn, that the firft
ftick or ftone he took into his hand to aid
and affift him in procuring thofe objects,
by performing a portion of his labour, fulfilled the fame duty in which every branch
of the capital of a mercantile nation is now
engaged.

1. *Of Land, including Mines and Fifheries, as
a Source of National Wealth.*

In the earlieft ftages of fociety, men acquire that portion of wealth they derive
from the furface of the earth, in the fame
manner as, in every ftage of fociety, they
attain that part of their wealth which proceeds from the ocean. Their exertions
are not made to increafe the quantity,
but to appropriate and adapt for ufe
                                        the

the portions of thofe things nature has
formed, for which their wants and their
appetites give them a defire.

In this ftate of his exiftence, therefore,
man derives a greater proportion of what
forms his wealth from land than in fubfequent ftages of fociety, when the aid of labour and capital are called in, not only to
appropriate and render fit for ufe, but to me-
liorate the quality, and increafe the quantity of thofe commodities for which his defires create a demand.

This, however, is but of fhort continu-
ance ; for nature, whilft fhe has implanted
in him the feeds of an unbounded variety of
defires, has every where fcattered, with fo
fparing a hand, the means of fatisfying them,
that the affiftance of labour and capital is
early called in to perform the moft important duty allotted to them through any ftage
of

of fociety, that of increafing the quantity of
thofe productions of nature which form the
objects of our defire; and from that moment, the natural produce of the earth gives
way to thofe productions, which the induftry of man, by improvement in cultivation,
procures in augmented quantity and fuperior quality.

In treating of the increafe of wealth, therefore, we fhall again be called upon to confider this fubject. At prefent it is only neceffary to obferve, that, with the fingle exception of the œconomical fyftem long prevalent in France, every thing ufeful to man,
produced by land, whether fpontaneoufly
or extracted by art, has been deemed, under
all fyftems of political œconomy, to add to
the wealth of a country.

It was, indeed, the principal tenet of the
œconomifts, that the earth is the fole fource
of riches, which are multiplied by agriculture;

culture * ; but, by a ſtrange mode of reaſoning, they exclude that part of the produce of the earth which is reſerved for
feed, and for furniſhing the nouriſhment of
the cultivator, from forming any portion
of national wealth †. This part of the
produce

* *Que le Souverain et la Nation ne perdent jamais de vue, que la terre eſt l'unique ſource des richeſſes, et que c'eſt l'agriculture que les multiplie.* " Let the Sovereign and the Nation con-
" ſtantly keep in view, that the earth is the ſole ſource of
" riches; and that agriculture is what multiplies them."
Maxime économique d'un royaume agricole. Phyſiocratie, p. 107.

† *Il y en a environ la moitié qui ſe conſomme immédiatement et en nature chez les cultivateurs. On ne peut donc imputer à cette moitié, qui n'eſt pas commerçable, ni l'augmentation des prix, ni l'augmentation des dépenſes cauſée par le renchériſſement. Ainſi elle ne doit pas entrer dans le calcul du changement de prix dont il s'agit ici, puis qu'elle n'entre pas dans le commerce, et que la conſommation qui en eſt faite conſtamment chez les cultivateurs, n'augmente ni ne diminue, dans les changemens du prix, les frais d'exploitation de la culture.* " About one-half (of what is produ-
" ced) is conſumed immediately, in the nouriſhment
" of the cultivators. To that half, then, which is not the
" ſubject of traffic, cannot be imputed the augmentation
" either of the value, or of the expenditure, occaſioned by
" the riſe of price. Accordingly, it ought not to enter
" into

produce was by them deemed neceffary to
fecure the production of future wealth, and,
to ufe their own language, they regard it
not as wealth, but as a machine that muft
be carefully preferved, for the continual reproduction of wealth *.

So thoroughly do this fect of Philofophers attach their idea of public wealth to
what conftitutes the mafs of individual
riches, that it is another of their maxims to
confider

" into the calculation of the change of value, which is
" the thing at prefent in queftion ; fince it is not the fub-
" ject of commerce, and fince the confumption of it, which
" conftantly takes place among the cultivators, neither
" augments nor diminifhes, by alteration of price, the ex-
" pence of improvement and cultivation." *Phyfiocratie,*
p. 188.

* *Les avances de l'agriculture d'un royaume, doivent être en-
vifagées comme un immeuble, qu'il faut conferver précieufement pour
la production de l'impôt, du revenue, et de la fubfiftance de toutes les
claffes de citoyens.* " The advances made in the cultivation
" of a kingdom ought to be confidered as an invariable
" quantity, which muft be carefully preferved for the pro-
" duction of the impofts, of the revenue, and of the fub-
" fiftence of every clafs of citizens." *Phyfiocratie,* p. 109.

confider the cheapnefs of the production of the earth as of no advantage to the people *. For they deem the revenue that is the wealth of the country, to be great in proportion as the value of the productions of the earth are high. Abundance, and high price, are, according to them, equally neceffary to form wealth † ;—two things Monfieur QUESNAY, had he underftood the nature of value, would have known to be no more capable of co-exiftence than heat and cold.

It is, however, this idea which appears to make them exclude that part of the produce

---

* *Le bon marché des denrées n'eft pas avantageux au petit peuple.* " The cheapnefs of commodities is not advantageous to the " common people." *Phyfiocratie,* p. 162.

† *Telle eft la valeur vénale, tel eft le revenu. Abondance et non valeur n'eft pas richeffe. Difette et cherté eft mifere. Abondance et cherté eft opulence.* " The revenue is always great in pro- " portion as the exchangeable value of commodities is " high. Abundance and cheapnefs do not conftitute riches. " Scarcity and dearth are mifery. Abundance and dear- " nefs are opulence." *Phyfiocratie,* p. 116.

produce of the earth which is applicable to feed and the nourifhment of the cultivator, from forming a part of national wealth. They confidered it as an invariable quantity, which can never be brought into the market; which could not of courfe influence price ; which they did not, therefore, deem a portion of wealth or riches,—two things they viewed invariably as one and the fame.

Even on their own principles, they are obvioufly fo far wrong, as they exclude what is appropriated to the nourifhment of the cultivator; for it is the feed alone that can by poffibility be deemed an invariable quantity, as, undoubtedly in practice, fcarcity, which always increafes price, forms an encouragement to the cultivator to fell ; and thus diminifhes what is appropriated for his fuftenance, in the fame manner as it does that of any other labourer.

It muft be remarked, too, that it is an undeniable

undeniable inference from this doctrine,
(which excludes the part of the produce applicable to feed and the fuſtenance of the
cultivator from forming a part of national
wealth), that the more you can reduce the
maintenance of the huſbandman,—as the
more will remain to be carried to the market, and of courſe to the account of net
produce, ſo the greater muſt be the national wealth. Thus the wealth of the
nation is made to depend upon depriving
the moſt important claſs of its inhabitants
of a part of the objects of their deſire.

But it does not ſeem to require much argument to ſet aſide this opinion. If the
diſtinction betwixt public wealth and private riches is founded in truth; if wealth
has been rightly defined to conſiſt of all
thoſe objects for which men poſſeſs a deſire, it is impoſſible to diſcover why that
which is applicable to the ſatisfaction of
the deſires of the huſbandman, ſhould not
as truly form a portion of our wealth, as
that

that which is fubfervient to the defires of
any other labourer. Neither can we, with
any propriety, exclude that part of the annual produce referved for feed, from forming a portion of wealth, merely becaufe it
is not employed in fatisfying our immediate defires, but is devoted to the formation of that which is to adminifter to them
at a more remote period.

It is on thefe grounds that the whole of
the fruits of the earth, as well as the produce of mines and fifheries, muft be confidered as component parts of public wealth.

2. *Of Labour, as a Source of Wealth.*

THAT fpecies of labour which has been
defcribed as employed in meliorating the
quality, and increafing the quantity, of the
natural produce of the furface of the earth,
has univerfally been confidered and acknowledged as a fource of wealth. That it

is

is pre-eminently fo, cannot be doubted by any one who reflects on the quantity of food and materials for clothing, that art enables man to extract from a very fmall part of the furface of the earth; and compares it with what nature any where affords. What a contraft betwixt the fituation of the folitary favage, who, with difficulty, extracts his maintenance from a diftrict around him; and that of a peafant in a cultivated country, who draws from a few fields wherewithal to maintain many of his own fpecies! The inhabitant of the country of the Iroquois, or of any other American nation, who lives on the produce of the chace, can hardly be fuppofed to collect his food from a range of lefs than fifty acres; whilft, in China, the rice field is fuppofed to yield three crops a-year, each returning one hundred fold, producing on fifty acres nourifhment fufficient for five hundred peafants.

In the vicinity of London, we know that the value of the produce of an acre under garden

garden culture, may be moderately calculated at L. 200 *. Thus the produce of
fifty acres, hardly fufficient in a ftate of
nature to furnifh the precarious fuftenance
of a poor American, becomes competent to
enable an inhabitant of this country to enjoy all the refinements of European luxury.

Notwithftanding the fuperiority which
the labour of the hufbandman enjoys over
that of all other labourers in the production

---

* The following eftimate was made by a gardener who
occupied nine acres fituated about two miles farther from
market, as his opinion of the produce of the foil at the
Neat-houfes before mentioned, to wit,

The radifhes, - - -	L. 10
Cauliflowers, frequently L. 70 or more, but fay	60
Cabbages, - - - -	30
Celery, the firft crop not unfrequently upwards	
of L. 60, but fay - - -	50
Endive, - - - -	30
Celery, fecond crop, - - -	40
	L. 220

This he ftated as an eftimate rather under the mark. MID-
DLETON's Report on the County of Middlefex, p. 264. See
alfo p. 267.

duction of national wealth, it does not appear that every other species of labour can with justice or propriety be considered as totally unproductive. This opinion, however, is expressly maintained by the œconomists, who hold that even the labour of the artificer and the manufacturer is totally unproductive. These philosophers uniformly regard a thing as wealth in proportion to its value *.   Arguing on this principle, they assume (what in none of their writings they prove), that the value added by the manufacturer to the raw material, during his day's work, is exactly equal to the value of the food, clothing, &c. he has consumed ; and then they infer (what, if they are right in this assumption, is undoubted), that during the course of the day

he

---

* *Posons maintenant en principe, que la valeur vénale est la base de toute richesse, que son accroissement est accroissement de richesse.*
" Let us lay down as a principle, that value in exchange
" is the basis of wealth, and that its increase constitutes an
" increase of wealth." *Philosophie Rurale, ou Economie Générale et Politique de l'Agriculture.*   See also note, p. 127.

he can have added nothing of value to the
ftock of the nation.

The ingenious men, who hold thefe
opinions, diftinguifhed for a clofe, fubtile
and nervous manner of maintaining them,
have not, with all their ingenuity, done fo
much to fupport this doctrine, as the Author of the Wealth of Nations, by the
manner he has attempted to refute it.

" The capital error of this fyftem," fays
Dr Smith, " feems to lie in its reprefenting
" the clafs of artificers, manufacturers and
" merchants, as altogether barren and un-
" productive. The following obfervations
" may ferve to fhew the impropriety of
" this reprefentation.

" 1. This clafs, it is acknowledged, re-
" produces annually the value of its own
" annual confumption, and continues, at
" leaft the exiftence of the ftock or capital
" which maintains and employs it. But upon
" this

" this account alone the denomination of
" barren or unproductive fhould feem to be
" very improperly applied to it. We fhould
" not call a marriage barren or unproduc-
" tive, though it produced only *a fon and a*
" *daughter, to replace the father and mother ;*
" and though it did not increafe the num-
" ber of the human fpecies, but only conti-
" nued it as it was before. Farmers and
" country labourers, indeed, over and above
" the ftock which maintains and employs
" them, reproduce annually a neat produce,
" a free rent to the landlord. As a mar-
" riage which affords three children, is cer-
" tainly more productive than one which
" affords only two ; fo the labour of farm-
" ers and country labourers is certainly
" more productive than that of merchants,
" artificers and manufacturers. The fupe-
" rior produce of the one clafs, however,
" does not render the other barren or un-
" productive*." Now this comparifon really appears, inftead of a refutation, to be a
confirmation

* Wealth of Nations, vol. ii. p. 272. 4to edit.

confirmation of the doctrine of the œconomifts ; and even to carry along with it
an avowal of the opinion, that manufacturing labour is not productive of an increafe of wealth.

A marriage which only produces two,
cannot increafe the numbers of the human
fpecies ; for thefe two (as is obferved) can
only fupply the places of the father and
mother. The inference, therefore, appears
to be, that as fuch a marriage can only
continue, and nowife contribute to the increafe of, the human fpecies, fo manufacturing labour, as the œconomifts ftrictly
hold, can only preferve the wealth of the
nation undiminifhed, notwithftanding the
confumption of the manufacturer ; but can
nowife contribute to its increafe.

" 2. It feems, upon this account, alto-
" gether improper to confider artificers,
" manufacturers and merchants, in the
" fame light as menial fervants. The la-
" bour

" bour of menial fervants does not conti-
" nue the exiftence of the fund which
" maintains and employs them. Their
" maintenance and employment is altoge-
" ther at the expence of their mafters, and
" the work which they perform is not of a
" nature to repay that expence. That work
" confifts in fervices which perifh general-
" ly in the very inftant of their perform-
" ance, and does not fix or realize itfelf in
" any vendible commodity which can re-
" place the value of their wages and main-
" tenance. The labour, on the contra-
" ry, of artificers, manufacturers and mer-
" chants, naturally does fix and realize it-
" felf in fome fuch vendible commodity.
" It is upon this account, that in the chap-
" ter in which I treat of productive and
" unproductive labour, I have claffed arti-
" ficers, manufacturers and merchants, a-
" mong the productive labourers, and me-
" nial fervants among the barren or un-
" productive *."

Here,

* Wealth of Nations, vol. ii. p. 273. 4to edit.

Here, without stating any further objection to the opinion that is meant to be refuted, the outline is given of that distinction betwixt productive and unproductive labour, which is maintained by the Author; the merits of which must be considered in the proper place.

" 3. It seems upon every suppofition im-
" proper to say, that the labour of artifi-
" cers, manufacturers and merchants, does
" not increase the real revenue of the fo-
" ciety. Though we should suppofe, for
" example, as it seems to be suppofed in
" this system, that the value of the daily,
" monthly and yearly confumption of this
" class, was exactly equal to that of its
" daily, monthly and yearly production;
" yet it would not from thence follow, that
" its labour added nothing to the real re-
" venue, to the real value of the annual
" produce of the land and labour of the fo-
" ciety.   An artificer, for example, who,
" in the first six months after harvest, exe-
" cutes L. 10 worth of work, though he
                              " should,

" fhould, in the fame time, confume L. 10
" worth of corn and other neceffaries, yet
" really adds the value of L. 10 to the an-
" nual produce of the land and labour of
" the fociety. While he has been confuming
" a half-yearly revenue of L. 10 worth
" of corn and other neceffaries, he has pro-
" duced an equal value of work, capable of
" purchafing either to himfelf, or to fome
" other perfon an equal half-yearly reve-
" nue. The value, therefore, of what has
" been confumed and produced during thefe
" fix months, is equal, not to L. 10, but to
" L. 20. It is poffible, indeed, that no more
" than L. 10 worth of this value may ever
" have exifted at any one moment of time.
" But if the L. 10 worth of corn, and other
" neceffaries which were confumed by the
" artificer, had been confumed by a foldier
" or by a menial fervant, the value of that
" part of the annual produce which exifted
" at the end of the fix months, would have
" been L. 10 lefs than it actually is in con-
" fequence of the labour of the artificer.
                                    " Though

" Though the value of what the artificer
" produces, therefore, fhould not, at any
" one moment of time, be fuppofed greater
" than the value he confumes, yet at every
" moment of time, the actually exifting va-
" lue of goods in the market, is, in confe-
" quence of what he produces, greater than
" it otherwife would be *."

The wealth of the nation is undoubtedly
greater, at every moment of time, than it
would be if the manufacturer was fuppofed
to confume, without working, or adding
any value to the raw material; but on the
hypothefis here ftated, that the workman,
in the firft fix months after harveft, fhould
execute L. 10 worth of work, and that in
the fame time he fhould confume L. 10
worth of corn and other neceffaries, as he
has fubtracted from the national capital a
fum equal to that which he has added to it,
if wealth is regarded as dependent on exchangeable value, it is difficult to perceive
how he fhould be deemed to have increafed

* Wealth of Nations, ubi fupra.

fed the national ftock by fuch an exiftence.

Triumphantly, however, as this leading
tenet of the œconomifts feems to have with-
ftood this attack, it is impoffible to fubfcribe to the opinion, that the labour of the
manufacturer and the artift are totally unproductive of wealth.

There are two modes of viewing this
fubject.   Wealth may be regarded as conftituted by price or exchangeable value; or
it may be viewed in the real light in which
it ought to be confidered, as confifting in
the abundance of the objects of man's defire.

If we regard wealth to be conftituted by
exchangeable value, and agree in the maxim, that value is the bafis of all riches,
and that an increafe of value is an increafe
of riches, there feems to be an end of the
queftion; for, in that view of the fubject,

it

it is as impoſſible to contend, that the labour
of the manufacturer or artiſt does not add
ſomething to the wealth of the nation, as
it is impoſſible to believe that a painter,
whoſe works have ſold for thouſands of
pounds, and the value of which has been
known to have increaſed for a century after
his death, added nothing more to the value
of the canvas than the value of his ſuſte-
nance, and an equivalent for the expence
of his education.

If, on the other hand, wealth is conſidered as it ought to be, as conſiſting of the
greateſt poſſible abundance of the objects of
men's deſires, this queſtion requires a little
further inveſtigation.

It may be ſaid, that abundance, in proportion to demand, according to this opinion, conſtitutes wealth; but that abundance, in proportion to demand, muſt always diminiſh price. It may even be ſaid,
that it has been explained, how, if puſhed

to

to an extreme, it muft extinguifh value; that
as long, however, as exchangeable value exifts unextinguifhed by public opulence, the
loweft poffible price of all the productions of
art muft be the fuftenance of the artift; for
without receiving this he could not exift:
and it may be alleged, that, on this principle, it therefore feems, that the wages
which denote the greateft degree of public
opulence in works of art, are thofe which
equal in value the fubfiftence of the artift.

The value really added by the manufacturer to the raw material, in the prefent
ftate of things, is, in this view of the fubject, conceived to proceed from the fcarcity of manufacturing fkill. Like the price of
monopoly, it is the higheft that can be got.
The talent of the artift being rare, from
the fmall number of them that arrive at
perfection in the arts, is fuppofed to impofe
a tax upon the public, which would not exift if the nation had a greater number of
artifts; that is, if it poffeffed greater opulence

lence in them : and it is undoubtedly true, that it is poffible to imagine talents fo multiplied, and the number of artifts fo abundant, as to reduce the wages of painters and fculptors to be no more than what is equivalent to their fuftenance ; and that, in this ftate, a nation would enjoy the greateft poffible degree of opulence in the productions of art, confiftent with the existence of exchangeable value.

But this is, unfortunately, a fituation which can exift only in imagination. The monopoly arifing from fkill, talent, and genius, is not an evil proceeding from the abfurd regulations of man; it is ftamped on the human fpecies by the hand of nature, and muft exift as long as genius adorns the world.

There is great difference in the value of land. One field poffeffes much more intrinfic fertility than another ; and it is true, that if a happy convulfion of nature, was at once to render the whole face of the earth equally fertile, we fhould ceafe to remark on the fertility

fertility of that favourite fpot, on the fame principle that we fhould ceafe to value the labour of the manufacturer and the artift, if he was equalled in fkill, tafte and dexterity, by every common labourer. But as long as the world remains conftituted as it is, we muft continue to admire the fertility of the field, and to confider the labour of the manufacturer and the artift as productive.

It muft alfo be remarked that, even if the nature of things were fo far altered that the works of the manufacturer and artift fhould become fo abundant in proportion to the demand for them as univerfally to reduce the wages of manufacturers and artifts to what in value was merely equivalent to their fuftenance, (if wealth truly confifts in the abundance of the objects of man's defire), we fhould be obliged, as long as the love of conveniency and tafte is incident to mankind, to confider the manufacturer and artift as productive labourers,

on

on the fame principle that we have regarded water as an article of public wealth.

In truth, it is only from the circumftance
of confounding wealth and riches, and confidering wealth, in the courfe of their reafoning, at one time as depending on exchangeable value, and at another as conftituted by
the abundance of the objects of man's defire,
that this doctrine of the œconomifts can
for a moment be maintained. For fuppofing that an artift or manufacturer added
only the value of his maintenance to the
raw material, if wealth is to be underftood
in its true fenfe, his labour, even in this
cafe, muft be confidered as productive
of wealth. The nourifhment on which
he fubfifts is wealth, becaufe it is an object
of man's defire. In fatisfying the defire of
the labourer, it has fulfilled the duty it is
deftined to perform; whilft, on the other
hand, by the form given to the raw material
by his induftry, a diftinct portion of wealth
remains ready, to fatisfy the defire of fome
other

other individual : fo that, admitting that at no one period there exifted, in confequence of his induftry, an additional value, ftill it is evident that, in confequence of the induftry of the manufacturer, there is a portion of defire fatisfied, and of courfe a portion of wealth created, which would not otherwife have exifted.

Thefe philofophers hold, (and it is a necef-fary inference from their doctrine), that it is immaterial to a country whether a web of cloth is exported in exchange for foreign commodities, or whether the fame commodities are acquired by exporting the wool of which the cloth is made, and the food on which the weaver has exifted. Nay, they even conceive, that the exportation of the raw materials is the moft advantage-ous *. There is obvioufly, however, a mate-

rial

* *Si l'on confidere fimplement le commerce d'exportation dans un royaume agricole, qui peut devenir d'un grand commerce exteri-eur des denrées du cru, lequel doit être favorifé preferablement à tout autre.*" " If one confiders merely the commerce of
" exportation

rial difference; for, in the former cafe, the country acquires as much of foreign commodity as in the latter; and, befides that, one of its inhabitants is maintained: that is, he has enjoyed his fhare of national wealth, by obtaining the objects of his defire.

By the Author of the Wealth of Nations, the manufacturer and the artift are indeed admitted to be productive labourers; and, in this refpect the diftinction he makes betwixt productive and unproductive labour, is lefs repugnant to the prevalent opinions of men; but a little examination will fhew that it is not more confonant to reafon.

He confiders as unproductive labourers all thofe whofe " fervices perifh in the very " inftant of their performance, and does " not fix or realize itfelf in any vendible " commodity,

" exportation in an agricultural kingdom, that can ac-
" quire a great external commerce, by difpofing of its
" raw materials, which ought to be favoured in preference
" of every other fpecies of commerce." *Philofophie Ru-rale*, p. 371.

" commodity, which can replace the value " of their wages and maintenance *." Productive labour, on the contrary, he defcribes as " fixing and realizing itfelf in fome par- " ticular fubject and vendible commodity. " It is as it were a certain quantity of la- " bour ftocked and ftored up, to be em- " ployed, if neceflary, upon fome other oc- " cafion. That fubject, or, which is the " fame thing, the price of that fubject, can " afterwards, if neceflary, put into motion " a quantity of labour equal to that which " had originally produced it †."

Unfortunately, however, a little confideration makes this diftinction appear nowife founded on the nature of labour, but merely dependant upon the ufe that is made of its produce. Thus the fame labour may appear either productive or unproductive,
according

---

* Wealth of Nations, vol. ii. p. 273. 4to edit.

† Ibid. vol. i. p. 401.

according to the ufe fubfequently made of
the commodity on which it was beftowed.
If my cook, for example, makes a tart which
I immediately confume, he is confidered as
an unproductive labourer; and the act of
making the tart as unproductive labour;
becaufe *that fervice has perifhed at the moment of its performance;* but if the fame
labour is performed in a paftry cook's
fhop, it becomes productive labour, becaufe
*it is a quantity of labour ftocked and ftored up,
to be employed, if neceffary, upon fome other occafion; the price of it, if neceffary, can afterwards put into motion a quantity of labour
equal to that which had originally produced it.*   Again: A piece of cloth burnt
immediately after it was formed, would
inevitably beftow, according to this definition, the character of unproductive on
the labour of the cloth-manufacturer. Thus
a tart being placed in a cook's fhop, would
give to the labour of the cook the character of productive, and the cloth being put

in

in the fire, beftows that of unproductive on the labour of the manufacturer.

This extraordinary diftinction, founded on the mere durability of the fervices performed, claffes as unproductive labourers fome of thofe who are occupied in rendering the moft important fervices to fociety. Thus the Sovereign, and all who are employed in the maintenance of the religion, the juftice, or the defence of the ftate, as well as thofe whofe fkill and care are occupied in fuperintending the health and education of the fociety, are alike deemed unproductive labourers *

If exchangeable value is to be confidered as the bafis of wealth,—it is needlefs to ufe much argument to explain the errors of this doctrine. The practice of mankind, in eftimating thefe fervices, if we

can

* Wealth of Nations, vol. 1. p. 401. 4to edit.

can judge by what is paid for them, bears fufficient teftimony of its inaccuracy.

If, on the other hand, wealth is regarded in its true light, as confifting of the abundance of the objects of man's defire, it is impoffible to difcern why that fhould not be confidered as wealth which tends to the fatisfaction of man's immediate defires, as well as that which is ftocked and ftored up for the fatisfaction of his future defires; and, in truth, there is no one who has cri-ticifed the diftinction, which refts the va-lue of commodities on their durability, with greater acrimony than the perfon who wifhes to make the diftinction betwixt pro-ductive and unproductive labour depend merely upon the duration of its produce. " We do not (fays he) reckon that trade dif-" advantageous, which confifts in the ex-" change of the hardware of England for the " wines of France, and yet hardware is a very " durable commodity, and was it not for " this continual exportation, might, too, be " accumulated

" accumulated for ages together, to the in-
" credible augmentation of the pots and
" pans of the country *." Again : It is a
lofing trade, it is faid, " which a workman
" carries on with the ale-houfe ; and the
" trade which a manufacturing nation
" would naturally carry on with a wine
" country, may be confidered as a trade of
" the fame nature. I anfwer, That the
" trade with the ale-houfe is not neceffari-
" ly a lofing trade †."

It appears, therefore, impoffible to contend, that the labour of the manufacturer
and artift, or even the labour of that clafs
whofe fervices perifh at the moment, are
not, as well as that of the hufbandman, to
be confidered as productive of wealth. The
comparative degree of utility of different
defcriptions of labour in producing wealth,
is a fubject which will be more properly
difcuffed in treating of the means of increafing wealth.

3. Of

* Wealth of Nations, vol. ii. p. 15. 4to edit.
† Ibid. p. 80.

3. *Of Capital, as a Source of Wealth.*

In treating of land as a fource of wealth, it was unneceffary to enter into any difcuffion of the means by which it contributes towards the public ftock. Thefe it evidently derives from the produce of Mines and Fifheries, and from the materials for food and clothing that abound on the face of the earth. This difcuffion was equally unneceffary in treating of labour as a fource of wealth. It is clear, that the labour of the hufbandman contributes to the formation of wealth, by means of the increafed fertility he creates; and though it has been difputed whether the manufacturer and menial fervant produce wealth, by adapting and preparing the raw material for our convenient confumption, yet it is felf-evident, that if they increafe the wealth of the nation, it is by giving form to the raw material, and preparing it for ufe.

By

By what means Capital or Stock contributes towards wealth is not fo apparent. What is the nature of the profit of ftock? and how does it originate? are queftions the anfwers to which do not immediately fuggeft themfelves. They are, indeed, queftions that have feldom been difcuffed by thofe who have treated on political œconomy; and, important as they are, they feem nowhere to have received a fatisfactory folution.

The Author of the Wealth of Nations appears to confider the profit of ftock, as paid out of, and therefore derived from, the value added by the workman to the raw material. He ftates, that—" As foon " as ftock has accumulated in the hands of " particular perfons, fome of them will na- " turally employ it in fetting to work in- " duftrious people, whom they will fupply " with materials and fubfiftence, in order " to make a profit by the fale of their " work, or by what their labour adds to
" the

" the value of the materials.   In exchan-
" ging the complete manufacture, either
" for money, for labour, or for other goods,
" over and above what may be fufficient
" to pay the price of the materials, and
" the wages of the workmen, fomething
" muft be given for the profits of the un-
" dertaker of the work who hazards his
" ftock in this adventure.   The value
" which the workmen add to the mate-
" rials, therefore, refolves itfelf, in this
" cafe, into two parts, of which the one
" pays their wages, the other the profits of
" their employer upon the whole ftock of
" materials and wages which he advan-
" ced *," And again, " The labour of a
" manufacturer adds generally to the value
" of the materials which he works upon,
" that of his own maintenance and of his
" mafter's profit †."
                                            Above

* Wealth of Nations, vol. i. p. 57. 4to edit.

† Ibid. p. 400. The following paffage alfo clearly fhows
that Dr SMITH thought the profit of ftock was a value added
                                            by

Above a century ago, Mr LOCKE ſtated pretty nearly the ſame opinion. " Land" (ſays he) " produces naturally ſomething " new and profitable, and of value to man- " kind; but money is a barren thing and " produces nothing; but by compact trans- " fers that profit that was the reward of " one man's labour into another man's " pocket *."

If this, however, was a juſt and accurate idea of the profit of capital, it would fol- low

by the labourer: " The ſtock which is lent at intereſt is " always confidered as a capital by the lender. He ex- " pects that in due time it is to be reſtored to him, and " that in the mean time the borrower is to pay him a " certain annual rent for the uſe of it. The borrower may " uſe it either as a capital, or as a ſtock referved for " immediate confumption. If he uſes it as a capital, he " employs it in the maintenance of productive labourers, " who reproduce the value with a profit." Wealth of Nations, vol. i. p. 426.

* Some Confiderations of the Confequence of lowering Intereſt, and raiſing the Value of Money. Edition 1692, p. 53.

low that the profit of ſtock muſt be a deri-
vative, and not an original ſource of revenue ; and capital could not therefore be
conſidered as a ſource of wealth, its profit
being only a transfer from the pocket of
the labourer into that of the proprietor of
ſtock.

The ingenious Author of the Treatiſe on
the Formation and Diſtribution of Riches,
ſeems to think, that a proprietor of ſtock
is entitled to a compenſation for what his
capital would have produced him, had he
employed it in the acquiſition of land *.
But this in practice is known not even to
furniſh a rule for the quantum of profit,
and certainly gives no idea, how or from
whence it originates.

Capital is ſo variouſly employed, that in
order to convey a juſt and diſtinct idea of
the mode in which, under all circumſtances,

* *Reflection ſur la Formation et Diſtribution des Richeſſes. Par*
M. TURGOT. § 60,

ces, it becomes entitled to a profit, it is neceſſary to enumerate the different uſes to which it may be devoted.

1. It may be employed by the manufacturer in building and obtaining machinery.

2. It may be ʻemployed in procuring and conveying to the manufacture the raw materials, in advance of wages, or conveying the manufactured commodity to the market, and furniſhing it to the conſumer ; that is, in the home-trade.

3. It may be employed either in the importation of the commodities of another country, or the exportation of home-manufactures ; that is, in foreign trade.

4. It may be employed in Agriculture.

5. There is a part of the capital of every country employed merely for the purpoſe

pofe of circulation ; a greater or a fmaller
proportion of which is neceffary for conducting the tranfactions of every member
of the community.

In enumerating the various modes in
which capital may be employed, with a
view to confider how it becomes entitled
to a profit, it is unneceffary to ftate that of
lending it on landed, and that of lending it
on perfonal fecurity.   If lent to the proprietor of land, the owner of the capital becomes, under certain conditions, a partner
and joint proprietor in the land.   If lent to
a perfon who has no land, the proprietor
of the capital, under fimilar conditions, becomes a fharer either in the profits of pro-
feffional labour, or of ftock, according as
the borrower derives his revenue from his
labour or his capital.   Thus the profit
which capital lent out acquires, is a tranf-
fer from one to another of what already
exifts, and can not, therefore, properly, be
faid to be produced.

It

It appears, then, that every means of employing capital, fo as to produce a profit, is defcribed under fome one of thefe five modes enumerated by which capital becomes entitled to a profit. On examination, we fhall find, that even when fo employed, part of its profit, in fome cafes, may be more properly faid to be ac-quired than produced.

Now, it is apprehended, that in every inftance where capital is fo employed as to produce a profit, it uniformly arifes, either —*from its fupplanting a portion of labour, which would otherwife be performed by the hand of man ;* or —*from its performing a portion of labour, which is beyond the reach of the perfonal exertion of man to accomplifh.*

1. *Of*

1. *Of the Method in which that Portion of Capital produces its Profit, which is employed in building and obtaining Machinery.*

THERE is no part of the capital of a country, that more obvioufly derives its profit from fupplanting a portion of labour that would otherwife be performed by man, or from performing a portion which is beyond the reach of his perfonal exertion, than that which is vefted in machinery. That man ufes capital in the form of machinery to fupplant labour, is one of the peculiarities and diftinguifhing features of his character. If it was not for this fingular faculty, his efforts to provide for his wants, like thofe of the other animals, would be bounded by what his hands, his teeth, and his feet, could enable him to accomplifh.

That we may perceive how the profit of capital thus employed arifes from fupplant-

ing

ing labour, let us confider the effect of capital vefted in machinery, in that firft employment of man, the cultivation of the ground.   The moment he places a portion of capital in the acquifition of a fpade, one man muft obvioufly, in the courfe of a day, be able, with his fpade, to prepare as much land for receiving feed, as fifty could, by the ufe of their nails.   Thus, this portion of capital fupplants the neceffity of the labour of forty-nine men.   In the progrefs of things, a portion of the national capital comes to be invefted in a plough ; and one man, with his plough, will prepare as much land for the reception of feed as perhaps fix could with their fpades.   Thus, that portion of capital invefted in a plough, fupplants the neceffity either of the labour of five diggers, or of two hundred and ninety-nine men reduced by abfolute want of capital to ufe their nails.

Again : if we confider the employment of capital in the formation of machinery,

in one of the operations the moſt familiar,
—that of making ſtockings ; the wires employed in knitting, the firſt means of ſtock-
ing-making, affords a ſimple inſtance of a
portion of capital employed in executing
labour, beyond the reach of the power of
man to accompliſh ; as, without ſuch aſſiſt-
ance, we' could hardly ſuppoſe him capable
of making a pair of ſtockings. But, in the
further progreſs of this art, a part of the
capital of the country becomes veſted in a
ſtocking-loom * ; and the profit of the
ſtock ſo employed, is derived from the
ſtocking-loom's ſupplanting the labour
of a number of knitters.   That this
is the ſource of the profit ariſing from
the machine, appears clearly from the
circumſtance,

* It is contended in France, that the firſt ſtocking-loom
was introduced by JEAN HINDRET, in the year 1656, in
his manufactory at the Chatteau de Madrid Bois de Bou-
loigne. The Frame-work Knitters Company, attributing
the invention to WILLIAM LEE of St John's Coliege, Cam-
bridge, have adopted, as one of the ſupporters to their
arms, a Maſter of Arts in his gown and cap. See ANDER-
SON's Hiſtory of Commerce, and *Encyclopedie*, Article *Bas*.

circumftance, that the wages of thofe knitters whofe labour it fupplants, form, on the one hand, the meafure of the utmoft poffible extent the proprietor of the machine can charge; and, on the other, the ground on which mankind judge of the utility of the invention.

Suppofing, for example, one man with a loom fhould be capable of making three pair of ftockings a-day, and that it fhould require fix knitters to perform the fame work with equal elegance, in the fame time; it is obvious, that the proprietor of the loom might demand, for making his three pair of ftockings, the wages of five knitters, and that he would receive them; becaufe the confumer, by dealing with him rather than the knitters, would fave in the purchafe of the ftockings the wages of one knitter. But if, on the contrary, a ftock-ing-loom was only capable of making one pair of ftockings in three days, as, from the hypothefis that three pair of ftockings could

could be finifhed by fix knitters in one day, it follows, that one knitter would make a pair of ftockings in two days; the proprietor of the loom could not difpofe of his ftockings; becaufe he would be obliged to charge one day's wages more than was paid to the knitters; and the machine, though it executed the ftockings in the greateft perfection, would be fet afide as ufelefs, merely becaufe incapable of fupplanting any portion of labour.

The fmall profit which the proprietors of machinery generally acquire, when compared with the wages of labour, which the machine fupplants, may perhaps create a fufpicion of the rectitude of this opinion. Some fire-engines, for inftance, draw more water from a coal-pit in one day, than could be conveyed on the fhoulders of three hundred men, even affifted by the machinery of buckets; and a fire engine undoubtedly performs its labour at a much fmaller expençe than the amount

of

of the wages of thofe whofe labour it thus fupplants. This is, in truth, the cafe with all machinery. All machines muft execute the labour, that was antecedently performed, at a cheaper rate than it could be done by the hand of man ; otherwife they would inevitably fhare the fate of the fuppofed ftocking-loom which could manufacture only one pair of ftockings in three days, and be laid afide as ufelefs.

The actual profit drawn for the ufe of any machine, when univerfally adopted, muft be regulated on the fame principle with the hire of a field, or the payment of an artift, or the price of any other commodity ; that is, by the proportion betwixt the quantity of machines that can be eafily procured, and the demand for them. But that the profit of ftock employed in machinery is paid out of a fund that would otherwife be deftined to pay the wages of the labour it fupplants, is evident ; becaufe, if the proprietors of all the capital fo employed,

ployed, would combine to charge a greater
fum for the ufe of the machines than the
wages of the labour fupplanted, they would
be inftantly fet afide, and the fame portion
of the revenue of the nation again employed in the payment of wages, that was fo directed before the machines were invented.

The cafe of a patent, or exclufive privilege of the ufe of a machine, ufually granted, as the law of England now permits, for
fourteen years, to reward an ingenious invention, will tend further to illuftrate
this.

If fuch a privilege is given for the invention of a machine, which performs, by
the labour of one man, a quantity of work
that ufed to take the labour of four; as the
poffeffion of the exclufive privilege prevents any competition in doing the work,
but what proceeds from the labour of the
four workmen, their wages, as long as the
patent continues, muft obvioufly form the
meafure

meafure of the patentee's charge; that is, to fecure employment, he has only to charge a little lefs than the wages of the labour which the machine fupplants. But when the patent expires, other machines of the fame nature are brought into competition; and then his charge muft be regulated on the fame principle as every other, according to the abundance of machines, or, (what is the fame thing), according to the facility of procuring machines in proportion to the demand for them. This alteration, however, in the rule of charging, does not prevent the profit of the machine being received out of a fund of the fame nature of that which it was paid from before the expiration of the patent; to wit, from a part of the revenue of the country, deftined, antecedent to the invention of the machine, to pay the wages of the labour it fupplants *.

Though,

---

* The theory of the Author of the Wealth of Nations made him regard the profit of ftock as derived from the labour of the productive manufacturer; yet there are paffages in his work that ftrongly tend to confirm the opinion

Though, in confirmation of this opinion, it is impoſſible to cite the theory of any learned

tion here maintained.   For example : " Both in the
" coarſe and in the fine woollen manufacture, the ma-
" chinery employed was much more imperfect in thoſe
" ancient than it is in the preſent times.   It has ſince
" received three very capital improvements, beſides,
" probably, many ſmaller ones, of which it may be
" difficult to aſcertain either the number or the import-
" ance.   The three capital improvements are, firſt, The
" exchange of the rock and ſpindle for the ſpinning-wheel,
" which, with the ſame quantity of labour, will perform
" more than double the quantity of work. Secondly, The uſe
" of ſeveral very ingenious machines, which facilitate and
" abridge, in a ſtill greater proportion, the winding of
" the worſted and woollen yarn, or the proper manage-
" ment of the warp and woof, before they are put in-
" to the loom ; an operation which, previous to the inven-
" tion of thoſe machines, muſt have been extremely tedious
" and troubleſome.   Thirdly, The employment of the
" fulling-mill, for thickening the cloth, inſtead of treading
" it in water.   Neither wind nor water mills of any kind,
" were known in England ſo early as the beginning of the
" ſixteenth century, nor, ſo far as I know, in any other
" part of Europe north of the Alps.   They had been in-
" troduced into Italy ſome time before.

" The conſideration of theſe circumſtances may, per-
" haps, in ſome meaſure, explain to us why the real price

" both

learned author who has treated of political œconomy, it has, however, in its favour, what is perhaps fully better; it derives ample teſtimony of its truth from the con-duct of the unlettered manufacturers them-ſelves, as is ſufficiently evinced by the riots that have taken place on the intro-duction of various pieces of machinery, and particularly at the time the ingenious machines for carding and ſpinning were firſt ſet a-going.

2. *Of*

" both of the coarſe and of the fine manufacture, was ſo
" much higher in thoſe ancient than it is in the preſent
" times. *It coſt a greater quantity of labour to bring the goods*
" *to market.*" Wealth of Nations, vol. 1. p. 310. 4to edit.
See alſo p. 306.

2. *Of the Method in which that Portion of Ca-*
pital produces its Profit, which is employ-
ed in procuring and conveying to the Ma-
nufacturer the raw Materials, in advance
of Wages; or in conveying the manufactured
Commodity to the Market, and furnishing
it to the Consumer;—that is, in the Home
Trade.

If it has been made evident, that the
share of the capital of a country vested in
machinery derives its profit from supplanting labour, a little consideration will make
it equally clear, that the stock employed
in procuring and conveying to the manufacturer the raw materials in advance of
wages, or in conveying the manufactured
commodity to the market, and furnishing
it to the consumers, derives the profit it
produces from the same source. The term
produces, is here purposely used; because it
will appear, on analysing the grounds on
which

which the proprietors of this portion of national capital become poffeffed of their profit, that they are entitled to acquire a profit, befides that which their ftock can be properly faid to produce.

That we may poffefs a clear view of the manner in which this part of the national capital becomes entitled to its profit, let us fuppofe that all at once it was abftracted from any fociety, and that each confumer was obliged to perform himfelf the fervices he now derives from the capital which is employed in procuring and conveying to the manufacture the raw materials in advance of wages, or in conveying the manufactured commodity to the market, and furnifhing it to the confumer.

It is impoffible, confiftent with brevity, accurately to trace all the fteps a confumer would be obliged to purfue to acquire any commodity, if this part of the capital of a country was abftracted ; and, fortunately,

it

it is only neceſſary to deſcribe it generally,
ſo as, by giving a view of the nature of the
duty he would perform, to exhibit the method in which capital thus acquires its profit.

As the national capital at preſent ſtands
appropriated, if a pair of ſtockings is wanted, they may be had by the conſumer at
the ſhop of the hoſier.   But if the part of
the national capital which is employed in
conducting them into that ſituation, was
abſtracted from any ſociety, the conſumer would be obliged, in the firſt inſtance, to quit his uſual occupation, and re-
pair to the ſheep-farmers, for the purpoſe
of procuring a quantity of wool.   Having
bought and paid for the wool, he would be
then under the neceſſity of conveying it to
the carder and ſpinner, whoſe wages he muſt
advance.   He would next be obliged to go in
queſt of the thread, when ſpun, to convey
it to be dyed, and to pay the wages of the
dyer.   Finally, he muſt undertake the taſk of
conveying

conveying the thread from the dyer to the
ſtocking-maker, of paying him his wages,
and of carrying the ſtockings home.

On examining the taſk thus impoſed on
the conſumer, it ſeems to conſiſt in two
different duties.

1. He is compelled, by abſtracting this
part of the national capital, to withdraw
from his own ſtock the money with which
he pays the wool, that with which he pays
the carder and ſpinner, and that with
which he pays the dyer, ſome time before
he acquires the uſe of the ſtockings, which
muſt create a loſs of the profit he might
derive by retaining this portion of capital
in his own employ.

2. He is obliged to perform the labour
requiſite for ſelecting the wool, the labour
of carrying it to be carded and ſpun, the
labour of conveying it to the dyer, and,
laſtly, that of taking it to the ſtocking-maker, and from thence home.

Now,

Now, thefe two duties, that would be thus impofed on the confumer, by abftracting the portion of capital employed in procuring and conveying to the manufacturer the raw materials in advance of wages, or in conveying the manufactured commodity to the market, and furnifhing it to the confumer, give a juft view of what is the fource of the profit of capital fo employed.

1. It feems entitled to a profit, on account of the confumer's being faved the neceffity of an advance for payment of the wool, &c.   But this profit cannot properly be faid to be produced by the capital fo employed; the capital thus engaged in the home trade can only be confidered as having a right to acquire it; for this profit is evidently produced by the flock which is by this means allowed to remain in the hands of the confumer, and arifes from the rent of land, if the confumer fo employs his capital,—from agri-

culture,

culture, if he employs it in cultivating the land,—or from fupplanting fome other fpecies of labour, if he employs it as ftock in trade.

2. It is entitled to a profit, becaufe it exempts the confumer from the fecond clafs of duties that have been enumerated. This profit it may be properly faid to produce; and this is obvioufly produced by fupplanting that labour which he would otherwife be compelled to perform.

Like the labour fupplanted by ftock vefted in a machine, the value of thefe duties combined, forms, on the one hand, the meafure of the utmoft poffible extent the proprietor of this portion of capital can charge; and, on the other, the ground on which mankind muft judge of the utility of its being fo employed.

For example: let us fuppofe that the confumer has made of profit from the money

ney which the exiftence of this capital enables him to retain in his own employ, and which he would otherwife have been obliged to advance for the purchafe of wool, &c. long before getting his ftockings into his poffeffion, the fum of fixpence ; and let us further fuppofe, that the confumer values the labour it faves him, at five fhillings : the utmoft poffible charge the proprietor of the capital could make, over and above the payment of the wool, and wages of the fpinner, dyer, and weaver, would be fomething under five fhillings and fixpence ; for if it exceeded this fum, the confumer would perform the duties himfelf, and the capital allotted to be fo employed would be regarded as ufelefs.

Again ; though the char ge might amount to five fhillings and fixpence, as long as the competition in performing the duty remained folely betwixt the confumer of the ftockings and one proprietor of ftock, yet, as the price of performing the labour fupplanted by a machine is at once fettled

on

on a different principle, when a number of
machines come into competition ; fo when
a number of different proprietors of ftock
prefent themfelves for performing thefe duties, the actual charge is at once regulated
in the fame manner as the charge for the
machine, when a number of machines come
into competition ; and, indeed, on the fame
principle as the price of all other things,
it is determined by the quantity of ftock
contending for the performance of thefe
duties in proportion to the demand for it.

Finally ; it muft be remarked, that though
the proprietor of capital fo employed, faves,
by the ufe of it, the labour of the confumer,
he by no means fubftitutes in its place an e-
qual portion of his own ; which proves that
it is his capital, and not himfelf, that performs it.   He, by means of his capital, perhaps, does the bufinefs of three hundred confumers by one journey ; and carts, boats,
and a variety of other machinery, all tending to fupplant labour, are applicable to the
large

large fcale in which he deals, from which a
confumer could derive no benefit in procuring for himfelf the fmall quantity adapted
to the fatisfaction of his individual defires.

3. *Of the Method in which that Portion of Ca-*
   pital produces its Profit, which is employed
   either in the Importation of the Commodities
   of another Country, or the Exportation of
   Home Manufactures;—that is, in Foreign
   Trade.

ON this fubject it is fortunately unneceffary to enter into fo long a detail. The fame
reafoning we have ufed to fhew that capital embarked in every branch of the home
trade uniformly derives its profit from
fupplanting a certain portion of labour, is
equally applicable to capital embarked in
foreign trade. As the portion of labour fupplanted by this defcription of capital is much
greater, if the competition exifted folely betwixt a fingle proprietor of ftock and the
confumer, his charge might be much higher.

Foreign

Foreign trade is the exchange of the commodities of one diftant part of the world for thofe of another, by which the defires of man are gratified with things which the habits of induftry in another country enable the inhabitants to produce at a cheaper rate or of a better quality, or with things that he could not obtain from the foil around him, or in the climate in which he lives.

As, in every cafe of trade, whether foreign, or domeftic, the confumer, if there exifted no capital, muft himfelf, in detail, pay for, or perform, every expence or portion of labour requifite to bring any commodity into his poffeffion in the fhape in which he defires it ; if the raw material grows at a diftance from him, and many of the fteps in the procefs of giving it form, are conducted at a diftance from one another, the portion of labour which the ufe of capital fupplants muft be greater.   But the profit of capital employed in foreign trade, though

though it arifes from fupplanting labour, comes to be regulated, not by the value of the labour it fupplants, but, as in all other cafes, by the competition among the proprietors of capital; and it will be great or fmall in proportion to the quantity of capital that prefents itfelf for performing the duty, and the demand for it.

Foreign trade, it muft alfo be remarked, in the fhipping it employs, furnifhes the great example of capital engaged in performing that fpecies of labour which is beyond the reach of the powers of man to accomplifh; for man, even with the fmalleft quantity of any commodity, is incapable of fwimming from iflands to the continent,—from the old to the new world, —and of performing thofe long voyages which the modern fkill in navigation enables the feaman to undertake.

The duty, however, which capital thus performs, and by which it produces its profit.

fit, is fo obvioufly of the fame nature, that it requires no explanation to fhew that it confifts in labour *.

4. *Of the Method in which that Portion of Capital produces its Profit which is employed in Agriculture.*

LABOUR is the only means of improving the fertility of the earth.—

" Curfed is the ground for thy fake. In " forrow fhalt thou eat of it all the days of " thy life. Thorns alfo and thiftles fhall " it bring forth to thee: and thou fhalt " eat the herb of the field. In the fweat of " thy face fhalt thou eat bread †."

And true it is, that by the exertions of the labour of man alone are food and materials

for

* The imagination of VOLTAIRE has put into the mouth of the Philofopher, in the Dialogue betwixt a Philofopher and a Comptroller of Finance, the following fentiment: "*Le* " *commerce fait le même effet que le travail des mains.*"

† Genefis, chap. iii.

for clothing extracted from the earth in fufficient quantity to fupply his wants.

In fhewing that ftock vefted in machinery draws its profit folely from the circumftance of fupplanting labour, the effect of
the fpade and the plough, in which the hufbandman vefts part of his capital, has been
already traced.   It has been fhewn, that it
alone derives its profit from fupplanting a
portion of the labour that he would otherwife be obliged to perform ; and the fame
reafoning is applicable to explain how the
whole of his capital, vefted in horfes, carts,
or any other machinery, derives its profit
from the fame circumftance.

" In a farm where all the neceffary build-
" ings, fences, drains, communications, &c.
" are in the moft perfect good order, the
" fame number of labourers and labouring
" cattle will raife a much greater produce,
" than in one of equal extent and equally
" good ground, but not furnifhed with equal
                    " conveniencies."

" conveniencies *."—Thus—" An impro-
" ved farm may very juftly be regarded in
" the fame light as thofe ufeful machines
" which facilitate and abridge labour †."
Though the Author of the Wealth of Nations did not perceive that capital vefted either in agriculture or in machinery derives
its profit from fupplanting labour; yet it
is evident from the paffage here quoted,
that he felt the fimilarity of their effects;
and if, inftead of regarding the effect of a
machine as facilitating labour, or as increafing the productive powers of labour ‡,
(as he expreffes it), he had perceived that
capital vefted in machinery acquires its
profit by fupplanting labour, he muft have
attributed

* Wealth of Nations, vol. 1. p. 343. 4to edit.

† Ibid. vol. 1. p. 335.

‡ It is a ftrange confufion of ideas that has led Dr
SMITH to defcribe the operation of capital as increafing the
productive powers of labour. The fame procefs of reafoning would lead a man to defcribe the effect of fhortening
a circuitous road between any two given places, from ten
miles to five miles, *as doubling the velocity of the walker.*

attributed the origin of the profit he here defcribes to the fame circumftance.

But, indeed, all capital vefted in any department of agriculture alike derives its profit from this fource.

If the farmer employs ftock or capital in manuring, that is, in mixing of foils, to increafe fertility, it is clearly labour which he performs; and the benefit he derives from it as obvioufly confifts in fupplanting labour he would otherwife be under the neceffity of performing, to procure the fame quantity of produce. If by fuch procefs he can double the fertility of his field, the labour of one acre fupplies the produce that would have been drawn from the labour of two; and, by the fertility thus beftowed, fupplants the neceffity of one-half of the labour antecedently requifite.

If he vefts his capital either in feed of a particular quality, or in a ftock of cattle

and

and fheep of a peculiar fattening kind, he does this, that, with the fame labour, he may grow more corn, or produce more beef or mutton. So truly does man's nourifhment depend on the fweat of his face, that he can derive aid or affiftance from nothing in increafing the fertility of the ground, but in proportion as it performs or fupplants a part of the labour which he muft otherwife of neceffity fubmit to.

5. *Of the Method in which that Portion of National Capital produces a Profit which is employed in conducting Circulation.*

In confidering how that portion of the national capital employed in conducting circulation produces a profit, it is neceffary clearly to diftinguifh what forms circulating capital, from the goods that are circulated by means of capital; and this becomes the more fo, becaufe we are accuftomed to fee thefe two things, however different,

ferent, almoſt uniformly confounded, by thoſe who have treated on the ſubjeſt *.

In the manner in which the circulation of moſt European countries is at preſent conducted, the circulating capital may be properly regarded as compoſed either of the coin, or of the ſubſtitutes for coin, which banking, and the modern facilities of conveying credit, have created.   To theſe, therefore, we confine our views ; conceiving them to form what may be, with ſtrict propriety, denominated the Circulating Capital of a Country : and a little examination

---

* In the Wealth of Nations, the circulating capital of a country is ſtated to be compoſed of four parts. The firſt is deſcribed as conſiſting of the money, by means of which all the others are circulated and diſtributed ; the Author thus plainly confeſſing, that the other three articles of which he imagined circulating capital to be compoſed. are not employed in circulating, but are actually goods to be circulated.   They are, in fact, portions of what is reſerved for conſumption.   Wealth of Nations, p. 326.

tion will fuffice to fhew, that gold and filver, as coin, are alone eftimated by man
for their utility in fupplanting labour, as
well as that the advantage which the public derives from the improved method of
circulation, by means of banks, is founded
on the fame principle.

Money is of ufe to mankind in two different capacities; as an inftrument of exchange; and as a practical ftandard, by
which the value of all commodities is meafured and expreffed. To convey a clear
idea how the portion of the national capital employed in executing thefe two duties is
profitable merely from the circumftance of
its fupplanting labour, perhaps no better method can be followed, than that which was
purfued in examining the foundation of the
profit of capital employed in the home
trade.

Let us, then, confider what would be the
effect of withdrawing from any fociety that

part of its capital which is employed in conducting the circulation of goods, and in forming a practical standard, by which the value of commodities is meafured and expreffed.

The moment this portion of the national capital is abftracted from any fociety, the exchange of thofe things which nature or art enables one man to produce with greater eafe or of better quality, for thofe things which fimilar circumftances enable another to produce with greater advantage, muft be conducted by barter.

A farmer, for example, who had in his barn a quantity of wheat, much greater than the confumption of his family, and who de-ftined the overplus to fupply the other arti-cles neceffary for their clothing and nourifh-ment, if he wanted a pair of fhoes, would be obliged to proceed with a quantity of his wheat to a fhoemaker, to endeavour to negotiate an exchange ; but as it might
probably

probably happen, that the firſt ſhoemaker
he accoſted, had already, in return for ſhoes,
obtained all the wheat he meant to con-
ſume, he would be under the neceſſity of
remaining without ſhoes, till he could find
a ſhoemaker who wanted wheat.

If, unfortunately, the whole profeſſion
were already ſupplied with wheat; to obtain a pair of ſhoes, he would be under
the neceſſity of endeavouring to diſcover
what was the article the ſhoemaker wiſhed to procure; and if, on inquiry, it
appeared that beer was the commodity
with which the ſhoemaker wiſhed to be
ſupplied, the farmer muſt then endeavour
to procure from the brewer a quantity of beer in exchange for his wheat, as a
preliminary to his future negotiation with
the ſhoemaker.

But the brewer might alſo be ſupplied with wheat; which would oblige the
farmer, in the firſt inſtance, to endeavour

to exchange his wheat for fome commo
dity the brewer wanted, that with it he
might purchafe the beer, with which he
afterwards meant to acquire his fhoes.

Tedious as this procefs may appear, it is
one of the fimpleft cafes that could be ftated, for the purpofe of pointing out and
explaining the laborious path which every man, if the circulating capital of a
country was abftracted, would be obliged to tread, in endeavouring to fupply
his wants by parting with his fuperfluities;
for it is plain, that the courfe would
often be infinitely more tedious and intri-
cate, before the goods of one man could be
repeatedly bartered, till they at length became exchanged for that particular commodity which another wanted.

Neither is this the fole fource of the labour that would be impofed on man, by
withdrawing the capital employed in the
conduct of circulation. As there would
then

then exift no general ftandard by which the value of commodities was ufually efti-mated, an inquiry muft of neceffity take place, in fettling the terms of every parti-cular exchange, to afcertain the relative value of the commodities.

For example: if the brewer to whom the farmer applied, wifhed to have fome wheat, and it fo happened, that neither the farmer had antecedently exchanged wheat for beer, nor the brewer beer for wheat, they would be at a lofs to fix the quantity of wheat that fhould be given for a gallon of beer. If, indeed, each had luckily already procured a leg of the fame fheep in exchange for the commodity they refpectively poffeffed, they might then difcover the relative value of the wheat and the beer, becaufe two things equal to one and the fame thing are equal to one another; but as it would probably happen, that the farmer and brewer had never exchanged wheat and beer for the fame commodity, they could not have re-courfe to this eafy mode of deciding the

portion

portion of wheat that ought to be parted
with for the acquifition of a given quantity of beer. The courfe, therefore, the farmer would have to purfue, even after he
had undergone the labour neceffary to difcover a brewer who wanted wheat, might
be infinitely laborious, before he could
trace out, through the medium of various
exchanges, fome one interchange, that afforded a point of comparifon betwixt the
value of the wheat and the beer.

If this, however, could not be difcovered,
he would be obliged, as the only means of
afcertaining the terms of the exchange, to
inftitute an inquiry into the proportion betwixt the demand for, and the quantity of
the beer, and alfo into the demand for, and
quantity of the wheat; thefe being the circumftances on which the relative value of
all commodities depends.

The beer being procured, it is plain
he might be under the neceffity of repeat-
ing

ing the fame operation in negotiating the exchange for the fhoes.

Thus it is obvious, that the portion of the capital of a country employed in conduct-ing circulation, is not only profitably em-ployed, by faving the labour of man, in its character of an inftrument for conducting exchanges, but alfo in its capacity of a ftandard, for meafuring the value of com-modities.

It is not, perhaps, at firft fight fo apparent, that circulating capital is profitable to mankind from the circumftance of fup-planting labour, as it is that the profit of a machine is derived from that fource ; but there is in reality no part of the capital of a nation that fupplants a greater portion of labour, certainly none the benefit of which in fupplanting labour is more univerfally enjoyed.

The labour of the manufacturer fixes
and

and realizes itfelf in fome vendible commodity.   Its exiftence as productive labour is
therefore more eafily difcernible than the
labour of the menial fervant, whofe fervices generally perifh at the inftant of performance. The labour of a manufacturing
machine, in like manner, fixes itfelf in fome
vendible commodity, which makes the origin of its profit more apparent than that of
circulating capital, whofe fervices, like that
of the menial fervant, perifh at the inftant
of their performance ; but which, like his,
too, remain at all times prepared to fupplant the neceffity of another portion of labour, which the mafter muft otherwife perform *.

Though

---

* Neither the labour performed by the menial fervant,
nor that of which the neceffity is fupplanted by circulating
capital, do naturally ftock, or ftore themfelves up in fuch a
manner as to be transferred from one to another for a defined value. The profit of the one and the other alike
arifes from faving the labour of the owner or mafter. The
fimilarity is indeed fuch, that it is natural to fuppofe the
fame circumftances which led the one to be deemed unproductive.

Though coin, employed as circulating capital, has been thus eagerly fought after, not for the fake of the gold and filver it contains, but merely on account of the labour it fupplants ; like other means of fupplanting labour, it requires, though an inferior, yet a certain portion of labour to procure it. To carry it about, when procured, is alfo, from its bulk and weight, laborious. To fave thefe remaining portions of labour, in conducting the circulation of a country, various modifications of banks have been fucceffively introduced, highly beneficial to the community in which they have

productive, would naturally create the fame impreffion with relation to the other. Accordingly, the Author of the Wealth of Nations, who conceives the labour of the menial fervant to be unproductive, informs us, that " the " gold and filver money which circulates in any country, " and by means of which the produce of its land and la- " bour is annually circulated, and diftributed to the pro- " per confumers, is, in the fame manner as the ready mo- " ney of the dealer, all dead ftock. It is a very valuable " part of the capital of the country, which produces no- " thing to the country." Wealth of Nations, vol. i. p. 388. 4to edit.

have been eftablifhed, from their fupplanting the labour, formerly performed by the
Sovereign, of procuring coin, and that performed by the fubjeəts, of making payments in it * ; and alfo from their executing,

* There are various paffages in Mr Thornton's Book
on Paper Credit, which may be cited in confirmation of the
propofition, that fupplanting of labour is the great objeət
in the introduətion of all fubftitutes for coin.—For example:

" To fpeak firft of Bills of Exchange.—It is ob-
" vious, that however portable gold may be in com-
" parifon of any other article which might be made a
" meafure of value, to carry it in quantities to a
" great diftance muft prove incommodious.   Let it be
" fuppofed that there are in London ten manufaəturers,
" who fell their article to ten fhopkeepers in York, by
" whom it is retailed ; and that there are in York ten ma-
" nufaəturers of another commodity, who fell it to ten
" fhopkeepers in London. There would be no occafion for
" the ten fhopkeepers in London to fend yearly to York
" guineas for the payment of the York manufaətures, and
" for the ten York fhopkeepers to fend yearly as many
" guineas to London." He then proceeds to fhew the ufe
of bills of exchange in fupplanting labour.   See p. 24.

Again, p. 54. " But further, if bills and bank-notes
" were extinguifhed, other fubftitutes than gold would un-
" queftionably be found.   Recourfe would be had to de-
                                                    " vices

ting, with a machine of little value, the labour antecedently performed by a very expenfive inftrument.

From this laft circumftance it is, that moft countries undoubtedly derive what has been efteemed the greateft benefit they enjoy from the modern improved method of conducting the circulation of commodities. Yet it feems to be to the defire of man to fupplant labour that we are indebted for the invention; for banks, we are told, were firft introduced into Swedeland *, where the money being all of cop-

per,

" vices of various kinds, by which men *would fave them-*
" *felves the trouble of counting, weighing, and tranfporting*
" *guineas, in all the larger operations of commerce.*" See
alfo the defcription he gives, p. 55. of the method in
which London bankers make payments to one another,
calculated for no other purpofe but to fupplant the neceffity of a portion of labour which their clerks would otherwife be obliged to perform.

* " The ufe of banks has been the beft method yet prac-
" tifed for the increafe of money. Banks have been long
" ufed

per, it was highly inconvenient, by reafon of
its weight and bulk, to carry it about in fuch
quantities as was neceffary to conduct exchanges.

In truth, though a country may derive
much benefit from having a cheaper medium of exchange, infomuch, that if there
is a fcarcity of capital, it will by this means
have more for other ufes ; yet this confideration never could form the motive of any
individual, for preferring one medium of
exchange to another. To the feller of a
commodity, the value of the medium of
exchange is perfectly indifferent, provided
he is fure it is in equal eftimation with
thofe from whom he fubfequently means

to

" ufed in Italy ; but, as I am informed, the invention of
" them was owing to Swedeland. Their money was copper,
" which was inconvenient by reafon of its weight and bulk.
" To remedy this inconveniency, a bank was fet up, where
" the money might be pledged, and credit given to the
" value, which paffed in payments." Law on Money and
Trade. Glafgow edit. p. 67.

to purchafe. A man can alone have an intereft in the value of what he produces, and
what he confumes; but coin or its fubftitutes are never confumed: they only pafs
from one to another, for the purpofe of faving
labour in the conduct of exchange; and the
only immediate intereft that he who ac-
cepts a given quantity of any medium of
exchange can have, is, that it fhould fave
as much labour as poffible. It is on this
principle that filver is preferred to an equal
value of copper; that gold, in making large
payments, is preferred to both; and that
bills of exchange, fupplant, with advantage, the ufe of the metals in extended
commercial concerns.

Had the ingenious Abbé MORELLET written for the purpofe of illuftrating what is
here ftated, he could not have given a more
defirable definition of paper-currency than
the following: " We underftand by paper-
" money, every acknowledgment of debt
" or obligation; in a word, every ftipula-
" tion,

" tion, by writing, betwixt a debtor and
" creditor, which obliges the former to
" pay, and authorifes the latter to exact a
" value; and which being capable of con-
" veyance, becomes a means of transfer-
" ring the property of thefe values from
" one to another, without tranfporting the
" things valuable in fubftance.

" It is plain, that this definition applies
" to all notes, bills, and every fpecies of
" bank-credit ; to fecurities granted by Go-
" vernments for money borrowed, as well
" as to all fecurities for money advanced in
" fpeculations of commerce or finance : fi-
" nally, to credit given by one individual to
" another, in the form of bills of exchange,
" promiffory-notes, orders, &c. &c. *."

But it is not alone when employed in the
ufeful and beneficial purpofes of commerce,
manufacture,

* *Profpectus d'un Nouveaux Dictionnaire de Commerce,*
p. 184. For the original fee APPENDIX, No. III.

manufacture, agriculture, and the conduct of exchanges, that capital ferves man, by fupplanting or performing labour. After the explanation given, without involving the reader in any additional detail, his own imagination will at once fuggeft how thefe immenfe capitals, fquandered in the modern conduct of mifchievous, but perhaps unavoidable warfare, are alone profitable to the community, upon the fame principle.

From this fhort examination it appears, that capital, whether fixed or circulating, whether embarked in the home or in foreign trade, far from being employed in putting labour into motion, or in adding to the productive powers of labour *, is, on the contrary, alone ufeful or profitable to mankind, from the circumftance of its either *fupplanting the neceffity of a portion of labour, that would otherwife be performed by the hand*

* Wealth of Nations, vol. 1. p. 437,—441,—445. 4to edit. ; and in many other paffages.

*hand of man,—or of its executing a portion of
labour, beyond the reach of the powers of man
to accomplish:* and this is not a mere criti-
cifm on words, but a diftinction in itfelf
moft important.

The idea, that capital puts labour into motion, that it adds to the productive powers
of labour, gives rife to the opinion that labour (which it will afterwards be fhewn is
the great means of increafing wealth) is
every where proportioned to the quantity
of exifting capital *; that the general induftry of a country is always proportioned
to the capital that employs it † ; and therefore authorifes the inference, that the increafe of capital is the fovereign and unbounded means of augmenting wealth.
Whereas the opinion, that capital can alone
be employed with utility and advantage in
fupplanting or performing labour, naturally

* Wealth of Nations, vol. i. p. 3. 4to edit.
† Ibid. vol. ii. p. 37.

rally fuggefts the inference, that a country cannot be benefited by the poffeffion of a greater portion of capital than
can be employed in performing and fupplanting labour, in the produ&ion and formation of thofe things for which there exifts a demand.

Having thus analyfed and explained the
nature and origin of the profit on ftock,
having attempted to make manifeft,—that
as land produces profit by means of its
produce,—and that as labour produces profit by increafing the quantity, and meliorating the quality, of the produ&ions of
nature, and by giving it form adapted for
confumption,—fo capital is produ&ive of
profit, either by fupplanting a portion of labour which would otherwife be performed
by the hand of man, or by performing a
portion of labour which is beyond the
reach of his powers to accomplifh ; in
purfuance of the plan adopted, we fhould be
naturally led to inveftigate, how far the
profit

profit of ſtock, the nature of which has been explained, is to be ranked, along with the produce of land and the exertions of labour, as a ſource of wealth.

But the inveſtigation in which we have been engaged, ſeems to preclude the neceſ-ſity of entering into any detail on this ſub-ject ; for if we have been ſuccefsful in ſhew-ing, that labour in all its varieties is more or lefs productive of wealth, it follows, that capital, the profit of which ariſes from per-forming, with great advantage to mankind, labour, which has already been proved to contribute towards wealth, muſt alſo be re-garded as a ſource of wealth.

CHAP.

CHAP. IV.

OF THE POSSIBILITY OF INCREASING WEALTH BY ANY OTHER MEANS THAN THOSE BY WHICH IT IS PRODUCED.

THE fources of national wealth having been examined and afcertained, it would feem that we might proceed, without further inveftigation, to confider the different effects of the produce of land,—of the exertions of labour, and of capital in fupplanting and performing labour, in increafing wealth; thefe being the fole fources of wealth, and therefore the only means of increafing it. For as animals are alone

multiplied

multiplied by the means by which they
are produced ; as vegetable fubftances
alfo can alone be increafed by the means
by which they are produced, as a greater quantity of metals, and other productions from the bowels of the earth,
can alone be acquired by an increafe of
that labour which procures them; and as
a greater quantity of raw materials can a-
lone acquire the form that adapts them for
confumption, by a more frequent repeti-
tion, or fkilful exertion, of the labour that
gives them form ; fo wealth, it might be
reafonably inferred, could alone be increafed by the means by which it is produced.

But popular prejudice, which has ever
regarded the fum-total of individual riches
to be fynonymous with public wealth, and
which has conceived every means of increafing the riches of individuals to be a
means of increafing public wealth, has
pointed out parfimony or accumulation by
a man's depriving himfelf of the objects of
defire, to which his fortune entitles him,
(the

(the ufual means of increafing private fortune), as the moft active means of increafing public wealth.

When we reflect that this abftinence
from expenditure, and confequent accumulation, neither tends to increafe the produce of land, to augment the exertions of
labour, nor to perform a portion of labour
that muft otherwife be executed by the
hand of man ; it feems that we might be entitled at once to pronounce, that accumulation may be a method of transferring wealth
from A, B and C, to D ; but that it cannot be a method of increafing public
wealth, becaufe wealth can alone be increafed by the fame means by which it is
produced.

But when the public prejudice is confirmed by men moft admired for talents;
when we are told by the moft efteemed
authority, that every prodigal is a public
enemy, and every frugal man a public benefactor ;

nefactor * ; that parfimony, and not induftry, increafes capital, (meaning wealth †) ;
and that, as frugality increafes, and prodigality diminifhes, the public capital ; fo the
conduct of thofe whofe expence juft equals
their revenue, neither increafes nor diminifhes it ‡ ; it becomes neceffary to enter
into a more minute examination of this
opinion ‖ ; and the more fo, as it has given
birth to an erroneous fyftem of legiflation,
which, if perfifted in, muft infallibly ruin
the country that adopts or perfeveres in
it.

The means by which ftock or capital acquires a profit, have been already inveftigated.

* Wealth of Nations, vol. 1. p. 414. 4to edit.

† Ibid. vol. 1. p. 410.

‡ Ibid. p. 421.

‖ This opinion concerning the falutary effects of parfimony, is held by many other writers on political œconomy ; more particularly by TURGOT, in his Treatife on the
Formation and Diftribution of Riches. See from paragraph 49. to paragraph 83.

ted. It has been fhewn, that it is uniformly profitable to man, by fupplanting the
neceffity of a portion of labour he muft
otherwife perform, or by performing a
portion of labour beyond the reach of his
powers; and it does not require much confideration to difcover what it is that exe-
cutes this labour : for it is obvioufly a part
of the produce of the earth, or a part of the
earth itfelf, to which either nature or art
has given a form that adapts it for the purpofe of fupplanting labour.

If capital, however, in all its varieties, is
neither more nor lefs than a part of the
produce of the earth, or a part of the earth
itfelf, to which either nature or art has given a form that adapts it for fupplanting
or performing a portion of labour; let us
confider, whether there are not bounds to
the quantity of its revenue, which a country can, confiftent with its welfare, beftow
in this fort of expenditure, that is appropriate to the execution of this duty.

For

For the fake of perfpicuity, we fhall begin by confidering the effects of accumulation in a fimple ftate of fociety, where
capital has not yet affumed all that variety of form, which man, in the progrefs of
fociety, gives it, for the purpofe of performing labour ; though the fame obfervations will afterwards be found applicable to
focieties fuch as modern Europe prefents to
our view, where capital floats in all the variety of channels to which extended commerce deftines it, and where even the natural channels, in which all property would
fluctuate, are deranged by overgrown financial arrangements.

When fociety exifts in that ftate where
man is chiefly occupied in agriculture, or
the cultivation of the land, his property
can alone confift in the land he poffeffes,—
in the grain he annually produces, and the
breeding ftock whofe produce is reared
for confumption,—and, laftly, in the animals and utenfils he employs, to enable him

to

to produce and confume his wealth with lefs labour; that is, in a more fatisfactory and comfortable manner to himfelf. In fuch a ftate, his property, therefore, divides itfelf into three different branches.

1. The land he cultivates.

2. The ftock he referves for immediate and remote confumption; under which is comprehended the produce of his farm, whether vegetable or animal.

3. His capital, confifting of the animals or machines he employs to fupplant labour in the cultivation of his farm, or in the convenient confumption of its produce.

That this laft part of his wealth is highly beneficial to himfelf, as well as to the fociety in which he lives, is undoubted; it fupplants a portion of labour which muft otherwife be executed by the hand of man, and may even execute a portion of labour beyond

yond the reach of the perfonal exertions of man to accomplifh. If therefore, he is not poffeffed of a fufficiency of thofe animals, inftruments and machines, which form his capital, it will moft clearly be commendable, and in the higheft degree advantageous to fociety, that he fhould augment the exertions of his induftry, for the purpofe of procuring them ; and if he cannot otherwife effect this augmentation, it may even be prudent and beneficial that he fhould abridge a portion of his immediate confumption, for the fake of increafing his capital ; that is, that he fhould allot a part of the live ftock and grain he otherwife would immediately confume and enjoy, to purchafe what would enable him, at a future period, to produce and confume more with greater eafe and fatisfaction to himfelf.

If, on the other hand, however, he is already in poffeffion of as much capital, as, in the exifting ftate of his knowledge, he

can

can ufe for the purpofe of fupplanting labour in cultivating the quantity of land he
poffeffes, it can neither be advantageous for
himfelf nor for the public that he fhould
abridge his confumption of food, clothing, and the other objects of his defire,
for the purpofe of accumulating a much
greater quantity of capital, (that is of live
and dead ftock, for performing labour),
than can by poffibility be employed in fupplanting labour.   The extenfion of his
lands, or the invention of new means of
fupplanting labour, would juftify a defire
for increafing his capital ; but, otherwife,
accumulation, by deprivation of expenditure, muft be detrimental to himfelf as well
as to the public.

To the farmer it muft be difadvantageous, becaufe he deprives himfelf and his family of what they naturally defire, and
would otherwife enjoy, for the purpofe either of acquiring a larger quantity of labouring cattle than he could ufefully employ,

ploy, (the maintenance of which demands farther facrifices of what his family would wifh to enjoy), or of accumulating a hoard of fpades, ploughs, and other utenfils of hufbandry, with which he was acquainted, infinitely greater than he could ufe;—thus depriving himfelf of fubftantial enjoyments, for the purpofe of acquiring an additional quantity of that of which an increafe, after a certain portion is obtained, can be of no further utility.

To the public it is ftill more difadvantageous, becaufe it diverts the channel of its induftry from a path, in which it muft be ufeful, to a path in which, unlefs there is either an acquifition of territory, or a difcovery of new means of fupplanting or performing labour by capital, it is ufelefs to mankind.

It creates, indeed, a demand for the labour of the blackfmith, of the carpenter, and of other mechanics who are employed

in

in giving to raw materials the form that adapts them for fupplanting labour; and it will thus alter the proportion betwixt the demand for, and quantity of, this fort of labour, in fuch a manner as, by increafing the value of it, to encourage its augmentation. But as this increafe of value, and confequent encouragement given to this fpecies of labour, muft occafion a diminution of expenditure, in things that would be immediately confumed, it muft reduce their value by the portion of demand it abftracts from them, (as has been already fhewn *), in a greater degree than it increafes the value of that labour, or of thofe commodities, to the acquifition of which it is perverted; that is, it muft produce a greater diminution of encouragement to the providing of food, clothing, and thofe other articles which would have been confumed, had it not been for this avidity of accumulating capital, than it gives augmentation of encouragement to the forming of thofe things, which, if they could

* See p. 86, 87.

could all be ufed, would tend to fupplant labour.

But further, to difplay the full extent of the evil that muft arife from indulging this baneful paffion for accumulation, that has been falfely denominated a virtue, it is ne-ceffary here to explain the fingular effect which the demand it creates muft have on individual riches.

It has already been made evident, that a fudden demand for any confumeable com-modity, by increafing its value, encourages an augmented production, and tends, there-fore, to increafe wealth, though its effect is always counteracted by the more import-ant diminution of the value of other com-modities, (from which the fudden rife of the value of any one commodity abftracts a portion of demand).; becaufe the check given to production, by the abftraction of demand, has a more powerful effect in di-minifhing wealth, than the encouragement
arifing

arifing from an extenfion of demand has in
augmenting it.   This was illuftrated, by
fhewing the effect which doubling the
demand for fugar would have, where the
means of fatisfying that increafed demand
were to be found by abftracting a part of
the expenditure of the fociety in butchers-
meat, wine and muftard *.

In confidering that fubject, it appeared,
that, though the diminution of individual
riches, in the articles of wine, muftard and
butchers-meat, would be great, this would,
in fome degree, though inadequately, be
compenfated by an increafe in the value of
fugar, and the confequent augmentation of
the riches of individuals in that article.

But if this abftraction of demand from
the articles of butchers-meat, wine and
muftard, had been occafioned by the defire
of the farmer to accumulate capital; that
is, to hoard up a quantity of ploughs and
other inftruments of agriculture, greater
than

* See page 87,

than could be ufed ; then, as the quantity of thefe articles would be increafed in proportion to the demand for them, their value muft be diminifhed, as well as that of the butchers-meat, wine and muftard, from whence the demand is abftracted. Thus a diminution of value muft be produced, not only in the articles for which parfimony occafions an abftraction of demand, but even in the article for which it creates a demand ; and public wealth muft feverely feel the effects of the difcouragement by this means given to the production of both.

The public muft, therefore, fuffer by this love of accumulation, if pufhed beyond its due bounds ; — 1. By the creation of a quantity of capital more than is requifite ;—and, 2. By abftracting a portion of encouragement to future reproduction.—

1. *By the creation of a quantity of capital more than is requifite* for the moment, a thing, however much efteemed, is produced in fuch a quantity, that the whole cannot be employed,—

ployed,—a part ceafes to be an object of defire; and as things, when no longer fcarce,
can form no part of individual riches, fo,
when no longer objects of defire, they form
neither a portion of individual riches nor of
wealth.—The fineft palaces in the world
ftand empty at Delhi, unoccupied and un-
defired; and the fpacious warehoufes at
Antwerp, ferve only as monuments of her
departed commerce.

2. *By abſtraẛing a portion of encouragement
to future reproduẛion*, a diminution muft be
occafioned in the wealth to be produced;
for, as long as the nature of men remains
unchanged, the knowledge of what has been
confumed, and of the degree of avidity difplayed in the market for the different articles of confumption, muft imperioufly regulate the nature of what is fubfequently
produced. This, indeed, may be affumed
as a propofition univerfally admitted; inaf-
much as even thofe who hold deprivation of
expenditure, and confequent accumulation,
to be a mode of increafing wealth, acknowledge

ledge (with unaccountable inconfiftency)
that the whole quantity of induftry annually employed to bring any commodity to market, fuits itfelf to the effectual demand *.

If, however, deprivation of expenditure,
and confequent accumulation, far from being a means of increafing the wealth of the
nation, muft, in this fimple ftate of fociety,
by difcouraging production, inevitably tend
to its diminution, it feems difficult to difcover what alteration the circumftances
of a country undergo in the progrefs of
wealth, which can fo far change the nature
of things, as to make accumulation a means
of increafing wealth.

It has been obferved, that the property
man poffeffes in that ftate of fociety to
which allufion has been made, naturally
claffes itfelf under three different heads.

1. The land he cultivates.
                                    2. The

* Wealth of Nations, vol. 1. p. 70. 4to edit.

2. The ſtock he reſerves for immediate and remote conſumption ; under which is comprehended the produce of his farm, whether vegetable or animal.

3. His capital, conſiſting of the animals or machines he employs to ſupplant labour in the cultivation of his farm, or in the convenient conſumption of its produce.

In the progreſs of wealth, the firſt article of the ſociety's property, the land the farmer cultivates, becomes, from improvement, more productive ; the improved ſyſtem of cultivation requires more capital, but there can be no ſyſtem of culture that can benefit by an unlimited application of capital :—*As much has been done for that field as poſſible*, is an expreſſion that ſubſiſts in the phraſeology of the farmer in all ſtates of ſociety ; and, in every ſtate of ſociety alike, means, that as much capital has been employed in the improvement of that field as the preſent ſtate of the knowledge of mankind enables him to lay out with advantage ;

vantage; that is, with any profpect of increafing its produce.

The increafed produce of land, occafioned by the wife application of labour and
capital, of courfe increafes in a great degree
the vegetable and animal fubftances referved for immediate or remote confumption,
which forms the fecond branch of the property of a fociety; and it is this branch of
the property of mankind that alone appears
capable of unlimited increafe; the more
man augments it, the more muft the human
fpecies abound in opulence, or in numbers.
The affluent member of an opulent fociety,
confumes more by reducing his nourifhment
into a form fuitable to his palate, by felect-
ing, to compofe his clothing, the parts of
the productions of nature moft kindly to
his feeling, and pleafing to his eye; and by
difpofing of a part of what is produced, in
exchange for commodities of a diftant
country, which affluence enables him, and
habit teaches him to enjoy. If, even by
all thefe various methods, the increafed
produce

produce is not confumed, experience fhews that abundance of the neceffaries of life has a direct tendency to increafe population, and by this means to reftore the proportion betwixt the demand and the quantity of the increafed commodities ; thus maintaining their value notwithftanding their abundance, and perpetuating the encouragement to reproduction.

The third clafs or defcription of the property of a fociety, its Capital, confifting of all the various means of fupplanting labour, and of performing labour which could not be accomplifhed by the perfonal exertions of man, is, in the progrefs of wealth and knowledge, alfo fubject to wonderful increafe; as the fhipping, the navigable canals, the roads, the machines for tranfporting and for fabricating, and the warehoufes for preferving commodities, as well as the capital employed in circulating them, fufficiently denote *.

But

* Nothing can more forcibly exhibit the great augmentation that has taken place during the laft century in the

capital

But this defcription of property has its limits, beyond which it cannot, with advantage,

capital which in this country is employed in conducting circulation, in confequence of its increafed opulence, than the following advertifement inferted in the Poft Boy of the 20th March 1708, and repeated in the fame paper, March 23. 25. and 27.

" London, March 20. Whereas, there have been feve-
" ral falfe and malicious reports induftrioufly fpread
" abroad, reflecting on Sir RICHARD HOARE, goldfmith,
" for occafioning and promoting a run for money on the
" Bank of England ; and in particular, feveral of the Di-
" rectors of the faid Bank reporting, That the faid Sir RI-
" CHARD fent to the Bank for ten of their notes, of L. 10
" each, with a defign to fend feveral perfons with the faid
" notes to receive the money thereon, fo as to effect his ill
" defigns, and to bring a difreputation on the Bank, and
" occafion a difturbance in the city of London : This is to
" fatisfy all perfons, that the Right Honourable the Lord
" ASHBURNAM, father of the Honourable Major ASHBUR-
" NAM, major of the firft troop of her Majefty's Life
" Guards, who was ordered to march for Scotland,
" fending to the faid Sir RICHARD HOARE for a large
" quantity of gold, and for ten bank-notes, of L. 10
" each, for the faid Major, to take with him to bear
" his expences : The gold was fent to his Lordfhip
" accordingly, and Sir RICHARD's fervant went to the
" Bank for ten notes, of L. 10 each, which the cafhier of
" the

vantage, be increafed. In every ftate of fociety, a certain quantity of capital, proportioned to the exifting ftate of the knowledge of mankind, may be ufefully and
profitably employed in fupplanting and
performing labour in the courfe of rear-
ing, giving form to, and circulating the
raw materials produced. Man's invention,
in the means of fupplanting labour, may
give fcope, in the progrefs of fociety, for
the employment of an increafed quantity;
but

" the Bank refufed to give. But if Sir RICHARD had in-
" tended to promote a run for money on the Bank, he
" could have done it in a more effectual manner, having
" by him, all the time that the great demand for money
" was on the Bank, feveral thoufand pounds in notes pay-
" able by the Bank; and alfo, there was brought to Sir
" RICHARD, by feveral gentlemen, in the time of the run
" on the bank, notes payable by the faid Bank, amounting
" to a great many thoufands of pounds, which he was de-
" fired to take, and receive the money prefently from the
" Bank; which he refufed to do till the great demand on
" the Bank for money was over.

" N. B. That the reports againft Sir RICHARD have
" been more malicious than herein is mentioned, which he
" forbears to infert for brevity's fake."

but there muft be, at all times, a point determined by the exifting ftate of knowledge in the art of fupplanting and performing labour with capital, beyond which capital cannot profitably be increafed, and beyond which it will not naturally increafe; becaufe the quantity, when it exceeds that point, muft increafe in proportion to the demand for it, and its value muft of confequence diminifh in fuch a manner, as effectually to check its augmentation. It is wonderful how the Author of the Wealth of Nations, who fuccefsfully ridicules the indefinite accumulation of circulating capital, by comparing it to the amaffing of an unlimited number of pots and pans *, did not perceive that the fame ridicule is applicable to the unlimited increafe of every branch of that defcription of the property of a country which conftitutes its capital.

Fortunately, however, for mankind, the mechanifm of fociety is fo arranged, that the mifchief done by the parfimony and difpofition

* Wealth of Nations, vol. ii. p. 15. 4to edit.

pofition to accumulation of one individual is almoft uniformly counteracted by
the prodigality of fome other; fo that in
practice nothing is found more nearly
commenfurate than the expenditure and
revenue of every fociety. This inquiry,
therefore, if mankind were left to regulate
their conduct by their inclinations, would
be rather a matter of curiofity than utility; for if the effects of parfimony are
uniformly counteracted by prodigality, the
public wealth can be neither increafed nor
diminifhed by it.

As an object of curiofity, it would, at all
events, be interefting to inveftigate, whether parfimony was entitled to all the prai-
fes lavifhed upon it by the learned and the
ingenious. But the impreffion thefe opinions
have, in our own times, made on the conduct of legiflation, has given to this inveftigation a degree of importance which
makes it highly interefting.

Statefmen

Statefmen and Legiflators, (who, like o-
thers, have confidered every means of increafing the fortunes of individuals as a
means of increafing public wealth), taught
to admire the effect of parfimony and accumulation in the conduct of private fortunes, have been naturally led to regard it as
a falutary means of increafing the public
fortune, or relieving from embarraffment
the public treafury *.

On this principle, the Republic of Holland, fo early as the year 1655, was induced

---

* " On the fame principle that guided the determina-
" tion of the Parliament of 1786, another act was paffed
" in 1792, which provided, That on all future loans (in
" addition to the taxes to be impofed for paying the inte-
" reft of the fame), a furplus of one pound per cent. per
" annum, on the capital created, fhould be raifed for the
" redemption of that capital. *This was an idea conceived*
" *in that fpirit of inflexible integrity and œconomy, of which na-*
" *tions rarely afford an example ; though, like the fame virtue in*
" *private life, it is calculated to promote, in the higheft degree,*
" *their credit and their profperity.*"   Brief Examination into
the Increafe of the Revenue, Commerce, &c. of Great
Britain, by GEORGE ROSE, p. 19.

ced to fet afide an annual revenue, to be permanently accumulated, for the public benefit. This example was, in the year 1685, followed by Pope Innocent XI.; and an arrangement of a fimilar nature took place in the management of the Treafury of England in the year 1717, which was afterwards extended in the year 1727, when an annual fum of no lefs than L. 1,200,000 was devoted to accumulation at compound intereft.

All thefe different fums, however, fet afide for accumulation, (or Sinking Funds as they are called);—that of the province of Holland in the year 1655,—that of Pope Innocent the XI., in the year 1685,—as well as that eftablifhed in England in the year 1717 and 1727,—arofe from favings in confequence of reductions of intereft; for mankind had not yet become fo enamoured of the idea of accumulation, as to embolden any Legiflature to impofe burdens on the public for the avowed purpofe.

How,

How and why this firſt attempt to force
accumulation by law in England died away,
will be afterwards conſidered. In point of
fact, we are told, by one of the ableſt and
moſt reſpectable advocates in favour of this
fyſtem of increaſing the wealth of a nation
by acumulation, that, foon after the year
1730, this fund fet afide for accumulation,
which, if it " could have efcaped the hand of
" violence, would have made Great Britain
" the envy and terror of the world, was pre-
" maturely deſtroyed by the hand of its own
" parent * ;" and after that period, though
there exiſted the name of a Sinking Fund,
and though fums were from time to time employed to purchaſe up portions of the public debt, the plan of a regular forced accumulation, by the authority of Government, with a view to public benefit, was
for

* See an Appeal to the Public on the Subject of the
National Debt, by Dr PRICE, p. 37.

for many years relinquifhed in practice *.
This fyftem was, however, again revived
in the year 1786, when, in the Houfe of
Commons, it was ftated,—and certainly at
the time truly ftated,—to be the common
confent of all, that L. 1,000,000 fhould
be

* Sums paid off by the Sinking Fund eftablifhed in 1717
and 1727, and afterwards augmented, by the reduction
of intereft, betwixt the year 1750 and the year 1757.

Year.				Year.			
1723,	L. 1,204,786	3	4½	1738,	L. 1,000,000	0	0
1724,	333,447	18	4	1751,	368,771	2	4
1727,	650,453	2	8½	1752,	821,270	13	9
1728.	1,000,000	0	0	1765,	870,888	5	5½
1729,	1,275,027	17	10½	1766,	870,888	5	5½
1730,	1,000,000	0	0	1767,	2,616,776	10	11
1731,	1,000,419	16	4	1768,	1,750,000	0	0
1732,	1,000,000	0	0	1769,	875,000	0	0
1733,	913,115	15	3½	1770,	1,500,000	0	0
1734,	86,884	4	8¼	1772,	1,500,000	0	0
1736,	1,000,000	0	0	1774,	1,000,000	0	0
1737,	1,000,000	0	0	1775,	1,000,000	0	0

Amount of the National Debt at different Periods up to the
Year 1775.

Year.		Year.	
1688,	L. 664,263	1748,	L. 78,293,312
1702,	16,394,702	1755,	74,571,840
1715,	54,145,363	1762,	146,682,844
1727,	52,092,235	1775,	135,943,051
1739,	46,954,623		

be fet afide to accumulate for national benefit.

A law was accordingly foon afterwards made, by which L. 1,000,000 was devoted to be accumulated quarterly, till fuch time as, together with the annuities which were to fall into the public, it amounted to L. 4,000,000 *per annum* *. And in the year 1792, after ably ftating the profperity which the duration of peace and tranquillity had fecured for this country, the fame Minifter, who propofed the accumulating fund in 1786, introduced a propofal for increafing the fum devoted to accumulation in the following terms :—

" Having ftated the increafe of revenue,
" and fhewn that it has been accompanied
" by a proportionate increafe of the national
" wealth, commerce and manufactures, I
" feel that it is natural to afk, What have
" been the peculiar circumftances to which
" thefe effects are to be afcribed?
" The

* Cap. xxxi. an. 26. Geo. III.

" The firſt, and moſt obvious anſwer,
" which every man's mind will ſuggeſt to
" this queſtion, is, that it ariſes from the
" natural induſtry and energy of the coun-
" try : but what is it which has enabled
" that induſtry and energy to act with ſuch
" peculiar vigour, and ſo far beyond the
" example of former periods ? The im-
" provement which has been made in the
" mode of carrying on almoſt every branch
" of manufacture, and the degree to which
" labour has been abridged, by the inven-
" tion and application of machinery, have
" undoubtedly had a conſiderable ſhare in
" producing ſuch important effects. We
" have, beſides, ſeen, during theſe periods,
" more than at any former time, the effect
" of one circumſtance which has princi-
" pally tended to raiſe this country to its
" mercantile pre-eminence ;—I mean that
" peculiar degree of credit, which, by a
" twofold operation, at once gives addi-
" tional facility and extent to the tranſac-
" tions of our merchants at home, and en-
" ables

" ables them to obtain a proportional fupe-
" riority in markets abroad. This advan-
" tage has been moft confpicuous during
" the latter part of the period to which I
" have referred, and it is conftantly in-
" creafing, in proportion to the profperity
" which it contributes to create.

" In addition to all this, the exploring and
" enterprifing fpirit of our merchants has
" been feen in the extenfion of our naviga-
" tion and our fifheries, and the acquifitions
" of new markets in different parts of the
" world ; and undoubtedly thofe efforts
" have been not a little affifted by the ad-
" ditional intercourfe with France in con-
" fequence of the Commercial Treaty ; an
" intercourfe which, though probably
" checked and abated by the diftractions
" now prevailing in that kingdom, has fur-
" nifhed a great additional incitement to
" induftry and exertion.

" But there is ftill another caufe, even
" more

" more fatisfactory than thefe, becaufe it is
" of a ftill more extenfive and permanent
" nature; that conftant accumulation of
" capital;—That continual tendency to in-
" creafe, the operation of which is univer-
" fally feen in a greater·or lefs proportion,
" wherever it is not obftructed by fome pu-
" blic calamity, or by fome miftaken and
" mifchievous policy; but which muft be
" confpicuous and rapid, indeed, in any
" country which has once arrived at an
" advanced ftate of commercial profperity.
" Simple and obvious as this principle is,
" and felt and obferved as it muft have
" been in a greater or lefs degree, even
" from the earlieft periods, I doubt whe-
" ther it has ever been fully developed and
" fufficiently explained, but in the wri-
" tings of an Author of our own times,
" now unfortunately no more, (I mean the
" Author of the celebrated Treatife on the
" Wealth of Nations), whofe extenfive
" knowledge of detail, and depth of philo-
" fophical refearch, will, I believe, furnifh
                              " the

" the beft folution to every queftion con-
" nected with the hiftory of commerce, or
" with the fyftem of political œconomy.
" This accumulation of capital arifes from
" the continual application of a part, at
" leaft, of the profit obtained in each year, to
" increafe the total amount of capital to be
" employed in a fimilar manner, and with
" continued profit, in the year following.
" The great mafs of the property of the
" nation is thus conftantly increafing at
" compound intereft ; the progrefs of
" which, in any confiderable period, is
" what, at firft view, would appear incre-
" dible.   Great as have been the effects of
" this caufe already, they muft be greater
" in future ; for its powers are augmented
" in proportion as they are exerted.   It
" acts with a velocity continually accele-
" rated, with a force continually increa-
" fed.

    " Mobilitate viget, viresque acquirit eundo *."

This

* See Mr Pitt's Speech, printed by authority for G. G.
and J. Robinsons, 1792, p. 36.

This was the prelude to a legiflative arrangement, which devoted the annual million to be accumulated till it produced
L. 3,000,000 *per annum* over and above
the yearly million, and the produce of the
annuities which would fall into the public;
and alfo to a provifion, compelling one *per
cent.* to be fet afide annually for accumulation on the capital of all debt which fhould
in future be contracted.

L. 400,000 additional was likewife given
to the accumulating fund this year, which
laid the foundation of another annual grant
of L. 200,000.

But the effects of this admiration of the
benefits derived from a fyftem of accumulation did not terminate here. The fame
Minifter, in the year 1799, impofed an Income Tax, which he calculated would produce L. 10,000,000 annually * ; and an act

was

* See Appendix, No. IV. being the Computation of Income by Mr Pitt, as ftated by Lord Auckland, in his
Speech,

was paſſed, appropriating the produce of this tax on the return of peace to accumulation, till it ſhould amount to a ſum ſufficient to redeem the debt ſubſequently to be contraincluded during the war.

The accumulating fund created in the year 1786, together with the addition derived from the arrangement made in the year 1792, by this time amounted annually to a ſum ſuch as enabled the public to foreſee, that before the probable return of peace, it would produce L. 5,000,000 annually.

Under the law of this country, therefore, as it was then conſtituted, had this income tax produced L. 10,000,000, L. 15,000,000 of the revenue of the country would, on the return of peace, have been devoted to accumulation.

This

Speech, printed by authority, 1799. And alſo by Mr ROSE, Appendix, No. 7. of his Brief Examination.

This ftatement will not, in fubftance, be contradicted either by Mr Pitt * or his admirers †. He took credit to himfelf for the device ; and they uniformly afferted, that the merits of the plan, which they ftated to be of more importance to Great Britain than the poffeffion of all the mines of America, would hand down his name

---

* See Refolution on the State of Finance, 19th and 20th, propofed by Mr Pitt, and agreed to by the Houfe of Commons, 1801.

† " But the farther refulting advantages are infinite-
" ly more important. It is not amongft the leaft of thofe
" advantages, that by the prefent plan, the falutary effects
" of the finking fund are greatly accelerated. The fums
" of different defcriptions to be referved and applied by
" the Commiffioners for the redemption of the national
" debt, will, in the firft year of peace, be not lefs than *fif-*
" *teen millions, or nearly* L. 50,000 *a-day,* for three hun-
" dred days in the year. The operation of fuch a fum
" brought daily into the market to purchafe ftock, which
" is to be extinguifhed, and not to return to, cannot fail to
" have an effect in favour of our public credit, as much
" beyond all calculation as it will be beyond all experi-
" ence." See the Subftance of Lord Auckland's Speech,
printed by authority, p. 22.

name with glory to pofterity *.—This, too, was the object of thofe daring projectors of the Tower of Babel, who are recorded in facred hiftory to have faid, " Go " to, let us build us a tower whofe top may " reach unto heaven, and let us make us a " name." And ftriking as the fimilarity may be in the object, there will be found a ftill more glaring refemblance in the defign.

Had an opportunity exifted, in profound peace, of applying this fum of L. 15,000,000, but for two years, to the ufes to which by law it was appropriated, the ruin it muft have produced would have practically exhibited and explained the folly of the attempt. But as we have had no opportunity of learning from experience the confequences of the meafure, it will require

---

* See CHALMERS's Eftimate of the Strength of Great Britain, p. 183. See alfo the Brief Examination into the Increafe of the Revenue, Commerce, &c. by Mr ROSE.

quire a little inveſtigation to diſplay them.

Before, however, proceeding to this inquiry, leſt the reader ſhould be diſpoſed to think, with the generality of mankind, that what is true in figures, and the reſult of accurate calculation, muſt be true in practice, and poſſible in execution; he is deſired to reflect, that one penny put out, at our Saviour's birth, at 5 per cent. compound intereſt, would, before this time, have increaſed to a greater ſum than could be contained in five hundred millions of earths, all of ſolid gold; and that this is a calculation as accurate, and as true, as any with which Parliament has been furniſhed in the progreſs of this deluſion *.

If

* " One penny put out at our Saviour's birth, to 5 per
" cent. compound intereſt, would, in the preſent year,
" 1781, have increaſed to a greater ſum than would be
" contained in two hundred millions of earths, all ſolid
" gold. But if put out to ſimple intereſt, it would, in the
" ſame

If L. 15,000,000 a-year extraordinary
were levied by the Government from the
revenue of its fubjects, to defray the charge
of warfare or any other extraordinary expenditure ; as this money would be expended in articles of confumption, as faft as affumed, the expence of the Government
would effectually counteract the effects of
the parfimony it renders neceffary, and
creates in the fubject. The only mifchief,
therefore, that could enfue, would arife
from

" fame time, have amounted to no more than 7 s. 6 d.
" All Governments that alienate funds deftined for reim-
" burfements, choofe to improve money in the laft rather
" than in the firft of thefe ways." Obfervations on Re-
verfionary Payments, &c. by RICHARD PRICE, D. D.
p. 228.

That the reader may fee a lively picture of the abfurd
length to which the fpeculations of increafing the wealth
of mankind, by accumulation of capital, have been carried,
we have, in APPENDIX, No. V. printed the teftament of
Mr FORTUNE RICARD, teacher of arithmetic at D——, read
and publifhed at the Court of Bailiwick of that town, the
19th Auguft 1794, tranflated by Dr PRICE.

from the extensive demand it must sudden-
ly occasion for one class of commodities,
and from the consequent abstraction of so
large a portion of the revenue of the subjects from the acquisition of those articles
in which it is usually expended ;—a mischief in itself nowife trifling, as recent experience has taught the merchants of this
country *.

Very different, however, must have been
the effect of raising fifteen millions for the
purpose of accumulation, or of forcibly converting fifteen millions of revenue into capital.   In this, as in the former case, there
would have ensued all the mischief occasioned by abstracting a portion of demand repre-
sented by fifteen millions a-year, from the
commodities which the subjects were accu-
stomed to acquire with this part of their revenue: but, in this cafe, there would unfortunately have existed no extraordinary expenditure, to counteract the full effects of this
forced parsimony ; for it would have been
difficult

* See page 91.

difficult to perfuade the proprietors of ftock, from whom fuch extenfive purchafes would have been made by the Commiffioners of the Sinking Fund, all at once to fpend, as revenue, that which habit had taught them to regard as capital ; or, in other words, all at once to ruin themfelves, in order to counteract the bad effects of this miferly policy in Government.

Unlefs, however, the ftockholder could have been perfuaded thus to expend his capital, fifteen millions a-year lefs muft have been expended in the different articles the country produced or manufactured ; that is, a portion of demand would at once have been withdrawn from commodities of Britifh growth or manufacture, nearly equal to the whole demand created by the foreign trade of the country in the year 1786, when the million was firft fet afide to accumulate, as the exports from England amounted in that year to the fum of L. 15,385,987.

But if it is true, (which all writers on political

political œconomy, however much they
may differ on other fubjects, concur in af-
ferting *), that the whole quantity of induftry employed to bring any commodity to
the market, naturally fuits itfelf to the effectual demand, and conftantly aims at bringing the precife quantity thither that is fufficient to fupply the demand; it follows,
that

* *Que la totalité des fommes du revenu rentre dans la circulation annuelle, et la parcoure dans toute fon étendue ; qu'il ne fe
forme point de fortunes pécuniares, ou du moins qu'il y ait compenfation entre celles qui fe forment et celles qui reviennent dans la circulation ; car autrement ces fortunes pécuniaires arrêteroient la
diftribution d'une partie du revenu annuel de la nation, et retiendroi-
ent le pécule du Royaume au préjudice de la rentrée des avances de
la culture, de la retribution du falaire des artifans, et de la confommation que doivent faire les différentes claffes d'hommes qui exercent
des profeffions lucratives : Cette interception du pécule diminueroit
la reproduction des revenus.* " It is neceffary that the fum-
" total of the revenue fhould enter into the annual cir-
" culation, and pervade it in its utmoft extent ; that no
" pecuniary fortunes be formed, or, at leaft, that there be
" a compenfation between thofe that are formed, and thofe
" which, from extravagance, return into the circulation ;
" for, otherwife, the amaffing of pecuniary fortunes would
" impede the diftribution of a part of the annual revenue
" of the nation, and hold back part of the circulation of
" the nation, to the prejudice of the advances neceffary for
" the

that this diminution of demand muft occafion a fimilar diminution of the productions
of the country.

Though the opinions of great and eminent
men are here referred to for eftablifhing the
pofition, that a diminution of demand muft
occafion a diminution of produce, that is,
of wealth ; it is not on authority alone that
this inference refts.   The reafons why it
muft happen have been ftated, and the progrefs

" the conduct of agriculture, of the recompence of the fa-
" lary of the artifans, and of the confumption incident to
" the different claffes of men who exercife lucrative pro-
" feffions: and this reduction would inevitably diminifh
" the revenue reproduced." *Maximes Générales du Gouvernement Economique, par* QUESNAY.

*Le revenu eft donc le canevas de la dépenfe proprement dite.
Il importe que le revenu foit dépenfé, car toute épargne fur le revenu eft diminution de dépenfe, et par une fuite directe de production
et de revenu.* " The revenue, then properly fpeaking, is
" the groundwork of the expence. It is neceffary that the
" revenue fhould be expended ; for every faving in the re-
" venue occafions a diminution of expenditure, and, by
" direct confequence, of production and of future reve-
" nue." *Philofophie Rurale, ou Economie Générale et Politique
de l'Agriculture*, p. 48.   See alfo Wealth of Nations, vol. 1.
p. 70. 4to edit.

grefs that a diminution of demand would probably make, in curtailing the production of commodities, was traced out in the cafe of a fuppofed diminution of demand for butchers-meat, wine and muftard *; and the fame reafoning is applicable to every article of the produce of any country for which there exifts a failure of demand.

But if this effect neceffarily attends a diminution of demand, which not only reafon, but the authority of all eminent men, concurs in faying muft enfue ; an ab-ftraction of demand, to the extent of fif-teen millions, muft have occafioned a fimi-lar deficiency of annual production. It fol-lows, therefore, that three hundred mil-lions (calculating the value of the fifteen millions of produce which muft have been annihilated, at twenty years purchafe) of real wealth would have been extinguifh-ed, before this accumulating fund, with all its boafted activity, could have in all proba-bility converted one hundred millions of the revenue into capital.

In

* See page 87.

In truth, the effects of this diminution of demand to the extent of fifteen millions, would have been much more formidable than what is here reprefented; becaufe it has already been eftablifhed, that the diminution in value of every commodity, occafioned by the diminution of demand, muft be always much greater than the value of the demand abftracted *.

Difmal as the confequences of this experiment muft have been in diminifhing the reproduction and revenue, there appear, on the other hand, no good effects likely to have refulted from it in relation to the capital of the country, to counteract its evil effects on the revenue.

The ftockholders, who would have been tempted to fell by the offer of the Commiffioners of this Sinking Fund, would, it is evident, have had in their poffeffion fifteen millions of capital, upon the employment of which in fuch a manner as to return a profit,

* See page 89.

fit, their income, that is, their fubfiftence, muft have depended. To acquire a profit, we know that capital muft be employed to fup-plant or perform a portion of labour, in producing or giving form to commodities; and it is hardly poffible to fuppofe, that there could have exifted any new channels of fo employing capital, at a moment when there was forcibly created a diminution of demand for commodities, to the extent of fifteen millions.

So far from its being reafonable to fuppofe there could have exifted, under fuch circum-ftances, any opportunity of employing an additional quantity of capital, it is certain, that fo great a diminution of demand muft have thrown out of employ fome of that capital which was ufeful in fupplanting la-bour, in the progrefs of bringing to market thofe commodities, for which there could no longer have fubfifted a demand.

The only means, therefore, thofe ftock-holders could have had of forcing the capi-tal

tal in their hands into employment, muſt
have been by offering to ſupplant labour,
at a cheaper rate than that at which it was
antecedently performed.   A competition
would thus have ariſen ; the profit of capital muſt have been diminiſhed ; the intereſt
paid for ſtock or money muſt have fallen,
and of courſe the value of fixed annuities,
or Government ſecurities, muſt have riſen :
and this muſt have continued progreſſively,
till capital became ſo abundant, and its profits ſo diminiſhed, that the proprietors would
have been induced to remove it to other
countries, where higher profits might be
made ; and France would inevitably have
been amply ſupplied with capital, the want
of which is the great drawback on her induſtry.

Neither is it theory alone which points
out theſe evils, as the neceſſary reſult of
ſuch a meaſure ; for, as far as practice gives
us an opportunity of judging, the accuracy
of the inference is uniformly confirmed by
experience.   When Pope INNOCENT XI.
reduced

reduced the intereſt of his debt from
4 to 3 *per cent.*, and employed the ſum ſa-
ved to accumulate, but a ſhort time elapſed
till the new 3 *per cent.* fund ſold at one
hundred and twelve. In like manner, when
the intereſt of the national debt of England
was reduced, in 1717, from 6 to 5 *per
cent.*, and the ſaving devoted to accumulation; the conſequence was, that in 1727,
from the riſe of public ſecurities, there was
an opportunity of again reducing the intereſt from 4 to 3 per cent., and of applying
an additional ſum to accumulate. This, of
courſe, produced another riſe, and to ſuch
a degree, that in the year 1733, we learn
from authority, that " the ſinking fund
" was now grown to a great maturity, and
" produced annually about L. 1,200,000;
" and was become almoſt a terror to all the
" individual proprietors of the public debt.
" The high ſtate of credit, the low rate of
" intereſt of money, and the advanced price
" of all public ſtocks and funds above par,
" made the great monied companies, and
" all

" all their proprietors, apprehend nothing
" more than being obliged to receive their
" principal too faft; and it *became almoft the*
" *univerfal confent of mankind, that a million*
" *a-year was as much as the creditors of the*
" *public could bear to receive* in difcharge of
" part of their principal *."

Nothing can more forcibly illuftrate the
truth of the opinions which have been ftated, than what Sir ROBERT WALPOLE here
affirms.   If he had been aware of the nature and the foundation of the profit of
ftock ; if he had perceived the effects of
forced parfimony, not only in depreciating
thofe commodities from which it abftracts
a portion of demand, but even in depreciating that for which it creates a demand ;
if he had written on purpofe to fupport and
illuftrate the theory here built upon, he could
not have done it with more effect than by
ftating, " that a million a-year became as
                                    " much

* Confiderations concerning the Public Funds, the Public Revenues, and the Annual Supplies, by Sir ROBERT
WALPOLE, p. 56.

" much as the creditors of the public could
" bear to receive."

It is remarkable, too, that this is almoſt
the only fact in the whole pamphlet, to the
truth of which his adverſary, in his reply,
ſeems to ſubſcribe *.   And, indeed, Mr
HUME, nearly twenty years afterwards,
plainly ſhews, that he was aware of that
circumſtance, by ſtating, that " in times
" of peace and ſecurity, when alone it is
" poſſible

* " You tell us, that the public creditors were ſo far
" from making any proviſion for themſelves, either in
" their ſeparate or their corporate capacity, that the ſink-
" ing fund ſhould be applied to the diſcharge of their
" principal, that, whenever it hath been applied to this
" purpoſe, the only conteſt between them hath been, who
" ſhould not be paid.

" In another place you tell us, That the South Sea
" Company were ſo far from looking upon their being
" firſt paid off, as a privilege or beneficial preference, that
" they expreſsly provided againſt it : This, again, is very
" true, nor have we denied it." The Caſe of the Sinking
Fund, being a full reply to a late pamphlet, entitled, Some
Conſiderations, &c. p. 27.

" poffible to pay debt, the monied intereft
" are averfe to receive partial payments,
" which they know not how to difpofe of
" to advantage *."

Further, the doctrine here maintained
derives ftrong and ample confirmation from
the gradual and progreffive effect which
the following ftatement fhews the finking
fund to have had on the price of public fecurities during the laft peace.

STATEMENT, fhewing the Prices at which 3 *per cent.*
Stock was bought by the Sinking Fund, in every
Quarter, from the beginning of the Year 1787 to the
end of the Year 1792.

1787.		1788.		1789.	
Qr.	Pr.	Qr.	Pr.	Qr.	Pr.
2. ending Jan. 31.	74½	6. -	76	10. -	73½
3. - Apr. 30.	76	7. -	75½	11. -	74¼
4. - July 31.	74½	8. -	74½	12. -	76¼
5. - Oct. 31.	71½	9. -	74¼	13. -	80⅛

1790.		1791.		1792.	
Qr.	Pr.	Qr.	Pr.	Qr.	Pr.
14. ending Jan. 31.	78	18. -	79⅛	22. -	88¾
15. - Apr. 30.	78⅞	19. -	79¼	23. -	96½
16. - July 31.	73¼	20. -	81½	24. -	90½
17. - Oct. 31.	76⅞	21. -	88¼	25. -	90¼

Yet

* See a note to the firft edition of Mr HUME's Difcourfe on Public Credit, which is fuppreffed in the later
editions.

Yet during thefe fix years, one would have imagined, that fo many opportunities muft have occurred of employing capital in new channels, that the accumulating fund being abforbed in new adventures, could not have diminifhed the value, that is, the intereft of capital; for the number of inclofure bills, of road and canal bills, never was fo great in fo fhort a time *, whilft the

---

* TABLE, fhewing the Number of Acts of Parliament for Roads, Bridges, &c. which paffed in each of the following Years.

	1785	1786	1787	1788	1789	1790	1791	1792	Total.
Roads and bridges, -	31	40	30	37	36	30	44	54	302
Canals, harbours, &c. -	7	4	3	5	6	9	13	17	64
Inclofures, draining, &c. -	22	25	19	36	36	27	39	41	245
Paving and other parochial improvements, -	20	14	14	14	18	20	20	19	139
The total,	80	83	66	92	96	86	116	131	750

the increase of our exports *, of the tonnage of our shipping †, as well as the extension of machinery in every branch of manufacture, was equally remarkable ; and it is certain, that the increase of produce and manufactures must have required an additional capital to circulate them.

Experience, however, shews us, that this was not the case. Stocks rose from 74 to 96 ; that is, the interest or value of capital sunk from four pounds one shilling and one penny, to three pounds two shillings and sixpence *per annum;* yet there was then only L. 1,000,000 a-year set aside

for

* Amount of the Exports from Great Britain in the following years.

Year.	L.	Year.	L.	Year.	L.
1786,	16,300,725	1789,	20,013,297	1791,	22,731,994
1787,	18,296,166	1790,	20,120,120	1792,	24,905,200
1788,	18,124,082				

† Account of the Tonnage of British Shipping cleared outwards in the following years.

Year.	Tons.	Year.	Tons.	Year.	Tons.
1786,	982,132	1789,	1,343,800	1791,	1,333,106
1787,	1,104,711	1790,	1,260,828	1792,	1,396,003
1788,	1,243,200				

for accumulation, and the whole fum accumulated during the five years, amounted to L. 5,424,592 *; that is, to little more than a third of that which the temerity of Mr PITT projected, on the firft year of the return of peace, to abftract from expenditure in the acquifition of commodities the produce and growth of the country, and to convert into capital.

In the receipt of the income-tax, Mr PITT, however, was difappointed: it never much exceeded five millions and a half †. But if he had remained Minifter, and we had enjoyed peace, a fum to this amount would, till the year 1811, have been applicable to accumulation, over and above the fum

* Report of the Select Committee, relating to the Public Income and Expenditure, 1791 : Appendix X. No. 1.

† The receipt of the Income Tax for one year, ending 5th April 1801. amounted to L. 5,741,150.—See Refolutions voted by the Houfe of Commons.

sum of L. 5,585,572 *, applicable to that purpose at the time peace was restored; that is, a sum of upwards of L. 11,000,000 would have been annually withdrawn from expenditure on commodities, the produce and manufacture of the country, and applied by law to accumulation;—a system which never could have been carried into execution, without effecting the ruin of the country, both by the diminution it must have occasioned of its produce and manufactures, and by the means it must have afforded of aggrandizing our enemies, by furnishing them with capital.

The income tax has now been repealed, and the sinking fund is new-modelled by the 42. GEO. III. cap. 71. By this law, the Sinking Fund established in 1786, and that

* See No. 13. Accounts presented to the House of Commons, respecting the public funded debt, and the reduction thereof, 1802.

that of the year 1792, the Old and New
Sinking Funds, as they are called, are confolidated; the provifions concerning the
old finking fund, as to the application of
the intereft after it amounted to three millions, are done away; the annuities, as
they expired, are directed to be no longer
carried to the account of the Commiffioners; one *per cent.* on a new loan is rendered unneceffary; the L. 200,000 annually
granted is made a permanent grant; and
the produce of both the new and the old
fund is made applicable to accumulate at
compound intereft, till the debt, amounting, at the time of paffing the act, to
L. 488,987,656 *, is extinguifhed.

Even now, then, on the return of peace,
as the law ftands, there will be an accumulating fund of more than fix millions *per*
annum.

* See No. 13. Accounts prefented to the Houfe of Commons, refpecting the public funded debt, &c. 1802.

annum *. Six millions muft, therefore, be
withdrawn from the acquifition of commodities, the growth and manufacture of the
country, and forcibly converted into capital ; a fituation which will require much
attention from thofe who have the management of the country at the time.   It
is an experiment hitherto untried.   The accumulating fund has rifen to this magni-
tude during warfare ; and the effects of accumulation, during war, are more than
counteracted by the extraordinary expenditure it occafions. The accumulating fund
now provided by law, is nearly fix times
greater than any of which we have had
experience during peace.   Indeed, it a-
mounts, in one year, to a fum almoft equal
to all that was accumulated betwixt the
                                      year

* The fum to be expended in the prefent quarter, by
the Commiffioners of the Sinking Fund, is L. 1,668,161,
12 s. 1 d.

year 1717 and the year 1732 * ; which reduced the value of capital from 6 to 3 *per
cent. ;* for, in this laſt year, 3 *per cents.*
were at one hundred and one. It is larger,
too, than the ſum-total of what was accumulated during the laſt peace †, and
the 3 *per cents.* were then gradually raiſed
from ſixty to nearly one hundred ; that is,
the value of capital was reduced from 5 to
3 *per cent.*

Thoſe, therefore, who have the management of the Public Treaſury on the return
of peace, muſt be careful, on the one hand,
leſt, from the abſtraction of demand to the
amount of ſix millions, the price of commodities

* The ſum-total applied for this purpoſe, during that
period, amounted to L. 6,464,132. See Sinclair's Hiſtory
of Public Revenue, Part II. p. 122.

† The ſum iſſued to the Commiſſioners of the Sinking
Fund betwixt the 1ſt of Auguſt 1786, and the 1ſt of Auguſt 1791, amounted to L. 5,424,592. Report of the
Committee of the Houſe of Commons on the Public Expenditure, 1791 : App. X. No. 1.

modities be reduced to fuch a degree as to difcourage reproduction; they muft be cautious not to miftake, for the effects of abundance, that which in reality may be only the effect of failure of demand. On the other hand, they muft be fcrupuloufly attentive to the effects of this forced increafe of capital; for if 3 *per cents.* fhould by this means be quickly raifed to par, or, in other words, if the value of capital fhould be reduced from upwards of 5 *per cent.* to 3, and the fame caufes continue to operate its farther reduction, in the prefent fituation of Europe it will inevitably furnifh our enemies with what will render them moft formidable.

That both thefe confequences muft enfue is undoubted, and that, too, with a degree of unexpected rapidity. Of the abftraction of demand to the amount of fix millions a-year, from goods the growth and produce of the country, we have no experience; neither have we experience of the effects of forcibly adding fix millions annually

annually to the capital of the nation : but
fince there exifted an accumulating fund in
this country, fix millions have never been
accumulated by the public even in a courfe
of years, without creating fuch abundance
of capital in proportion to the demand for
it, as to reduce its value to 3 *per cent. per
annum.*

That the prefent fituation of the country
is different from what it was at any former
period, is moft certain. That it may, therefore, be able to fuftain a larger accumulation
than formerly, is probable ; but accumulation of capital muft at all times have its
bounds, beyond which if it is enforced, the
confequences which have been ftated muft
inevitably be produced.

We already know, that the value of capital may be reduced from 6 to 3 *per cent.*
by forced accumulation ; and it is impoffible to fay how low it may be brought, by
the continued progrefs of accumulation,
which

which increafes the quantity of capital; whilft, far from increafing, (by the effect it has of abftracting revenue from expenditure in confumable commodities, and confequently of abridging confumption), it inevitably diminifhes the demand for it.

If, indeed, the whole of the capital which muft by this means be created, could poffibly be kept within the country, it is demonftrable, that before any confiderable progrefs could be made in this fyftem of accumulation, the value of capital muft be reduced to a trifle.

How far fuch an abundance of capital, if produced univerfally over the world by the increafed induftry of man, directed to the production and formation of thofe things every way ufeful to fupplant and perform labour, *(the fole method in which the capital of a country ought to be increafed)*, would be beneficial, is a queftion we are not here called upon to agitate.

What

What is affirmed, and what we have attempted to eſtabliſh by argument, is, that a nation, in the circumſtances and ſituation of the Britiſh Empire, cannot, with impunity, either forcibly abſtract a ſum ſo large as has been propoſed, from expenditure in conſumable goods of its produce and manufacture; or forcibly accumulate its capital with ſuch rapidity.

For no nation, without injury to the progreſs of its wealth, can thus rapidly increaſe its capital, at the expence of abſtracting annually ſo large a ſum from expenditure in conſumable commodities; and, in the preſent ſituation of Europe, if this country could, by parſimony, render capital ſo abundant; as it is impoſſible to prevent the removal of it, it would be relatively injurious to our intereſt; for the ſituation of other nations, and thoſe, too, whoſe intereſts, at preſent, we would leaſt wiſh to promote, is ſuch, that they would

derive

derive more benefit from it than would refult to the Britifh Empire.

In truth, though Parliament has formally
announced, by an act of the Legiflature *,
the extinction of the national debt in forty-five years; or, in other words, the defign of abftracting from expenditure, and
forcibly converting into capital, within
that period, a fum amounting nearly to
five hundred millions ; that is, to more than
fix times what has been efteemed the a-
mount of the whole capital now employed
in the conduct of our foreign trade † ;—
that act, fooner or later, muft be reconfi-
dered : for the impoffibility of accumulating a penny till it amounts to the value
of five hundred millions of earths of folid
gold,

* See APPENDIX, No. VI. containing extracts of cap. 71.
42. GEO. III.

† See Mr PITT's Computation, APPENDIX, No. IV.

gold, is not more apparent, than the impoffibility, without the ruin of the country, of
abftracting from expenditure, in its goods
and manufactures, a revenue fo large as
L. 5,585,572, and that, too, annually increafing at compound intereft for forty-five
years *.

Nothing, indeed, can be more abfurd,
than the golden dreams with which Parliament and the nation have been amufed,
through the medium of the calculations
that have been formed on this fubject †.
Perhaps

* See APPENDIX, No. VII. where a ftatement is given
of the fum that, under this fyftem, if purfued, muft every
half year be abftracted from expenditure in goods the
produce and manufacture of the country, and forcibly
converted into capital during the forty-five years, which,
before the expiration of that term, will be found to amount
to upwards of L. 20,000,000 *per annum.*

† See APPENDIX, No. VIII. containing a ftatement
prefented to the Houfe of Commons 7th April 1802, of the
amount of ftock which will be purchafed in forty-five and
forty-fix years, at the feveral rates of intereft 3, 3¼, 3½, 3¾,
and 4 *per cent.* by a finking fund of L. 5,585,572 *per annum.*

Perhaps it may with reason be thought, that nothing could be more unfortunate than the faith that seems to be reposed in them.

For though the Sinking Fund, the off-spring of this delusion, never can, without ruining the country, be accumulated to an amount equal to the debt of the nation, yet its exiftence has greatly facilitated the contracting of debt ; that is, it has enabled those who had the management of the Government more completely to derange the natural and moft advantageous diftribution of the property of the country ; —that diftribution, which, giving to the poffeffor the greateft real intereft in the property he has to manage, affords the greateft encouragement to those exertions of induftry in the conduct of it, which alike benefit the proprietor and the public.

The extreme importance of the fubject alone

alone appears a fufficient apology for having gone fo much at length into the confideration of the legiflative provifions for
paying off the national debt. But, indeed,
it was neceffary, in giving an idea of the
origin and progrefs of wealth, to fhew that
it can alone be increafed by the means by
which it is produced ; and this could not be
effected without inveftigating the confequences of parfimony, (which has been hitherto confidered as the moft active means
of increafing wealth), and without fully
explaining why parfimony, when pufhed
beyond a certain extent, whether private, or
public, whether the effect of the depraved
tafte of individuals, or of an erroneous fyftem of legiflation, muft be fatal to the progrefs of public wealth.

Having now endeavoured to do away
the impreffion which prejudice has created
on this fubject, we are at liberty to proceed
to the confideration of how far, and in
what manner and proportions, the produce

of

of land, and of labour, whether performed by the hand of man or by capital, contributes to the increaſe of national wealth ; for as theſe conſtitute the ſole ſources of public wealth, ſo they muſt form the ſole means of increaſing it.

CHAP.

CHAP. V.

OF THE MEANS OF AUGMENTING WEALTH, AND THE CAUSES THAT REGULATE ITS INCREASE.

THOUGH land, labour and capital have been considered as forming the sources of the wealth of mankind, and though we have endeavoured to establish the opinion, that wealth can alone be increased by the means by which it is produced; it does not from thence follow, that land, labour and capital should each of them afford means of increasing wealth; far less that they should, in different stages of society, contribute towards

wards its increafe, in any thing like fimilar
proportions.

It has already been obferved, that in the
early ftate of his exiftence, man muft have
derived a greater proportion of his wealth
from land than at any fubfequent ftage of
fociety.   To the produce of the earth,
which nature prefented to his view, he muft
at firft have had recourfe for the fatisfaction of all his appetites and defires.

His bodily labour, in this ftate of fociety, muft, in its object, have been fimilar to
that of the other animals, calculated to
appropriate and prepare for confumption
thofe things which nature afforded; and,
under fuch circumftances, the fhare of his
labour muft have been fmall, indeed, which
could either be fupplanted or performed by
capital.   The club with which he deftroys
his prey; the wooden knife with which he
prepares it for confumption; the hook
with which he draws towards him, and ap-

propriates

propriates the fruit of trees; the hatchet of ſtone with which he obtains and faſhions thoſe his rude inſtruments; form nearly the whole capital that the hiſtory of ſavage nations diſplays to our view.

Thus circumſtanced, like the reſt of the animal creation, on nature he depends alone for the means of continuing his exiſtence. The fertility of ſome ſeaſons beſtows an ample, the ſterility of others affords only a ſcanty ſupply; and man ſeems little to ſurpaſs other animals, either in dexterity in ſecuring the objects his appetites ſuggeſt as deſirable, or in ingenuity in preſerving and adapting them for conſumption.

Even in this ſtate, however, as an animal cannot be captured and appropriated, or a quantity of fruit collected and conveyed home without labour, his wealth cannot be conſidered as excluſively proceeding from land, though this is obviouſly the great and
principal

principal fource from whence he acquires it.

But the moment man appears in the ftate of a fhepherd or an hufbandman, we perceive his labour, whether performed by his hands or capital, taking a new direction, and acting in a fphere peculiar to the human fpecies.

It is no longer employed, like that of the other animals, in fecuring or fafhioning the fcanty fupply which nature affords ; but points itfelf to the more important object, of increafing the quantity, and meliorating the quality, of thofe productions of nature that are moft defirable to him.

The fpontaneous produce of the earth, at firft the chief fource of his wealth, nowife contributes to the increafe of it ; for it is to his perfonal labour, and that performed by the capital he creates, to which he owes the augmented production of thofe things,

the

the firft fupply of which he derived from
nature.

The increafe of the wealth of mankind
may, therefore, be properly confidered
as arifing from labour, whether perfonal or
performed by capital, directed towards
the increafe of the quantity, and melioration of the quality, of the productions of nature ; and from that defcription of labour,
whether performed by his hands or by capital, from which, in a certain degree, he,
in common with other animals, derived the
objects of his defire from his earlieft exiftence ; to wit, from labour, directed towards
appropriating and adapting to confumption
what forms his wealth.

It muft be obferved, too, that this laft
fource of the increafe of the wealth of
mankind, is, in the progrefs of fociety, in
fome degree narrowed, as the productions
of the ocean are almoft the fole objects of
defire, that, in the progrefs of fociety, remain unappropriated.

In

In civilized fociety, therefore, with the exception of what he derives from the o-cean, the wealth of man can alone be in-creafed :—

1. By labour, whether perfonal or per-formed by capital, employed in increafing the quantity, and meliorating the quality, of the objects of his defire; that is, *by agriculture.*

2. By labour, whether perfonal or per-formed by capital, employed in giving form to, and adapting commodities for, confumption; that is, *by manufacturing in-duftry.*

Though we have already vindicated ma-nufacturing induftry, from the attempts of fome philofophers, to prove that it is total-ly unproductive of wealth, it in truth, how-ever, acts a very fubordinate part in the formation of the increafed wealth of every fociety,

fociety, unfhackled by legal reftrictions or forced diftributions of property.

It is evident, that the wealth arifing from giving form to, and adapting commodities for, confumption, muft depend upon the production of a fufficient quantity of raw materials to be fafhioned, as well as upon the exiftence of a fufficiency of food and neceffaries, for the fuftenance of thofe who are fo employed.

In civilized fociety, the multiplied relations which the varied diftributions of property create, tend to render the fubject more obfcure. Perhaps, therefore, there is no means of forming a more accurate idea of the relative importance of agricultural and manufacturing induftry, in increafing the wealth of a community, throughout the whole progrefs of fociety, than by confidering the relative importance of land and labour, in the formation of wealth, antecedent to the period in which man directed

his

his labour to the object of increafing the quantity, or meliorating the quality, of commodities: for agricultural induftry maintains, in all periods of fociety, the fame preeminent relation to manufacturing induftry, in the formation of wealth, that land then bore to labour; as man, in that ftate, derived from the fpontaneous productions of the earth, accurately and diftinctly, the fame defcription of wealth with which, at fubfequent periods of fociety, agricultural induftry exclufively furnifhes him. Whilft, in like manner, manufacturing induftry contributes to his wealth in every ftage of fociety, comparatively in the fame degree that labour, whether performed by his hands or by capital, did in that early and rude period of his exiftence.

In different civilized focieties, the diftribution of manufacturing induftry, employed in preparing the produce of the earth for confumption, is various. Great quantities of it, in fome communities, are expended

pended for the fatisfaction of the defires of a few, whilft the reft of the fociety unconfcioufly fuffer, not only from the lofs of the fhare of manufacturing induftry, in adapting for confumption what forms the objects of their defire ; but from a diverfion to the formation of thofe things that are calculated to flatter the whims of the luxurious, of a part of the labour and capital that would be more advantageoufly employed in agricultural induftry, for the purpofe of procuring an ample fupply of the neceffaries of life.

Though, from this circumftance, manufacturing induftry, in fome focieties, acquires an appearance of importance, yet the relation which, from the nature of things, agricultural and manufacturing induftry muft inevitably bear to one another, never can be altered.

In confidering the increafe of the wealth
of

of mankind, it is the caufes that regulate
the diftribution of induftry, and the confequences that arife from the manner in
which it is diftributed, that form by far
the moft interefting objects of fpeculation;
and it is thefe which will here form the
chief fubject of confideration.

Before, however, proceeding to this inveftigation, the relative importance of labour and capital in increafing wealth, whether employed in manufacturing or agricultural induftry, prefents a queftion which
forces itfelf into confideration by the manner in which it has been treated by almoft
all writers on political œconomy.

The dexterity that man acquires in performing labour, by confining himfelf to
one particular branch, has been dwelt upon
from the times of XENOPHON to the prefent day *.

This

* " Nor are thefe, which have been mentioned, the only
" reafons why the difhes fent from the king's table are
" grateful

This idea has, indeed, been carried fo far, that the legiſlation of ſome countries ſeems to have been conducted on the perſua-ſion,

" grateful to thoſe who receive them; they are in themſelves
" far more delicious to the taſte than others. And, indeed,
" it is not ſurpriſing that this ſhould be the caſe : for as
" other arts are practiſed to much greater advantage in
" large cities, ſo the king's viands are dreſſed in the moſt
" exquiſite manner. For, in ſmall towns, the ſame
" perſons are employed to make a bedſtead, a door, a
" plough, a table : — (frequently, too, the very ſame man is
" a houſe-builder, and thinks himſelf well off if he thus finds
" a ſufficient number of employers to enable him to earn
" a livelihood : it is impoſſible, however, that a man prac-
" tiſing a great variety of trades can be expert in them
" all) :—but in great cities, where there are many who
" have a demand for each article, an individual gets
" a ſufficient living by exerciſing a ſingle profeſſion :—
" and not even the whole of that; but one makes ſhoes for
" men, and another for women only. Sometimes, even,
" one man maintains himſelf by ſewing ſhoes, and another
" by cutting them out ; one by cutting and ſhaping gar-
" ments, and another, without interfering with any other
" part of the buſineſs, by joining the pieces together. A
" man, therefore, who confines himſelf to one ſimple depart-
" ment of workmanſhip, muſt of neceſſity execute it in the
" beſt manner. The caſe is preciſely the ſame with re-
" ſpect

fion, not only that labour was beſt performed
when the attention is confined to one particular branch ; but, on the belief that men
acquire additional dexterity, in executing
that

" ſpect to the preparing of food ; for he who has but one
" and the fame perfon for his bed-maker, his butler, his
" baker, his cook, and his caterer, muſt lay his account
" with being but indifferently ferved : but where the ſole
" occupation of one perfon is to manage the boiling, and
" of another the roaſting of the meat ; where one is enga-
" ged only in boiling, and another in frying fiſh ; where
" one makes bread, not of all forts, but reſtricts himſelf to
" the furniſhing of one ſpecies of an approved good qua-
" lity ; it feems to me, that, while the work is thus arran-
" ged, it muſt, in its feveral parts, be performed in the
" moſt perfect manner." Cyrop. Book viii.

This paffage in XENOPHON was pointed out to me by
my learned friend Profeffor DALZEL ; to whom I owe
likewife the above tranflation. See the original, APPEN-
DIX, No. IX.

" The advantages accruing to mankind, from their
" betaking themfelves feverally to different occupations,
" are very great and obvious ; for, thereby, each beco-
" ming expert and ſkilful in his own particular art, they
" are enabled to furniſh one another with the products of
" their refpective labours, performed in a much better
" manner, and with much lefs toil, than any one of them
" could do of himſelf." HARRIS's Effay on Money and
Coins, Part I. p. 16.

that fpecies of labour which they have feen performed from their earlieft infancy. On this principle, profeffions have been made hereditary, as was the cafe in Egypt, in fome parts of India, and in Peru. But the inconveniencies of this fyftem are apparent, and the idea has been generally reprobated.

Of late years, however, great weight has been laid upon the advantages attending the divifion of labour. The Author of the Wealth of Nations has, indeed, confidered this circumftance to be fo important, as to declare, that " it is the great mul-
" tiplication of the productions of all the
" different arts, in confequence of the di-
" vifion of labour, which occafions, in a
" well-governed fociety, that univerfal
" opulence which extends itfelf to the
" loweft ranks of the people *."

The

* Wealth of Nations, vol. 1. p. 13. 4to edit.

The extreme importance of the divifion of labour, in increafing wealth, is
an idea which appears to be derived from
contemplating the number of diftinct operations that contribute towards the formation of fome of our moft trifling manufactures, fuch as the trade of pin-making,
the profeffion which is, indeed, generally reforted to, to illuftrate the importance
of the divifion of labour.

Even in the conduct of this manufacture,
however, the advantage derived from any
degree of habitual dexterity, that can be
created by the divifion of labour, or from
the faving of time which would otherwife be loft in paffing from one fpecies
of work to another, nowife contributes towards expedition in forming the article, in
comparifon of the circumftance of fupplanting and performing labour by capital.
Without the machinery, which the faculty
that man poffeffes of fupplanting labour
by capital introduces, no great progrefs,
could

could have been made in the rapidity with which pins are formed ; and one man, with the ufe of this machinery, though he goes through and performs all the operations himfelf, muft, obvioufly, manufacture more pins in an hour, than would be formed in a month, or even in a year, by any number of men amongft whom the labour could be divided, if unaided by the circumftance of part of their labour being fupplanted and performed by capital,

It is in truth the great and diftinguifh-ing advantage which man poffeffes of fup-planting and performing labour by capital ; in conjunction with the power of directing his labour to the increafe of the quantity, and melioration of the quality, of the pro-ductions of nature ; (both faculties peculiar to the human fpecies), which form the means of procuring the wealth and com-forts enjoyed by civilized fociety.

In the annals of the tranfactions and ne-gotiations

gotiations that have taken place between different nations on the fubject of commercial arrangements, the danger of admitting a country to a commercial competition, becaufe the divifion of labour was there carried farther than in any other, is a thing unheard of : whilft the conftant and uniform ground of objection, urged by men whofe prejudices lead them to think that commerce may be conducted in a manner injurious to a nation, is the fuperiority that the one country has over the other, derived from dexterity in fupplanting and performing labour by capital *.

If, indeed, further confirmation was wanting, to eftablifh that this is the effential circumftance which gives birth to all improvement in the execution of labour, it is amply to be found in every ftatement that ever came from any man practically concerned

* See Appendix, No. X. containing extracts from two different memorials publifhed in France at the time of the Commercial Treaty with this country.

concerned in any branch of manufacture; as it is uniformly to the introduction of fome fort of machinery, to the effects of the application of chemiſtry to manufactures, or to the increaſe or command of capital enabling the manufacturers to reduce the price, and by this means creating an augmentation of demand, to which the extenſion of ſales is attributed * : but if the explanation that has been given of the nature of the profit of ſtock is juſt and ſatisfactory, it follows, that attributing the ſuccefs of a manufactory to the command of capital, is, in other words, attributing it to the circumſtance of labour being ſupplanted by capital ; as capital can alone be advantageouſly and profitably employed in performing this office.

It is regarding the diviſion of labour as the great ſource of human improvement, that

* See, on this ſubject, APPENDIX, No. XI. where various examples in ſupport of this opinion are extracted from different commercial publications.

that has led the Author of the Wealth of
Nations to ftate, that " the impoffibility of
" making fo complete and entire a fepara-
" tion of all the different branches of la-
" bour employed in agriculture, is perhaps
" the reafon why the improvement of the
" productive powers of labour in this art,
" does not always keep pace with their im-
" provement in manufactures * ;" whereas,
in reality, nothing exhibits in fo ftriking a
point of view the improvement of the human race in the dexterous execution of labour, as the expedition and fuccefs with
which, by two or three individuals, a large
field is prepared for the reception of feed,
compared with the time that it would coft
ten times the number of men to do the
fame work, if unaided by the operation of
capital in fupplanting labour; and with
the imperfect manner in which it would,
after all, be executed, if the work was to
be performed by the hand of man alone.

Nothing

* Wealth of Nations vol. ii. p. 8. 4to edit.

Nothing has a more powerful effect in misleading even the best and most accurate understandings, than an anxious desire to maintain a favourite opinion, or to support a favourite theory; and there is perhaps no stronger illustration of this unfortunate tendency, than what is to be derived from the strained manner in which it has been attempted to establish the opinion, that the division of labour is the cause of that universal opulence which fortunately prevails in many civilized societies.

To impress this belief, the introduction of machinery has been stated as originally owing to the division of labour, of which it is considered as a mere consequence.

But, in truth, the history of man shews us, that the simplest and most efficacious machines for supplanting labour,—(instruments with which habit has so familiarized us, that we hardly dignify them with the name of machinery),—are introduced, at an early

early period of fociety when the divifion of labour. is comparatively unpractifed and unknown, for the purpofe of fupplanting the perfonal labour of man in the conduct of agricultural induftry ;—an art which, though its pre-eminence in the production of wealth is acknowledged, (even by thofe who wifh to eftablifh, that the divifion of labour is the great fource of the increafed opulence of mankind), is in no period of fociety diftinguifhed by reaping benefit from the divifion of labour *.

Neither

---

* " The fuperiority which the induftry of the towns " has every where in Europe over that of the country, is " not altogether owing to corporations and corporation " laws. It is fupported by many other regulations. The " high duties upon foreign manufactures, and upon all " goods imported by alien merchants, all tend to the fame " purpofe. Corporation laws enable the inhabitants of " towns to raife their prices, without fearing to be under- " fold by the free competition of their own countrymen. " Thofe other regulations fecure them equally againft that " of foreigners. The enhancement of price occafioned by " both, is every where finally paid by the landlords, farm-

" ers,

Neither does it appear, that there is any ground for attributing to this circumſtance

T 3

the

" ers, and labourers of the country." Wealth of Nations, vol. 1. p. 159. 4to edit.

" Land, mines and fiſheries, require all both a fixed " and a circulating capital to cultivate them ; and their " produce replaces with a profit not only thoſe capitals, " but all the others in the fociety." Ibid. p. 338.

" This impoſſibility of making ſo complete and entire a " feparation of all the different branches of labour em- " ployed in agriculture, is, perhaps, the reaſon why the " improvement of the productive powers of labour in this " art, does not always keep pace with their improvement " in manufactures." Ibid. p. 8.

" It is the great multiplication of the productions of all " the different arts, in confequence of the diviſion of la- " bour, which occaſions, in a well-governed fociety, that " univerfal opulence which extends itſelf to the loweſt " ranks of the people." Ibid. p. 13.

Though, from the two firſt of theſe paſſages, it ap- pears, that land is confidered by the Author of the Wealth of Nations, as the great, and almoſt ſole, ſource of wealth ; and though, in the third paſſage, agriculture is ſtated to reap comparatively but little benefit from the diviſion of labour ; yet, in the laſt, the diviſion of labour is deemed to be the cauſe of that univerfal opulence, which, in a well-governed fociety, extends itſelf to the loweſt ranks of the people.

How can thefe opinions be reconciled ?

the modern improvements of machinery, in the conduct of manufacturing induſtry. The diviſion of labour tends to confine the attention, and of courſe the knowledge of the workman, to the performing of one ſimple operation ; whereas, the perfection of manufacturing machinery is to combine and embrace the execution of the greateſt poſſible variety of operation in the formation of a commodity, by the uſe of one machine *. It appears, therefore, that the habits of thinking, which the diviſion of labour tends to generate in the manufacturer, (if they have any effect on the invention

---

* Of this any one may be ſatisfied, who chooſes to look at the cottonmills now in uſe ; or at the machines formed on the model of that at Derby, for the erecting of which, in 1734, Parliament rewarded Sir Thomas Lombe — " This machine is ſaid to have contained 26,586 wheels, " and 97,746 movements, that work 73,726 yards of ſilk " at every turn of the wheel ; that is to ſay, 318,504,960 " yards in twenty-four hours, at three turns of the wheel " per minute." Advantages and Diſadvantages of Great Britain with regard to Commerce, p. 122. Lond. 1754,

vention and improvement of machinery), muſt be detrimental; as they are deſtructive of that train of thought which leads to the perfection of machinery.

The eagerneſs and anxiety of the Author of the Wealth of Nations, to enforce this his favourite opinion, has made him aſſert, that " a great part of the machines em-
" ployed in thoſe manufactures in which
" labour is moſt ſubdivided, were original-
" ly the inventions of common workmen,
" who being each of them employed in
" ſome very ſimple operation, naturally
" turned their thoughts towards finding
" out eaſier and readier methods of per-
" forming it *."

The inaccuracy of the fact cannot eſcape any one converſant with the hiſtory of machinery: but if it was true, it would unfortunately have, in ſome degree, the effect of overturning the very opinion it is meant to ſupport; as it would prove, that the divi-

ſion

* Wealth of Nations, vol. 1. p. 12. 4to edit.

fion of labour had not the fame happy effect in the improvement of machinery, that
is is faid to have in the manufacture of
other things ; common workmen, or men
who execute a variety of other work, having been more fortunate in inventing and
improving machines than machine-makers,
or men whofe labour is folely confined to
that particular employment.

The truth is, the divifion of labour contributes (as is well illuftrated in the paffage of XENOPHON formerly referred to *)
much more to the nice execution of fome
branches of refined manufacturing induftry, than, as is generally conceived, to any
branch of manufacturing induftry being
executed with great increafe of rapidity.
In this laft refpect, too, it may have fome
influence, in confequence of its tendency to
improve the dexterity of the workmen ; but
this circumftance co-operates, in fo fmall a
degree, with the power of performing labour by capital, in producing this effect as
nowife

* See page 282.

nowife materially to invalidate the general conclufion,—That it is to the characteriftic faculty which man poffeffes, from the earlieft period of his exiftence, of applying mechanical principles to the conftruction of tools and machines, calculated to perform and fupplant labour, and to his powers of ufing capital for the fame purpofe, in all his commercial relations, as well as in every tranfaction which requires the exertion of labour, that he owes the eafe and wonderful rapidity with which labour is executed; and, confequently, that extended opulence which expands itfelf throughout civilized fociety.

" It is evident, upon a moment's reflec-
" tion," (fays an anonymous writer, who feems to poffefs a thorough knowledge of all our manufactures), " that almoft every
" convenience and external comfort we en-
" joy, depends upon the fingular fkill of
" man, in the invention and ufe of ma-
" chines. By this fkill our fields are culti-
" vated, our habitations are raifed, our gar-
" ments are manufactured, our fhips are
" built,

" built, and knowledge is acquired and dif-
" fufed, in company with the general ad-
" vantages of commerce, from pole to pole.
" Read the hiftory of mankind ; confider
" the gradual fteps of civilization, from
" barbarifm to refinement, and you will
" not fail to difcover, that the progrefs of
" fociety, from its loweft and worft, to its
" higheft and moft perfect ftate, has been
" uniformly accompanied, and chiefly pro-
" moted, by the happy exertions of man,
" in the character of a mechanic or engi-
" neer.   Let all machines be deftroyed,
" and we are reduced in a moment to the
" condition of favages ; and in that ftate
" man may, indeed, exift a long time, with-
" out the aid of curious and complex ma-
" chines ; though, without them they can
" never rife above it *."

When Mr Hume, in the middle of laft
century, fuppofed that the progrefs of human induftry, in any country, was bounded

* Letters on the utility of employing Machines to fhorten Labour, printed 1780.

ed and confined by the check it muſt receive from the augmentation of wages, and
" that manufactures gradually ſhift their
" places, leaving thoſe countries and pro-
" vinces which they have already enrich-
" ed, and flying to others, whither they are
" allured by the cheapneſs of proviſions
" and labour, till they have enriched theſe
" alſo, and are again baniſhed by the ſame
" cauſes * ;" he did not ſufficiently attend
to the unlimited reſources that are to be
found in the ingenuity of man in inventing means of ſupplanting labour by capital ; for any poſſible augmentation of wages that increaſed opulence can occaſion, is
but a trifling drawback on the great advantages a country derives, not only from the
ingenuity of man in ſupplanting labour by
machinery, but from capital laid out in
roads, canals, bridges, incloſures, ſhipping ;
and employed in the conduct of home and
foreign trade, all of which is alike engaged
in ſupplanting the neceſſity of paying the
wages of labour.

The

* Diſcourſe on Money, p. 43. Edin. 1752.

The progrefs made of late years in Scotland, in the art of diftilling fpirits, affords
a ftrong illuftration and example of the vaft
refources of human ingenuity in abridging
labour by mechanical contrivances.

In the year 1785, a propofal was made
to collect the duty on the manufacture of
fpirits in Scotland, by way of licence, to
be paid annually for every ftill, according
to its fize, at a fixed rate per gallon, in lieu
of all other duties.

The London diftillers, men the moft experienced in their profeffion, who agreed to
the rate of the licence on the gallon, fuppofed to be equivalent to the former duties, declared themfelves from experience
fatisfied, that the time of working ftills
with benefit was limited to an extent perfectly well known, and that whoever exceeded thefe limits, would infallibly lofe,
upon his materials and the quality of the
goods, what he gained in point of time; and,
in conformity to their opinion, the duty was,

in

in the year 1786, fettled, upon the fuppofition that ftills could be difcharged about
feven times in a week.

Two years after this, in a memorial prefented to the Lords Commiffioners of the
Treafury, the fame men alleged, that the
Scotch diftillers had, by the ingenuity of
their contrivances, found means to difcharge their ftills upwards of forty times a
week; and we fince know, from a report
made to the Lords Commiffioners of the
Treafury, in the year 1799, that a forty-
three gallon ftill was brought to fuch a degree of perfection, as to be difcharged at
the rate of once in two minutes and three
quarters, which is almoft twenty-two times
in an hour *. It appears alfo from this report,
that

* " In a letter which I received a few days ago from
" Mr MILLAR, he informs me, That he has made a new
" ftill of the fame kind, that contains only forty gallons in
" the body, and three in the head, forty-three gallons in
" all; and that the ftate of working with this ftill is as
" follows: From the commencement of the charge till the
" word

that the operation of diftillation was capable of being performed in a ftill fhorter time, and that the quality of the fpirit was nowife injured by the rapidity of the operation *.

Yet, in the conduct of this wonderful improvement in the manufacture of fpirits, there was no aid derived from the divifion of labour, nor could it once be thought of as a poffible refource.

Illuftrations to the fame effect might be brought from the wonderful improvements made

" word is given to let off, two one-fourth minutes ;
" time of difcharging half a minute ; making the time of
" charging, running and difcharging, two three-fourth mi-
" nutes only, which is almoft twenty-two times in an
" hour." Memorial of Dr JEFFRAY refpecting the Diftillation of Spirits : Printed in the Appendix to the Report
on the Diftilleries of Scotland, 1799, p. 392.

    * " Believing then, as I do, that the quality of the fpi-
" rits is not neceffarily affected by the rapidity of the
" diftillation," &c, Ibid. p. 401.

made of late years in bleaching, dyeing,
fpinning, weaving, as well as in the manufacture of iron and copper, none of which
derive, in their details, the fmalleft benefit
from the divifion of labour.

Though the divifion of labour, therefore,
may tend to produce fuperior execution in
fome refined arts, it is with confidence we
again repeat, that the univerfal opulence
which extends itfelf over civilized fociety,
conferring " on the frugal European pea-
" fant, comforts and accommodations ex-
" ceeding thofe of many an African king,
" the abfolute mafter of the lives and liber-
" ties of thoufands of naked favages *," is
to be attributed to two circumftances, both
*peculiar to, and characteriftic of, the human
fpecies;—To the power man poffeffes, of directing his labour to the objects of increafing the
quantity, and meliorating the quality, of the
productions of nature ;—and to the power of
fupplanting*

* Wealth of Nations, vol. 1. p. 15.　4to edit.

*fupplanting and performing labour by capi-
tal.*

As thefe great fources of human improvement are common to all mankind, it
becomes an interefting object of inquiry,—
Why all civilized focieties have not derived equal benefit from them?—and, What
are the circumftances that retard the progrefs of induftry in fome countries, and
that guide its direction in all?

The effect of demand in regulating the
quantity, the nature and the quality, of
thofe things which are produced by the labour of man, has been already pointed out
and difplayed. If the world had only one
inhabitant, and if we could fuppofe that
the time of this folitary individual was fully occupied in procuring and forming for
himfelf the various objects of defire he
wifhed to enjoy; it is evident, that a fudden fancy to enjoy more of any one particular article than the portion of labour he
employed

employed in obtaining it was capable of furnifhing, would create a neceffity of his allotting, for this purpofe, a farther portion of the time which he fpent in procuring fome lefs preffing object of his defire, in order that he might acquire an additional quantity of the commodity of which he defigned to increafe his confumption.

Now, an increafed demand has a direct tendency to produce the fame effect in the arrangement of the labour of a fociety, that fuch a wifh would produce in regulating the conduct of an individual.

The advanced price, in confequence of an extenfion of demand, operates not alone as an encouragement to exertion in thofe who manufacture the commodity ; for it creates a neceffity of abridging the confumption of fome lefs preffing object of defire, in order that the goods which were appropriated to acquire it, may be applied to pay the advanced price of the commodity

dity for which there exifts an increafed demand ; and thus a quantity of labour is let
loofe from the manufacture of thofe things
for which the demand is abridged, at the
very time that its application is directed to,
and encouraged in, the formation of that
for which the demand is increafed. By this
means an alteration is produced in the arrangement of the labour of a fociety, precifely fimilar to that which would be produced in the conduct of an individual, (whofe
time was fully occupied in procuring for
himfelf the objects of his defire), by a wifh to
increafe his confumption of any one article.

It is thus, (as has been already explained *), that demand as effectually regulates
the diftribution of induftry in every fociety, as the wifhes and inclination of an individual decides his conduct, and directs
his efforts. Whatever, therefore, fixes or
determines the proportion of demand that
exifts for different articles of wealth in any
fociety,

* See page 108.

fociety, muft regulate the diftribution of its induftry.

Neither the private interefts or prejudices of particular orders of men, nor the policy of different governments, can fucceed in directing the induftry of a country into any particular channel, but through the medium of augmenting the demand for the commodities which that fpecies of induftry produces. The defpotic orders of a government, dictated by the vain fpeculations of its rulers, if not calculated to make an alteration in demand, can produce no permanent effect on the direction of human induftry. Pecuniary aid and affiftance given to the manufacturer, may create, and even fuftain, a lofing trade; but demand alone can create a flourifhing trade, or direct the permanent application of the induftry of a country into any particular channel.

The firft, and moft important ftep, therefore,

fore, in inveftigating the caufes of the direction which induftry takes in nations
which are, to a certain degree, advanced
in fkill, dexterity and judgment, in the
means of executing labour, is the difcovery
of what dictates the proportion of demand
for the various articles which are produced; and though this may not be at firft
fight apparent, yet a little attention to the
arrangements and conduct of men in civilized fociety, will, perhaps, authorife the
opinion, that it is not totally impoffible to
difcover what it is that caufes that variety
of demand for different articles, which is
obfervable not only in different countries,
but even in different places in the fame
country.

The firft, the univerfal, and the moft ardent defire of man, is to procure what
merely conftitutes food; the next is moft
undoubtedly to guard himfelf from the
inclemency of the feafon. Thefe defires
he feems to poffefs in common with all
other animals; and they are perhaps the
only

only feelings, in relation to wealth, that
nature directly implants ; for, on examination, we shall see reason to think all farther
desires with regard to wealth, (which are
peculiar to the human species), arise from
the circumstance of the possession of wealth,
which man alone, of all animals, seems to
have the faculty of increasing by his own
exertions.

We often see the poor man living on
coarse bread, made of inferior grain, satis-
fying his thirst with water, covering himself with tattered garments, lying on straw,
and enjoying, even in that state, content-
ment and felicity. Increase his wealth, his
desires extend themselves, and though, perhaps, it does not add materially to his hap-
piness, he eats bread made of better grain,
drinks some sort of liquor prepared by art,
covers himself with better clothing, procures a comfortable habitation, and, in proportion as he extends his wealth, he naturally enlarges his desires to views of comfort,

fort, in his clothing, as well as in other
articles.

But a demand for what conftitutes the
luxuries of life, can only exift on the part
of thofe who poffefs wealth beyond what
enables them to acquire the things which
the habits of mankind induce them to regard as neceffaries. For demand, in the
mercantile fenfe of the word, is not to be
confidered as a mere wifh or defire, but as
a defire attended with the means of fatisfying the object of it; it is the poffeffion of
thefe conjoined that conftitutes what the
Author of the Wealth of Nations has called
the Effectual Demander *; that is, the perfon with a view to whom the commodity
can, in fpeculation alone, be manufactured
or brought into the market.

Goods, indeed, may appear for once in a
market where there is no effectual demander;

* Wealth of Nations, vol. i. p. 68. 4to edit.

er; though that is not very probable, as the forefight of mankind generally operates as a preventive check; and by this means it happens, that without even an experiment, the extent and gradations of fortune feem univerfally to influence the quantity and quality of what is offered for fale.

Thus, if the whole ifland of Great Britain was fuddenly divided into fmall properties of one hundred pounds a-year each, no parliamentary regulations or encouragement could poffibly prevent the extinction of the manufacture of thofe coftly carriages, the purchafe of which might exhauft upwards of four years revenue of one of thofe limited fortunes. It is, on the other hand, obvious, that any regulation which could at once unite the property thus divided, into fortunes of ten thoufand a-year each, muft, independent of all encouragement, and in defiance of even very heavy taxation, inftant-

ly

ly reftore the demand for, and of courfe
the manufacture of, thofe vehicles.

The diftribution of property could not,
however, be changed from fortunes of
one hundred, to fortunes of ten thoufand a-year, without, in every inftance, reducing ninety-nine families, antecedently
poffeffed of one hundred a-year each, into a
ftate of dependence for fuftenance and employment upon each of thofe men, amongft
whom the property of the country by this
hypothefis would be divided.   The goods
which the man of ten thoufand a-year would
immediately apply to the acquifition of carriages and other luxuries, muft of courfe be
withdrawn from expenditure in thofe things
in the acquifition of which they were employed, when fortunes were divided into
one hundred pounds *per annum.*

Each of the individuals who, antecedent
to the fuppofed change in the arrangement
of property, poffeffed a hundred pounds a-
year, might naturally wifh and defire to
obtain

obtain the things to which he was habituated; but as this wiſh could no longer be
accompanied with the means of obtaining
the objeсt, it could no longer give riſe to a
demand. Of courſe, the demand for that
claſs of commodities muſt be diminiſhed;
and the reduсtion of their value, created
by this diminution of demand, muſt diſ-
courage that direсtion of induſtry, at a
time when, in conſequence of the ſuppoſed
new arrangement of property, the demand
for articles of luxury would raiſe the value of labour employed in the formation of
them; and thus effeсtually direсt the labour
of thoſe who were thrown out of employment, to that channel in which, by the
new arrangement of property, it was ſure
of being cheriſhed by a conſtant demand.

On the other hand, if the property had
remained divided into ſmall fortunes of
one hundred a-year each, what would have
been the conſequence?—Experience ſhews
us, that proprietors of this claſs live, in general, on their eſtates; indeed, want of means

to

to defray the neceffary expences of travel-
ling, confines them at home : and as there is
nothing fo falutary for the improvement of
a country, as the eye of a proprietor, confined to a fpace of territory which he can
himfelf manage ; fo likewife, the expenditure arifing from the refidence of the proprietors, muft naturally encourage the induftry of the country, and of courfe difcourage thofe refined manufactures, the refult of the accumulation of labour on raw
materials, which diftinguifh the induftry of
towns.

This view of the fubject inevitably leads
to the fufpicion, that it is the diftribution
of wealth which regulates the portion of
demand for different defcriptions of commodities, in as cogent a manner as demand
regulates the direction of the induftry of a
fociety, and of courfe the formation of
wealth.

Demand, as has been remarked, arifes
not

not only from having a wish or desire to possess a particular object, but from the desire of possessing being combined with the means of acquiring ; and it is here most important to remark, that though the mere wish or desire of possessing can never furnish the means of acquiring, yet a little observation on the conduct of men shews us, that the means of acquiring, very certainly and very rapidly instil the desire of possessing. It seems, therefore, an undeniable inference, (if demand proceeds from the desire of possessing, combined with the means of acquiring), that the distribution of wealth, which at once furnishes the means of acquiring, and instils the desire of possessing, must imperiously regulate the nature and extent of demand *.

But

* The general feeling of mankind, of the incompetency of a mere wish or desire, to constitute a demand, is forcibly expressed in the common and well-known proverb, *If wishes were horses, beggars would ride ;* and the rapidity with which the means of possessing communicates the desire of enjoyment, is expressed with equal energy in another proverb, *Put a beggar on horseback, he'll ride to the devil.*

But it is not general reafoning alone which produces a conviction, that the diftribution of wealth, in all focieties, muft ultimately regulate the formation of wealth. The fame conclufion may be deduced, by a ftill plainer and more familiar procefs, from an examination of the fituation, the habits, and the diftribution of the property of mankind ;—a view of the fubject which may be illuftrated by examples innumerable, uniformly evincing, that, in every fociety, it is the wealth of the confumers who refort to the market, and the manner in which it is diftributed amongft them, that univerfally decide both the quantity and quality of the goods that are expofed to fale.

We have often occafion to remark, in many of the fmall fifhing-towns of England, where the goods generally expofed in the fhops are of a nature adapted to the demand dictated by the property of the inhabitants, that the fummer feafon no foon-

er

er invites to the coaft a number of opulent
families, for the purpofe of bathing, than
there is transferred thither a quantity of
goods fuited to the demand which the fortunes of thofe who for a time vifit the place
create ; and the refidue of thefe goods is at
the end of the feafon conftantly removed,
becaufe the fortunes of the natives are not
fuch as to create a demand for commodities of that nature.

It is to be remarked, too, that for the good
of the place, as well as of thofe new fhopkeepers who refort to it, it is neceffary that
thofe who thus for a time refide in it fhould
not be too affluent ; for the taftes and habits
which extreme affluence generates, naturally induce thofe who poffefs it to bring from
a diftance their wines, and many other articles of their confumption, as well as to fend
to the capital for any new ornaments, or
additional articles of clothing, which the
tafte of the day may fuggeft as defirable ;
fo that not only the affluence of thofe who
refort

refort to the market, but even the degree of affluence, feems to decide on the nature and extent of the demand, which may be diminifhed as much by the extreme riches of the temporary vifitants as by their poverty.

It was the luxurious habits of the French Court, generated by extreme affluence, that, with juftice, gave rife to the complaint uniformly made by the inhabitants in and around Fountainbleau, that the fhort refidence of the Sovereign, in fummer, created an additional demand for nothing but eggs, milk and butter, as the courtiers brought almoft every other article of confumption along with them; and it is not improbable that fhopkeepers and traders in and around that town, are at prefent deriving more benefit from its being converted into an Englifh prifon, than they did from its being reforted to by the Court of France.

The curing of fifh is a means of increafing

fing food, and of courfe wealth, which has occupied the attention of many of the maritime powers of Europe. The legiflature of this country has, in particular, made repeated inquiries, enacted various regulations, and given, at different periods, very confiderable bounties for improving and encouraging the curing of herring.

The great object has been to imitate, and, if poffible, to rival the Dutch in this undertaking ; but the inquiries of committees, the regulations in confequence of their reports, the bounties and encouragements granted by law, the inftructions given by Dutchmen difperfed throughout our fifhing towns, to teach the procefs which has fucceeded in Holland, have all proved ineffectual. The herrings produced are as inferior in quality as ever, to thofe cured in that country, and muft remain fo, if there was even much greater encouragement given : for the confumers of the greateft part

of

of the herrings cured in this country are the pooreft of all men,—men abfolutely deprived of the power of poffeffing property, the flaves in our Weft India colonies ; whilft the confumers of the herrings cured in Holland are men of property and affluence in Germany and other parts of Europe, at whofe tables that fifh is introduced as an article of luxury.   Till, therefore, the Weft India proprietor becomes as nice about the victuals of his flaves, as a German Prince is about the luxuries produced at his table, this country can never expect to fee the curing of herring brought to an equal ftate of perfection as in Holland : for the fortunes of the confumers in Germany make the excellence of the commodity the fole recommendation in that market ; whilft the fituation of the flaves makes the cheapnefs the only recommendation in the Weft India market.

Let any man examine the wretched clothing fent from this country to cover thofe

thofe who are employed in the cultivation of the fugar-cane; and then let him
reflect, whether, if this was the chief
fource of demand for our linen and cloth,
any poffible bounty could induce our manufacturers to produce lawn, cambric, or
fine broad-cloth.

This nation is at prefent the greateft
commercial country in the world. There is
hardly any people, in any climate, with
whom our merchants have not dealings;
and if we examine the cargoes that are
made up to fuit the demands of different
nations, we fhall univerfally obferve, that
it is the diftribution of property, in each
country, that dictates the nature and quality of the goods that are fent to it.

In India, property is moft unequally divided. The poor man poffeffes the neceffaries, but has not wealth fufficient to fuggeft
a defire even for the comforts of life. The
rich poffefs not only wherewithal to pam-

per

per their appetites, but fufficient to fatisfy
their moft refined defires. Accordingly,
the cargoes which our India captains carry out, if meant for fale in the country,
and not for the fupply of the Company's
fervants, uniformly confift of the moft expenfive clock-work, of mirrors of the greateft fize, of fire-arms of the moft diftinguifhed workmanfhip, of luftres, and other orna-
mental articles, of a value even beyond
what any European market requires.

In the United States of America, on the
other hand, property is more equally divided than perhaps in any other country.
Almoft every man poffeffes not only the
means of procuring the mere neceffaries of
life, but his wealth is fuch as to extend his
demands to fome articles of comfort in
clothing, furniture, and habitation; and
there is hardly fuch a thing as a princely or
overgrown fortune. Accordingly, the goods
fent to the American market are all comparatively low-priced, things calculated to fecure comfort, not to attract admiration.

Send

Send to India a cargo of goods afforted for this market; they will find no fale. The poorer orders might, indeed, have a wifh for articles of this fort; but in a country where three half-crowns per month is the ufual allowance for wages, food and clothing, they cannot have the means of procuring them; and a wifh, unaccompanied with the means of obtaining a commodity, never can conftitute a demand. Neither could there exift, on the part of the native princes, any demand for fuch articles. They, indeed, have amply the means of obtaining them; but this, without the wifh or defire to poffefs them, cannot conftitute a demand; and thefe are not the commodities for which opulence creates a defire. The things for which riches dictate a demand are articles fcarce and rare, calculated to difplay fplendour, and excite admiration,—

" Non ufu plebeio trita voluptas *."

But

* PETRON. ARBITER, *Sat.* cap. CXIX. 8.

But the effect of the diftribution of property is not alone to be traced out by contemplating its influence in determining the
direction of manufacturing induftry : it
even goes fo far as to regulate and decide
the nature and condition of the animals
reared and brought to the market for the
food of man.

England is the only country in Europe
where wealth is fo diffufed, that the great
body of the manufacturers, that is, a great
proportion of the people, can afford to
enjoy a mixture of animal with vegetable
food for their nourifhment *.

Where the wealth of man admits of his
ufing

* That man can be nourifhed at a much cheaper rate
on vegetable than on animal food, is apparent, from the
circumftance of the large quantity of land requifite to raife
enough of animal food for his fuftenance, compared with
the fmall quantity of land that will produce a fufficiency
to maintain him on a vegetable diet. On this fubject, fee
APPENDIX, No. XII.

ufing a portion, but not of his enjoying a fuperabundance of animal food, it becomes defirable that it fhould be as fat as poffible ; as meat in this ftate goes furtheft to feafon, relifh, or *kitchen*, as it is vulgarly called, a quantity of potatoes, pulfe, or other vegetables. Accordingly in England, we find the fatteft and the greateft quantity of fat meat in the world; and no one who will read the numerous publications that have of late years appeared on agricultural fubjects, can entertain a doubt, that it is the eafe and affluence of the lower orders of the people, enabling them in part to fubfift on animal food, and the circumftance that fat meat goes furtheft in mixing with vegetables, from whence the demand for meat in this ftate arifes.

Of the new Leicefter breed of fheep, now fo much run upon, and fo famed, for what in the language of the grazier is called their *fatting quality*, proportionally fpeaking, none go to the London market;
that

that is, arrive at the table of the luxurious.   Leeds, Manchefter, Birmingham,
Wakefield, Newcaftle, the feats of our
manufactories, are the markets in which
they are eagerly fought after, and the places where they are in general confumed.
And if the wealth of the country was not
fo diftributed as to put it in the power of
this clafs of men to enjoy animal food,
there would be no demand for meat fed to
this extent ; becaufe that extreme degree of
fat is a quality, which, far from recom-
mending it to, would banifh it from, the
tables of thofe whofe opulence has trained
them on to delicacy and refinement of
tafte.

    " On going to market one day, to fell our
" fat cattle, (fays a refpectable and very
intelligent farmer), " I was overtaken by
" a gentleman from Scotland.   Farmer,
" faid the gentleman, You make your fheep
" fo fat that I could not eat the mutton.
" It matters not, Sir, replied I, becaufe we
                            " have

" have plenty of cuftomers for this kind of
" mutton ; and allow me to fay, it is very
" happy that the great confumption does
" not depend upon fuch as you.

" Afk the pitman, the keelman, the wool-
" comber, the weaver, the fabricators of me-
" tals, and all thofe various but valuable clafs
" of manufacturers which abound in diffe-
" rent parts of this ifland, which of the
" two kinds of mutton they prefer ? would
" they not readily anfwer, Take you the
" lean meat, large-boned, and black gravy,
" but give us the fmall-boned fat meat,
" with oil fwimming in the difh. And are
" not thefe the men that make the greateft
" confumption in fat mutton, beef * ?"
&c.

In fome parts of the fouth of Scotland,
the defire of imitating the improvements
of

* Obfervations on Live Stock, by GEORGE CULLEY,
p. 125, 126.

of their neighbours in England, has introduced the new breed of fheep, whofe pro-
penfity to fatten has made them fo much
fought after. On the banks of the Tweed,
in particular, fuch flocks are to be found.
But there are few parts of that country
where the lower orders habitually live on
animal food. Morpeth is accordingly the
market to which they are generally fent,
becaufe, fays the intelligent Author already quoted, " the natives of Scotland have
" not as yet learned to eat fat mutton, like
" the pitmen and keelmen about New-
" caftle." The truth is, the common people of that country do not poffefs wealth
fufficient to enable them to confume animal food, otherwife it would not require
much learning to give them a tafte for fat
meat ; for whenever they do acquire the
means of confuming a mixture of animal
with vegetable food, the tafte for meat in
that ftate at once difplays itfelf. The
proof of this is, that Glafgow and Paifley,
the only places in Scotland where the body

of

of the people poſſeſs that degree of opulence, are known to be the only markets for
very fat meat; that is, the markets where
the demand for meat in that ſtate enſures
a ſuperiority of price.

Innumerable illuſtrations might be
brought, uniformly tending to ſhew, that
the diſtribution of property determining
the nature of demand, alone regulates and
decides the channels in which the induſtry
of every ſociety exerts itſelf. Perhaps, however, there is not a more powerful method of
bringing home this great and leading truth
to the conception of every man, than by
taking a general view of the ſtate in which
property has exiſted in France and Great
Britain, the two countries in Europe moſt
diſtinguiſhed for opulence and refinement;
and then contemplating the method in
which the diſtribution of their reſpective
wealth has marked, diſtinguiſhed, and cha-
racterized, the induſtry of both theſe countries.

In

In Great Britain, as we have already obferved, wealth is more generally diffuſed
than in any other country. Though there
exiſt ſome great and overgrown fortunes,
they do not appear to have been formed at
the expence of entailing general poverty
on the community. The yeomen in ſome
parts of the country, the farmers and manufacturers in all, when compared with
thoſe of any European nation, have always
been diſtinguiſhed for the eaſe and even the
opulence which they enjoy *.

In France, on the other hand, the wealth
of the country for centuries was ſhared out
and confined amongſt the Nobility. They
had univerſally, too, the habits of ſacrificing
the intereſts of their daughters and younger
ſons to increaſe the wealth, and perpetuate
the power of their repreſentatives :—for
the victims of the female ſex, Convents furniſhed an aſylum and retreat ; whilſt Mona-
ſteries, Church-benefices, and the Army,
were

* Lord BACON's Hiſtory of HENRY VII.

were uniformly reforted to as means of providing for the younger fons.

"France" (fays a well-informed Author, who wrote in the middle of the laft century) "concentres in Verfailles and Paris, as "in a fingle point, all the powers which can "attract mankind—to Court, on account "of the greatnefs and honours, which can "be attained no where elfe, and which are "for none but thofe who live at it;—to Pa-"ris, in which are not only all the trea-"fures of the ftate, but where all thofe "fubjects of the ftate refide who are rich, "either through the public or their own "private revenue; fo that all the weal-"thy have fixed their habitation in this "town, from a preference owing to the "neighbourhood of the Court *." It is to be obferved, too, that the privileges and exemptions from taxation enjoyed by the Nobility, greatly added to the effects of the

* Remarks on the Advantages and Difadvantages of France and Great Britain with refpect to Commerce. 1754, p. 42.

the unequal divifion of property ; for by this means, in proportion as the public debt and the expences of the Court increafed, the unequal diftribution of riches became more marked and perceptible ; whilft the effects of this inequality appeared more forcibly from the extravagance of that Nobility in whofe hands the wealth of the country was concentrated : " That clafs, " who, in the fervice of the nation have al- " ways fpent the capital of their fortunes, " and who, when they are ruined, give way " to another fet of the fame clafs, who in " like manner fpend their capital *."

Indeed, in no country was there to be found a portion fo confiderable of its riches fhared out in large fortunes amongft fo fmall a number, the expenditure of which uniformly and conftantly took place on the fame fpot.

" The

* *Cette partie de la nation qui fert toujours avec le capital de fon bien, qui quand elle eft ruinée donne fa place à une autre qui fervira avec fon capital encore.* Efprit de Loix, Liv. xx. Chap. xx.

" The opulent man, who lives on his
" fortune, without any employment, con-
" fumes by himfelf, by his menial fer-
" vants, by his parafites, the national pro-
" dudtions of the firft neceffity. So far
" agriculture profits by his expenditure :
" but his pride and effeminacy employ, to
" provide him with lodging, with furni-
" ture, with clothing and equipage, the af-
" fiftance of all the arts that are natura-
" lized in France ; it is, then, the men of
" large fortune who furnifh the natural
" aliment of French induftry *."

In Paris, accordingly, (as, under fuch
circumftances, our theory would lead us to
expect), thofe who excelled as hair-dreffers,
as tailors, as milliners, the moft expert
hands

---

* *Le riche oifif confume par lui-même, par fes valets, par fes parafites, les denrées nationales de première neceffité. L'agriculture profite evidemment de ces dépenfes; le fafte et la moleffe, empruntent pour le loger, le meubler, le vétir, le voiturer, le fecours de tous les arts naturalifés en France ; il eft donc l'aliment propre de l'induftrie Françoife.* Ephémerides du Citoyen, Tom. II 1766. p. 133.

hands employed in painting china or carriages, and in cutting or setting diamonds,
embroiderers of clothes and furniture, &c.
received encouragement certainly equal, if
not superior, to those employed in the same
line in London; whilst we are told by Mr
ARTHUR YOUNG, that, from the information he could collect during his residence
in different parts of France, country labour was 76 *per cent*. cheaper there than
in England *.

This sufficiently shews, that the demand
for country labour, in proportion to the
number of labourers of this description,
was much inferior to what it is in this
country; and that the proportion betwixt
the

---

* Country labour being 76 *per cent*. cheaper in France
than in England, it may be inferred, that all those classes
that depend on labour, and are the most numerous in society, are 76 *per cent*. less at their ease, (if I may use the
expression), worse fed, worse clothed, and worse supported, both in sickness and in health, than the same classes in
England, notwithstanding the immense quantity of precious metals, and the imposing appearance of wealth in
France.

the demand for, and the number of, thofe
whofe profeffions are calculated to adminifter to the defires of the affluent, even
though their number was much greater,
muft have been equal, nay, fuperior, to
what it is in England.

But we know, that when the intereft of
men engages their attention to the formation or manufacture of any clafs of commodities, the alertnefs and dexterity in fupplanting labour by capital, which practice
generates in any particular branch of manufacture, uniformly lowers the price, at the
fame time that it improves the quality, of
the articles produced.—" For it is fo plain,
" that every man profiteth in that he moft
" intendeth, that it needeth not to be ftood
" upon. It is enough to point at it" *.

Accordingly, to eftablifh the comparative fuperiority, excellence, and cheapnefs,
of all articles in France which contribute
to the fplendid decoration either of the
perfons,

* Bacon's Effays, p. 83.

perfons, the tables, or the apartments of men of fortune, we need only appeal to thofe who have refided there, and who have enjoyed the fociety of the people of that country.

Even in England, no one can go into the drawing-rooms of the affluent, or attend St James's on a birth-day, without feeing this fuperiority fufficiently difplayed, by the quantity of French manufactures exhibited, notwithftanding the fevereft legal prohibitions, and thofe, too, enforced by the example of the Sovereign.

On the other hand, to prove the fuperiority which England difplays in the neatnefs and cheapnefs of all thofe articles which adminifter to the comforts of life, and which are within the reach of thofe who poffefs merely a competency ; it is only neceffary to call for the teftimony of any man who has even paffed through the two countries. The neatnefs of the houfes in
                                                                    and

and around London, and the fplendour of the hotels in Paris, have conftantly formed themes of remark to all travellers.

What is univerfally matter even of loofe obfervation among mankind, where intereft does not dictate the fentiment, is generally true, and may almoft always with certainty be relied upon. Here, however, it is unneceffary to truft merely to fuch a fource of information. For the effects of the diftribution of wealth on the refpective induftry of the two countries, is no where more ftrongly difplayed than in the documents and memorials which the negotiation for a commercial treaty called forth; and as this was evidently an occurrence calculated to intereft the Government of both countries, in acquiring the moft accurate knowledge of the fubject, they feem to furnifh a fource of information which may with confidence be depended upon.

From thefe it would appear, that when the

the commercial treaty between France and
England was adjufted, in the year 1786,
thofe who conducted it, as well as thofe
who were confulted on the fubject, uniformly conceived, that France had a decided advantage in the manufacture of every
thing for which affluence dictates a defire ;
and that England, on the contrary, excelled in the formation of all thofe articles which adminifter to the comfort of
fuch as enjoy but a moderate degree of
wealth *.

In

---

* See APPENDIX, No. XIII. containing extracts from
various papers and memorials, written at the time of the
commercial treaty with France, 1786.

From thefe, it appears,

1. That, in the article of cloth, the fine cloths of France
were preferable to the fine cloths of England ; whilft, on
the other hand, it was conceived, that the lower-priced
cloths of England could meet with no competition either
for quality or cheapnefs.

2. That, though France had a moft decided fuperiority
in the manufacture of rich filks, England was fuppofed

In reality, the diftribution of wealth not only regulates and directs the channels in which the induftry of every fociety is embarked, in fuch a manner as to decide upon the nature, condition and quality, of what is produced, but even in a great degree determines the progrefs of population throughout the world.

If

fed to have the advantage in making of ribbons, ftuffs mixed with filk, &c. &c.

3. That, in the article of linens, the fuperiority that France enjoyed was folely confined to the cambrics and finer forts

4. That, in articles of millinery, and things for the perfonal decorations of the luxurious, France had an undoubted pre-eminence.

5. That, in the manufacture of glafs, the fuperiority of France in making of looking-glaffes, was as decided as that of England in the formation of common glafs, and of articles of cryftal for general ufe.

6. That the china of France enjoyed an undifputed fuperiority; whilft the potteries and earthen ware of England were confidered as not to be rivalled.

7. That the fuperior tafte and excellence, as well as the cheapnefs, of all articles of jewellery and filverfmith work in France, was as decided as that of all articles of common hardware, the manufacture of England.

If it did not lead into a wider field than is confiftent with the object of our prefent inveftigation, it would be eafy to fhew, that as what a late ingenious author calls the pofitive check to population, (which he points out as common to man, with the reft of the animal and vegetable creation), to wit, the want of nourifhment, in reality arifes from the deficiency of the objects of man's defire, that is, of his wealth; fo what he has called the preventive check to population, and which he deems peculiar to man, is in every fociety, and in all its forms, univerfally to be traced home to the diftribution of wealth *.

Thus,

---

* ", The preventive check is peculiar to man, and arifes
" from that diftinctive fuperiority in his reafoning facul-
" ties, which enables him to calculate diftant confequen-
" ces. Plants and animals have apparently no doubts
" about the future fupport of their offspring. The checks
" to their indefinite increafe, therefore, are all pofitive.
" But man cannot look around him, and fee the diftrefs
" which frequently preffes upon thofe who have large fa-
" milies ; he cannot contemplate his prefent poffeffions or
" earnings, which he now nearly confumes himfelf, and
" calculate

Thus, as it is the labour of man, whether performed with his hands or by capital, employed in augmenting the quantity,
or in improving the quality, of the pro-

Y 3   ductions

" calculate the amount of each fhare, when, with very
" little addition, they muft be divided, perhaps, among fe-
" ven or eight, without feeling a doubt, whether, if he
" follow the bent of his inclinations, he may be able to
" fupport the offspring which he will probably bring into
" the world. In a ftate of equality, if fuch can exift, this
" would be the fimple queftion. In the prefent ftate of
" fociety other confiderations occur. Will he not lower
" his rank in life, and be obliged to give up, in great
" meafure, his former fociety ? Does any mode of em-
" ployment prefent itfelf, by which he may reafonably
" hope to maintain a family ? Will he not at any rate
" fubject himfelf to greater difficulties, and more fevere
" labour, than in his fingle ftate ? Will he not be unable
" to tranfmit to his children the fame advantages of edu-
" cation and improvement that he had himfelf poffeffed ?
" Does he even feel fecure, that fhould he have a large
" family, his utmoft exertions can fave them from rags
" and fqualid poverty, and their confequent degradation
" in the community ? And may he not be reduced to
" the grating neceffity of forfeiting his independence, and
" of being obliged to the fparing hand of charity for fup-
" port ?" Effay on the Principles of Population, by J. R.
MALTHUS.

ductions of nature, and in adapting them
for confumption, that forms the means of
increafing the wealth of mankind; fo it is
the diftribution of wealth, which, determining the nature of demand, regulates the
direction of labour, and diftributes it in
fuch a manner, as to caufe a variety in
the productions of induftry, conformable
to the wants and defires to which the habits created by the power of enjoyment
give birth.

For the diftribution of wealth not only
decides on the character of manufacturing
induftry, but on the proportion betwixt
the fhare of the labour of man which
is directed towards increafing the quantity
and meliorating the quality of the productions of nature, and the fhare which is
occupied in giving form to the materials produced.   When great inequality of
fortune prevails, the demand for labour
employed in giving forms adapted to the
tafte of the luxurious and the rich, encourages

rages that fpecies of induftry; whilft the extreme poverty of thofe who look for little beyond the neceffaries of life, occafioning no increafe of demand for things of this clafs, affords little encouragement to labour employed in augmenting the quantity, and meliorating the quality, of the productions of nature, and no inducement to improvement in that line of induftry.

Nothing can more clearly illuftrate this pofition, than a comparative view of the agriculture of France and England. The flourifhing ftate of agricultural labour in England, has long been a general topic of admiration; whilft we are told by the ingenious Author of the articles *Fermier* and *Grain*, in the *Encyclopédie* *, that in France, out of thirty-fix millions of acres under the plough, thirty millions are cultivated by tenantry who are fo poor, that the landlord is obliged to furnifh labouring cattle and feed, and often even to advance money,

* M. QUESNAY.

money, till the firft harveft, for payment of the expences of the farmer's living, and of his farming inftruments *.

On the principles here ftated, the caufes of deficiency in any particular line of induftry may in every country be eafily dif-covered, by an examination into the di-ftribution of the property of its inhabi-tants, and this appears to be all that is ufeful or neceffary. Any attempt to ftate the precife diftribution of wealth which tends moft to encourage the production of wealth, would be liable to the fame criti-cifm that the Author of the Wealth of Na-tions

* See APPENDIX, No. XIV. containing, 1. Defcriptions extracted from the *Ephémerides de Citoyen*, which give an idea of the fituation of lands cultivated by *metoyers*, under the culture practifed, as QUESNAY fuppofes, on thirty mil-lions of acres of the arable land of France. 2. A ftate-ment of the annual expenditure on one farm, and of the annual produce of another, in the Carfe of Gowrie, in Scotland; to which is added an account of the production of that diftrict.

By contrafting thefe ftatements, the reader will fee how much the wealth of a nation depends on the direction of its induftry.

tions has made on that table or formula, which the œconomifts prefented to the world as accurately difplaying the order of expenditure moft advantageous for a community. Dr SMITH has truly faid, that, as there are many regimens under which the human body enjoys health, fo a country may enjoy, to a certain degree, profperity under very different circum-ftances *.

In general, however, it may be obferved, that great inequality of fortune, by impo-verifhing the lower orders, has every where been the principal impediment to the in-creafe of public wealth. We know from experience, that no country of equal ex-tent ever enjoyed fo much wealth as what is diffufed over this ifland. We have a right, therefore, to conclude, that the di-ftribution of property has been more fa-vourable to the growth of wealth in this than in any other country. In the begin-ning of the feventeenth century, Lord BA-

CON,

* Wealth of Nations, vol. ii. p. 271. 4to edit.

con,accounting for the advantages obtained
by the Englifh in their wars with France,
afcribes them chiefly to the fuperior eafe
and opulence enjoyed by the common people * ; and it certainly appears, that with
ftill greater confidence, the fuperiority of
wealth

* " Let ftates that aim at greatnefs, take heed how
" their nobility and gentlemen do multiply too faft : for
" that maketh the common fubject grow to be a peafant
" and a bafe fwain driven out of heart, and in effect
" but a gentleman's labourer : even as you may fee in
" coppice-woods. If you leave your ftadles too thick, you
" fhall never have clean underwood, but fhrubs and
" bufhes.　So, in countries, if the gentlemen be too many,
" the commons will be bafe : and you will bring it to
" that, that not the hundredth poll will be fit for a hel-
" met ; efpecially as to the infantry, which is the nerve of
" an army ; and fo there will be great population and
" little ftrength.　This which I fpeak of has been no
" where better feen, than by comparing of England and
" France : whereof England, though far lefs in territory
" and population, hath been, neverthelefs, an over-match,
" in regard the middle people of England make good
" foldiers, which the peafants of France do not."　Lord
Bacon's Effays, p. 80.　See alfo his Life of Henry VII.

wealth we enjoy may be afcribed to the fame caufe.

The wealth of mankind, it has been ob-ferved *, can alone be increafed :—

1. By Labour, whether perfonal, or per-formed by capital, employed in increafing the quantity, and meliorating the quality, of the objeds of his defire; that is, *by agri-culture.*

2. By Labour, whether perfonal or per-formed by capital, employed in giving form to, and adapting commodities for, confumption; that is, *by manufacturing in-duftry.*

The fuperior efficacy of the application of capital, for the purpofe of executing eve-ry branch of labour, over the moft im-proved manual dexterity, has alfo been explained; and the degree in which the increafe

* See page 278,

increafe of public wealth is dependent on this circumftance, has been illuftrated and made manifeft *.

It becomes, therefore, of the greateft importance to remark, that though the channels of expence of men of large and extended fortunes, that inftil a defire for articles of tafte, are often as unbounded as the fanciful imagination of thofe who adminifter to the fatisfaction of their caprices ; yet their habits cannot poffibly fuggeft expenditure, for the purpofe of fupplanting labour they are never called on to perform. On the contrary, the habits of a man poffeffed of fmall fortune, which adds to thofe comforts his induftry enables him to acquire, naturally fuggefts the defire of fupplanting the labour he performs, whilft he finds, in his moderate wealth, means of executing that which benefits himfelf, and enriches the community to which he belongs.

The

* See page 282, &c.

The defcription of MONTESQUIEU of the Nobility of France, as living on their capital, might with juftice have been extended to thofe frequenters of all Courts who are born to inherit large fortunes ; for the real fource of increafing wealth is alone to be found amongft farmers, manufacturers, merchants, whofe habits open their eyes to farther means of fupplanting the labour they perform or fuperintend, and which their fmall, but increafing fortunes, enables them to execute, with benefit to their private, and with ftill greater advantage to the public fortune.

Thus the diftribution of wealth not only regulates and decides the channels in which the induftry of every country is embarked, and of courfe the articles in the production of which it excels ; but a proper diftribution of wealth infures the increafe of opulence, by fuftaining a regular progreffive demand in the home market, and ftill more effectually, by affording to
thofe

thofe whofe habits are likely to create a defire of fupplanting labour, the power of executing it *.

Neither

---

* Though we do not recollect any attempt to fhew why the opulence of the lower orders tends to accelerate the growth of national wealth, or any reafoning to prove that it muft have that effect; yet the fact, (as appears from the following extracts), has not efcaped the obfervation of the learned and ingenious.

" The device of King Henry VII. (whereof I have fpo-
" ken largely in the Hiftory of his Life), was profound
" and admirable in making farms and houfes of hufban-
" dry of a ftandard ; that is, maintained with fuch a pro-
" portion of land unto them, as may breed a fubject to
" live in convenient plenty, and no fervile condition : and
" to keep the plough in the hands of the owners, and not
" mere hirelings. And thus, indeed, you fhall attain to
" Virgil's character, which he gives to ancient Italy.

" *Terra——potens armis atque ubere glebæ.*"
                                        Bacon's Effays, p. 81.

" Above all things, good policy is to be ufed, that the
" treafure and monies in a ftate be not gathered into few
" hands. For, otherwife, a ftate may have a great ftock
" and yet ftarve. *And money is like muck, not good except it*
" *be fpread.*" Bacon's Effays, p. 39.

" Whether

Neither are thefe the only means by which a wife and fortunate diftribution of wealth tends to produce an increafe of the wealth of a country; for when, in confequence of the mode in which wealth is diftributed, induftry is once embarked in the production and formation of particular commodities, and dexterity is acquired in preparing for the market things for which the diftribution of the growing wealth of colonies and other countries create a defire; a new and increafing demand encourages and fuftains an extenfion of production greater than the wealth or the wifeft diftribution of wealth in any country,

" Whether a people can be called poor, when the com-" mon fort are well fed, clothed and lodged?" Querift, by the Bifhop of Cloyne.

Quand le commerce eft en peu de mains, on voit quelques fortunes prodigieufes eft beaucoup de mifère; lorfqu' enfin il eft plus étendu, l'opulence eft générale, les grandes fortunes rares. " When commerce is in few hands, one fees fome very " large fortunes in the midft of general poverty; but when " it gets into a greater number of hands, we fee general " opulence, and few large fortunes." *Difcours de M. De Voltaire, à fa reception à l'Academie Françaife.*

try, ifolated and cut off from all communications with others, could either authorife
or maintain.

For fkill in the means of fupplanting and
performing labour by capital, which habit
creates, and the power of executing it by
the poffeffion of capital, at all times infures
to countries practifed in different branches
of induftry, means of furnifhing the commodities for which growing opulence
creates a defire, at a cheaper rate than
they can be manufactured in a country
where either the progreffive increafe of
wealth, or a fudden change in the diftribution of it, has given birth to new defires.

It muft be obferved, too, that this new
fource of demand, as it creates an augmentation of production, and confequently of
wealth, inftils into the inhabitants of the
country, advanced in any peculiar line of
induftry, new defires, which in return
create a demand for things that the climate

mate or foil of the fociety rifing in opulence enables them exclufively to produce,
as well as for things that the habits of induftry, and the foil and climate of a fociety in which the diftribution of property is
altered, enables them to produce, of a better
quality, and at a cheaper rate.

It is thus that commerce, though not a
means of increafing wealth, muft be confidered as the caufe of increafed induftry ;
for, by promoting an interchange of commodities betwixt two countries, it becomes
a moft powerful agent in extending the demand for the commodities of each, enrich-
ing the one and the other, by exciting a
quantity of induftry that would otherwife
have remained dormant ; but which, when
thus brought into activity, augments the
productions of both.

To the œconomifts (who maintained
that value in exchange is the bafis of all
wealth, * that the increafe of price is the
increafe

* *Philofophie Rurale*, p. 60.

increafe of wealth, and that the riches of a country augment in proportion as the exchangeable value of its commodities increafes, *) commerce ought to have appeared a direct means of increafing wealth. A demand, on the part of England, for two thoufand pounds worth of any particular French wine, as it muft alter the proportion betwixt the demand for, and the quantity of it, muft increafe the value of the whole of that fort of wine. In like manner, a demand on the part of France, for two thoufand pounds worth of Englifh cloth in return, muft alter the proportion betwixt the demand for, and the quantity of it, in fuch a manner as to increafe the total value of that commodity.

It is impoffible, therefore, to difcern, how the œconomifts, who regarded exchangeable value as the bafis of wealth, fhould not have confidered commerce, which thus increafes the value of the commodities

* *Phyfiocratic,* p. 116.

modities of both countries, as a means of increafing wealth.

Yet this fect of philofophers, uniformly excluding from their view the effect which increafe of demand muft have in augmenting the exchangeable value of the goods of all countries, amongft which a commercial intercourfe exifts, and confining all their views of commerce to the mere act of exchange, have obftinately repeated throughout their writings, in forms innumerable, that commerce is only an exchange of equal value, for equal value *.

If wealth, however, has been properly confidered, as confifting in the abundance of the objects of the defires of mankind; if exchangeable value has been properly regarded alone as the means by which, in civilized fociety, mankind exprefs their preference for the various productions of human induftry, and thus regulate the channels

* See *Dialogues fur le Commerce et fur les Travaux des Artifans*, by QUESNAY. Printed in *Phyfiocratie*.

nels in which it is embarked; commerce cannot with confiftency be regarded as a direct
means of producing, and of courfe it cannot be deemed a means of increafing wealth.
It muft, however, appear, in a ftate practifed in the various branches of labour, to be
the great caufe of putting the means of increafing wealth into action.

It is from this circumftance that the
wealth of a country, in thefe days when
the commercial relations of nations extend themfelves over the globe, no longer
depends alone on the internal diftribution
of its wealth ; and that the progrefs of
wealth is now accelerated or retarded,
in proportion as the diftribution of the
growing wealth of rifing countries, or
changes in the diftribution of wealth in
focieties that have been long eftablifhed,
give birth to a great or fmall demand for
the commodities in the production of
which, in confequence of the internal arrangement

rangement of its own wealth, a country has been long practifed.

It is only neceffary to view the nature of the Britifh manufactures for which America furnifhes a demand, to be convinced, that the encouragement to Britifh induftry, afforded by demand from the United States, muft have been comparatively fmall indeed, had that country been univerfally cultivated by flaves, and parcelled out into eftates productive of large incomes, fuch as our Weft India colonies exhibit. On the other hand, the advantages that French induftry would have derived from fuch an arrangement of American property, are at once fuggefted, by reforting to the drawing-rooms, viewing the clothing, and confidering the expenditure, even of the Britifh Weft India planter.

If, in the changes which have taken place in the diftribution of European property, we had perceived (inftead of a tendency

dency to break down properties, and to emancipate from perfonal flavery, as well as from flavifh tenures) a gradual accumulation of wealth into large maffes, and a greater proportion of the lower orders reduced into a ftate of perfect flavery ; the encouragement Britifh induftry would have derived from European demand, muft have been very different from what has been experienced, even under all the turbulent events that have diftinguifhed modern times.

This view of the circumftances on which the progreffive wealth of European nations at prefent depends, muft afford matter of great confolation to every man who is ferioufly concerned for the profperity and aggrandifement of the Britifh Empire.

For, if it could be allowed to enjoy peace and tranquillity, there never was a period in which the property of mankind feemed almoft univerfally to be getting into an arrangement

rangement that infured a fimilar extenfion of demand for the produce of the peculiar fpecies of induftry in which any one coun‑ try by practice excelled.

And this flattering profpect, however much it may excite the envy of other Eu‑ ropean nations, cannot, with reafon or with impunity, induce them to abftain from, or throw impediments in the way of, com‑ mercial communication with us.

For, on the principles here ftated, it is ob‑ vious that commerce cannot exift betwixt any two countries, without equally exciting the induftry of both. No means can be devifed of *interchanging commodities* that will exclufively encourage the induftry of any one of the parties concerned ; and the foolifh objections to commercial communi‑ cation, that ignorant jealoufy fuggefts, muft ever retard the progrefs of the induftry of a country that makes them, as effectually

as

as that of the country, againſt the increaſe
of whoſe induſtry they are levelled.

Great Britain cannot exclude the laces
and cambrics of France, without obliging
the conſumers of thoſe articles, throughout the Britiſh diminions, (in conſequence
of the neceſſary riſe of price), to appropriate more goods to the purchaſe of theſe
commodities; leſs muſt of courſe remain
for the acquiſition of other things in the
home market. Further, ſuch a prohibition
neceſſarily abſtracts a demand, to the amount
of the value of the lace and cambric, from
thoſe commodities, in the manufacture of
which, practice has given England peculiar
dexterity, which France muſt have deſired
in return; for no degree of freedom in
commercial communication can ever convey goods from one country to another,
without an equivalent.

France, on the other hand, cannot exclude the hardware of Birmingham, or
the

the cloth of Leeds, without making the natives of that country appropriate more
commodities to the purchafe of hardware
and coarfe cloth. This of neceffity abftracts a portion of what would be employed in acquiring other objects of internal
induftry ; befides which, a demand to the
amount of the value of the hardware and
cloth, muft, by this means, be withdrawn
from the acquifition of articles of French
growth and manufacture, which England
would require in return *.

Impediments,

* The clamour made in France againft the Commercial Treaty in 1787, muft have been excited by the induftry of a few interefted individuals; for it is impoffible that
that country fhould not have derived equal benefit with
England from the intercourfe.

The following extract, from the feventh *mémoire* of M.
BOYETET, director of commerce in the years 1787 and
1788, fhews the amazing increafe of demand for wines
that took place immediately after the Treaty of Commerce.

*Les états qu'on a de la fortie des vins de Bourdeaux pour
l'Angleterre et l'Irelande, dans les fix premiers mois de cette année,
portent deux mille fept cent cinquante tonneaux de vin.*

Ceux

Impediments, therefore, to commercial
communication, muft ever retard the growing opulence of mankind, as much by difcouraging the induftry of the country
whofe folly occafions them, as by any effect they can have on the induftry of the
country they are meant to injure. The
quibbling policy of commercial negotiators,
who falfely and ignorantly pride themfelves
on taking advantage of each other, ought
alone

Ceux des fix derniers mois de l'année 1786, *portent mille cinq
cent quatre-vingt-trois tonneaux.*

*Il en réfulteroit une augmentation de fortie dans les fix premiers
mois de cette année, de mille cent foixante fept tonneaux de vin de
Bourdeaux.*

" The account of wines exported from Bourdeaux to
" England and Ireland, in the firft fix months of this year,
" ftates it to amount to two thoufand feven hundred and
" fifty hogfheads.

" In the laft fix months of the year 1786, there appear
" to have been only one thoufand five hundred and eigh-
" ty-three hogfheads exported.

" It follows, then, that in the firft fix months of this year,
" there has been an increafed exportation to the amount
" of one thoufand one hundred and fixty-feven hogfheads
" of claret."

alone to create the contempt it merits;
for human ingenuity cannot contrive a
means of conducting the commercial relations betwixt any two countries, that does
not alike promote the profperity of both.

If, in delineating the means and the
caufes of the progreffive increafe of wealth,
we have been fortunate enough to imprefs
conviction, it will follow:—

That man owes his wealth, or the accumulation of the objects of his defire, which
he alone of all animals poffeffes, to the
power of directing his labour to the increafing of the quantity, or the meliorating of
the quality, of the productions of nature;
and to the power of fupplanting and performing labour by capital;—faculties peculiar to, and characteriftic of, the human
fpecies:—

That though land, labour, and capital,
may be regarded as the fources of wealth,
the

the wealth of mankind is alone increaſed by labour, whether performed by the hand of man or by capital, employed in increaſing the quantity, and meliorating the quality, of the productions of nature ; and by labour, whether manual or performed by capital, employed in giving form to, and adapting raw materials for conſumption :—

That the direction which labour in every country takes, and of courſe the channels of induſtry in which it excels,—nay, the extent to which the exertions of its induſtry, and even its population, can be puſhed, depend upon the diſtribution of its wealth :—

That when once the peculiar character of the induſtry of a country is, by this means, fixed and decided, the progreſs of its opulence is accelerated or retarded in proportion as the diſtribution of wealth in other countries creates a demand for the articles

articles, in the production of which it excels :—And, laftly ;—

That all impediments thrown in the way of commercial communication, obftruct the increafe of wealth, as much by difcouraging the induftry of the country which gives rife to them, as by their effects on the induftry of the country they are meant to injure.

F I N I S.

APPEN-

APPENDIX.

APPENDIX.

———

No. I.   (Page 50).

" Il faut diftinguer les *biens* d'avec les *richef-*
fes.   Ceux-là ont une valeur ufuelle, et n'ont
point de valeur vénale.   Celles-ci ont une valeur ufuelle et une valeur vénale.   Il ne fuffit
pas à une nation d'avoir des *biens*.   Il faut
qu'elle tende à fe procurer de grandes *richeffes*,
pour fubvenir par le commerce à tous les befoins
différens des membres dont elle eft compofée."
Phyfiocratie, p. cxviij.

No. II.

No. II.   (Page 114).

THE fyftem which regards commerce as the fole fource of wealth, was long maintained by moft of the eminent men who treated on commercial fubjects ; as the following extracts (to which many others might be added) fufficiently fhew.

"IT is a general opinion, that the trade of England was never greater, and it may be true, that if it be fo, yet it will not abfolutely conclude, that the kingdom doth increafe in riches; for the trade may be very abundant, and yet by confumption and importance of more than is expected, the ftock may wafte.

"The balance would be a true folution of the queftion, if it could be rightly had : but by reafon it muft be made up by a medium of the books of rates, it will be very uncertain.

"Therefore we muft feek another rule that is
more

more fenfible, upon which we may all judge,
and that may be by the plenty or fcarcity of
money ; for it is a true rule, if money increafe,
the kingdom doth gain by trade ; if it be fcarce,
it lofeth."—Sir THOMAS ROE's Speech in Parliament, 1640.

" THOSE *trades* may be efteemed good, which
confume our products and manufactures, upon
which the value of our land and employment of
the poor depends ; that increafe our feamen and
navigation, upon which our ftrength depends ;
that fupply us with fuch commodities as we abfolutely want for carrying on our *trade*, or for
our fafety, or carry out more than bring in, upon which the increafe of riches depends.

" On the contrary, thofe that import more
than they export, or bring us in goods perfectly
manufactured, or any fort of goods that hinder
the expence of our own, or that carry our *wool*
or other materials, to enable foreign nations to
make manufactures, to be fpent in the room of
our own ; or bring in commodities that are not
of neceffary ufe, but tend to increafe idlenefs
and luxurious expences ; or are carried on by fo-
                                        reign

reign bottoms, or factors or merchants that are
foreigners, (not fo advantageous as when carried
on by our own fhips and people); or *trades* carried on by the exportation of *coin* or *bullion.*
Such heads as thefe may ferve as a touchftone
for the examination of *trades.*"—A Difcourfe of
Coin, Trade, and Paper Credit, p. 58. 1697.

" ALTHOUGH a kingdom may be enriched by
gifts received, or by purchafe taken from fome
other nations, yet thefe are things uncertain,
and of fmall confideration when they happen.
The ordinary means, therefore, to increafe our
wealth and treafure is by foreign trade, wherein
we muft ever obferve this rule, to fell more to
ftrangers yearly than we confume of theirs in
value. For fuppofe that when this kingdom is
plentifully ferved with the cloth, lead, tin, iron,
fifh, and other native commodities, we do yearly export the overplus to foreign countries, to
the value of twenty-two hundred thoufand
pounds; by which means we are enabled beyond the feas to buy and bring in foreign wares
for our ufe and confumption, to the value of
twenty hundred thoufand pounds. By this
order duly kept in our trading, we may reft affured,

fured, that the kingdom fhall be enriched yearly two hundred thoufand pounds, which muft be
brought to us in fo much treafure ; becaufe that
part of our ftock which is not returned to us in
wares, muft neceffarily be brought home in treafure."—England's Treafure by Foreign Trade,
by THOMAS MUN, p. 7.

" THAT the greatnefs of this kingdom depends upon foreign trade, is acknowledged, and
therefore the intereft of trade not unbecoming
perfons of the higheft rank ; and of this ftudy,
as well as others, it may be faid, there is an infinity in it ; none, though of the largeft intellects
and experience, being able to fathom its utmoft
depth.

" Among other things relating to trade, there
has been much difcourfe of the balance of trade;
the right underftanding whereof may be of fingular ufe, and ferve as a compafs to fteer by, in
the contemplation and propagation of trade for
public advantage.

" The balance of trade is commonly underftood two ways :

" 1. Gene-

" 1. Generally,—fomething whereby it may be known whether this kingdom gains or lofes by foreign trade.

" 2. Particularly,—fomething whereby we may know by what trades this kingdom gains, and by what trades it lofes.

" For the firft of thefe :

" It is the moft general received opinion, and that not ill-grounded, that this balance is to be taken by a ftrict fcrutiny of what proportion the value of the commodities exported out of this kingdom bear to thofe imported ; and if the exports exceed the imports, it is concluded the nation gets by the general courfe of its trade ; it being fuppofed that the overplus is imported in bullion, and fo adds to the treafure of the kingdom, gold and filver being taken for the meafure and ftandard of riches."—A Difcourfe of Trade, by Sir Josiah Child, p. 163 & 164.

" If we export any value of our manufactures for the confumption of a foreign nation, and import thence no goods at all for our own confumption,

fumption, it is certain, the whole price of our own manufactures exported muft be paid to us in money, and that all the money paid to us is our clear gain.

" The merchant, perhaps, does not get 20 *per cent.* by the goods he fends abroad ; yet if he fells his goods for the very price he paid for them, and brings back the whole price in money, and not in goods, to his native country, the merchant, in this cafe, gets nothing, but his country gets clear the whole value of the goods."—The Britifh Merchant, p. 23.

" If we have at any time imported from France, (for our own confumption), a greater value of goods and merchandifes than we exported for the confumption of that country, it is certain, that one way or other, we paid the balance in money ; and whether we paid this by exporting bullion out of England, or by drawing bullion from other nations indebted to us, into France, the cafe is the very fame, that whole balance was fo much lofs to this kingdom ; fo much we may be faid to have loft by our French commerce."—The Britifh Merchant, p. 34.

No. III.

No. III.   (Page 202).

" Nous entendons par *papiers de crédit,* toute *créance,* ou obligation ; en un mot, toute ſtipulation par écrit entre un débiteur et un *créancier* ou *porteur* de *créance,* qui oblige celui-là à payer, et autoriſe celui-ci à exiger une valeur, et qui pouvant être cédée et tranſportée, devient un moyen de tranſporter la propriété, de ces valeurs, d'un poſſeſſeur à un autre poſſeſſeur, ſans tranſporter les valeurs en nature.

" On voit que cette définition convient à tous les papiers, billets, actions des banques ; aux créances qui repreſentent des valeurs empruntées par les gouvernemens, ou des fonds d'entrepriſes de commerce, de finance, &c. et enfin, aux créances mêmes de particulier à particulier ; telles que les *lettres de change, promeſſes, billets à ordre,*" &c.

No. IV.

No. IV.   (Page 239).

COMPUTATION OF INCOME BY MR PITT.

	Annual Income.	Deduction for part under L. 60, which will pay nothing, and part under L. 200, which will pay an average $\frac{1}{50}$.	Taxable Income.
Landlords rents, 40,000,000 cultivated acres, estimated at 12 s. 6 d. per acre, - -	£.	£.	£.
	25,000,000	$\frac{1}{5}$ 5,000,000	20,000,000
Tenants rents at $\frac{3}{4}$ths,	19,000,000	$\frac{2}{3}$ 13,000,000	6,000,000
Tithes, - -	5,000,000	$\frac{1}{5}$ 1,000,000	4,000,000
Mines, navigation and timber, - -	3,000,000		3,000,000
Houses, - -	6,000,000	$\frac{1}{5}$ 1,000,000	5,000,000
Rents on inhabited houses, 4,500,000, Professions, - -	2,000,000		2,000,000
Scotland $\frac{1}{8}$th of England, - -	5,000,000		5,000,000
Income from professions beyond sea, -	5,000,000		5,000,000
Interest on funds, after deducting sums issued to Commissioners as sinking fund, and interest of capital redeemed, - -	15,000,000	$\frac{1}{5}$ 3,000,000	12,000,000
Profit on foreign trade, supposed 15 per centum on L. 80,000,000 capital insured, -	12,000,000		12,000,000
Ditto, home trade, at 15 per cent. -	18,000,000		28,000,000
Other trade, -	10,000,000		
			102,000,000

See appendix No. 4. to the substance of a speech by Lord Auckland, printed by authority, 1799. To the same purport, see appendix, No. 7. of Mr Rose's Examination, &c.

No. V. (Page 244).

The Teſtament of M. Fortuné Ricard, &c. tran-ſlated from the French by Dr Price.

" In the name of God, I Fortuné Ricard, teacher of arithmetic at D——, invoking the Holy Virgin, and St Fortune my patron, do make this my laſt-will as follows :

[" The executors, who have cauſed this will " to be printed, in order to fulfil the intentions " of the late M. Fortuné Ricard, do not think " it neceſſary to publiſh thoſe particular bequeſts " which concern only his own family. After " having diſpoſed of his patrimony among them " with wiſdom, he proceeds in the following " manner :"]

" It remains for me now to declare my inten-tions with regard to the promiſe of 500 livres, (L. 22 : 4 : 6), ſubſcribed on my behalf by M. P. banker

banker of this town. This fum proceeded originally from a prefent which was made me by Prosper
Ricard, my much honoured grandfather, when I
entered the eighth year of my age. At that age
he had taught me the principles of writing and
calculation. After having fhewn me, that a capital, with its accumulating intereft at 5 per
cent., would amount, at the end of one hundred
years, to more than one hundred and thirty-one
times the original fum ; and feeing that I liften-
ed to this lecture with the greateft attention, he
took 24 livres out of his pocket, and addreffed
me with an enthufiafm which is ftill prefent to
my mind. " My child, (faid he), remember,
" while thou liveft, that with œconomy and cal-
" culation nothing is impoffible for man. Here
" are 24 livres, which I give thee. Take them
" to a merchant in our neighbourhood, who will
" place them in trade out of regard to me. Eve-
" ry year thou fhalt add the intereft to the prin-
" cipal. At thy death, thou fhalt employ the
" produce in good works for the repofe of thy
" foul and my own." I have executed this order with fidelity ; and in the courfe of my life, I
have planned many projects for employing this
money. Having reached the feventy-firft year
                                        of

of my age, it amounts to 500 livres; but as I
muft, fome time or other, fet bounds to myfelf,
I now defire that it may be divided into five
portions, of 100 livres each, to which the interefts fhall be annually added, and the accumulated fums fhall be fucceffively applied to the following ufes;

" 1. In a hundred years, the firft fum of 100
livres will amount to more than 13,100 livres,
(L. 5822). From this fum, a prize of 4000
livres fhall be given for the beft theological differtation, to prove the lawfulnefs of putting out
money to intereft. Three medals, of 600 livres
each, fhall alfo be given for the three differta-
tions which fhall be adjudged the next in merit
to the prize differtation. The remainder of the
13,100 livres fhall be expended in printing the
prize differtation, and extracts from the others.
Copies of thefe fhall be fent, gratis, to all the
bifhops, clergy, and confeffors of the kingdom.
I had intended to have fent them alfo into foreign countries; but I obferve, that all the uni-
verfities of the Chriftian world, excepting thofe
of France, have folemnly recognifed the lawfulnefs of putting money to intereft, and that it
continues

continues neceffary only in this kingdom, to explain a queftion in morals, fo interefting to the
welfare of the ftate.

" 2. After two hundred years, a fecond fum of
100 livres, amounting, with its accumulated intereft, to more than 1,700,000 livres (L.756,500),
fhall be employed in eftablifhing a perpetual
fund, for fourfcore prizes, of 1000 livres each,
to be diftributed annually by the different aca-
demies of the kingdom, as follows : Fifteen prizes
for the moft diftinguifhed virtuous actions ; fifteen for works of fcience and literature ; ten for
folutions of queftions in arithmetic and calculation ; ten for fuch new proceffes in agriculture
as fhall produce the beft crops ; ten for mafter-
pieces in the fine arts ; and ten to encourage
races and other exercifes, proper to difplay the
force and agility of the body, and to reftore
amongft us a tafte for the gymnafium, which
was in fuch great efteem among the Greeks, and
which formerly made fo many heroes.

" 3. After three hundred years, from another
fum of 100 livres, increafed in that time to
more than two hundred and twenty-fix millions,
(L. 10,057,000),

(L. 10,057,000), there fhall be appropriated
196 millions, towards eftablifhing, in the moft
confiderable places in France, five hundred patriotic banks, for lending money without intereft ; the largeft of which fhall have a fund of
ten millions of livres, and the fmalleft a fund of
100,000 livres. Thefe banks fhall be managed
by a committee of the moft upright citizens in
each place, and the money fhall be employed in
loans, to fuccour the unfortunate, or advanced
towards promoting agriculture, trade, and induftry. The remaining thirty millions fhall be expended in founding twelve mufeums, in the cities of Paris, Lyons, Rouen, Bourdeaux, Rennes,
Lifle, Nancy, Tours, Dijon, Thouloufe, Aix, and
Grenoble. Each of thefe mufeums fhall be placed at the moft agreeable end of the city. Five
hundred thoufand livres fhall be expended upon
each building, and in the purchafe of grounds
which fhall belong to them, and be laid out into
botanical and fruit gardens, and alfo into kitchen gardens, and extenfive walks. To each
mufeum fhall be annexed an income of 100,000
livres ; and there fhall be lodged and boarded in
it forty literary men, and artifts of fuperior merit, who, at the time of meals, fhall be divided
into

into four tables, that their repafts may be chear-
ful, without being too noify. Each mufeum
fhall be provided with fix fecretaries, a de-
figner and engraver, and four carriages. There
fhall be alfo a hall for concerts, a theatre, a che-
mical laboratory, a cabinet of natural hiftory,
a hall for experimental philofophy, and a grand
gallery for a common library. A hundred thoufand livres fhall be expended on a feparate library for each of thefe eftablifhments. The fame
fum fhall be employed in providing them with
feparate cabinets of natural hiftory, and with
philofophical inftruments. And 10,000 livres
fhall be referved annually, for keeping up and
increafing thefe cabinets and philofophical inftruments.

" The libraries fhall always be open to the
public. Twenty members of the mufeum fhall
be engaged in giving public and gratuitous
courfes of lectures upon the foreign languages,
and upon all the arts and fciences. The other
twenty fhall be engaged in fuch other employ-
ments as may be moft ufeful. No one fhall be
admitted a member, till he has previoufly given
proof, not of his rank, defcent, or nobility, but

of

of his morals, and of his never having diſhonour-
ed his pen, by writing againſt religion and government, or by ſacrificing any member of the
community. On being admitted, he ſhall make
oath, " That he will prefer virtue, truth, and
" his country, to every thing ; and the general
" good of literature to his own fame." The
works of the members of the muſeum ſhall be
printed at the expence of the eſtabliſhment, and
when thoſe expences are reimburſed, the profits
ſhall belong to to the authors.

" 4. After four hundred years, the fourth ſum
of 100 livres, amounting, with intereſt, to near
30,000 millions, (L. 1,330,000,000), ſhall be employed in building one hundred towns, each containing one hundred and fifty thouſand ſouls,
in the moſt agreeable ſituations which can be
found in France. The means of peopling theſe
towns, of governing and making them flouriſh,
are explained in a memorial annexed to this
will. In a ſhort time there will reſult from
hence an addition of fifteen millions of inhabitants to the kingdom, and its conſumption will
be doubled ; for which ſervice I hope the œconomiſts will think themſelves obliged to me.

" I

" I am fenfible that all the fpecie in Europe is not equal to thefe 30,000 millions, and that it will be impoffible to make provifion in money for fuch immenfe fums. For this reafon, I leave it to the difcretion of my executors to exchange cafh at convenient feafons for landed and other real poffeffions. The revenue arifing from thofe poffeffions fhall either be laid out in cafh, or realized by further purchafes, fo that my bequefts may be fulfilled in their due time, without any difficulty.

" I am convinced, by the moft accurate calculations, that my arrangements, inftead of clogging, will give activity to the circulation of fpecie. Laying out the money I have ordered in the purchafe of eftates, will foon increafe their value ; and when thefe accumulating riches fhall have fo produced their effect, as that there can no longer be found in France a landholder who will fell his eftate, purchafers muft be fought for among the neighbouring nations.

" 5. Finally, with regard to the laft fum of 100 livres, amounting nearly, by the accumulation of five hundred years, to four millions of
millions

millions of livres, (one hundred and feventy-fix thoufands of millions Sterling), it fhall be dif-pofed of as follows :

" Six thoufand millions fhall be appropriated towards paying the national debt of France, up-on condition that the Kings, our good Lords and Mafters, fhall be entreated to order the Comp-trollers General of the Finances to undergo in future an examination in arithmetic before they enter upon their office.

" Twelve thoufand millions fhall likewife be employed in paying the public debts of England. It may be feen, that I reckon that both thofe na-tional debts will be doubled in this period ; not that I have any doubts of the talents of certain minifters to increafe them much more ; but their operations in this way are oppofed by an infini-ty of circumftances, which lead me to prefume, that thofe debts cannot be more than doubled. Befides, if they amount to a few thoufands of millions more, I declare that it is my intention that they fhould be entirely paid off, and that a projeÃ fo laudable fhould not remain unexecu-ted for a trifle more or lefs. I beg that the Englifh

lifh would not refufe this flight mark of the re-
membrance of a man, who was indeed born a
Frenchman, but who fincerely efteemed their
nation, and always was a particular admirer of
that magnificent work which NEWTON, their
countryman, has entitled Univerfal Arithmetic.
I earneftly defire, that, as an acknowledgment
for this legacy, the Englifh nation will confent
to call the French their *neighbours*, and not their
natural enemies; that they may be affured that
nature never made man an enemy to man ; and
that national hatreds, commercial prohibitions,
and, above all, *wars*, conftantly produce a mon-
ftrous error in calculations. But I dare not in
this inftance require any thing. We muft hope
for all we defire from Time ; and when we have
the happinefs of rendering a fervice, we muft
not deftroy its value, by annexing conditions to
it which may encumber thofe whom we wifh to
ferve.

" Thirty thoufand millions fhall be formed
into a fund, for producing an annual revenue of
fifteen hundred millions, to be divided in times
of peace among all the powers of Europe. In
time

time of war, the fhare of the aggreffor or aggref-
fors fhall be given to thofe who have been at-
tacked unjuftly, in order to engage Sovereigns,
if poffible, to reflect a little before they com-
mence unjuft hoftilities. This revenue fhall be
diftributed among the different nations in proportion to their population. Every ten years an
exact numeration fhall be taken, with a view to
this diftribution, which fhall be made by a diet
compofed of deputies from all the different nations ; but I direct that a larger proportion fhall
be diftributed to thofe Sovereigns who fhall apply for it, and appear to defire it with no other
view than to encourage population among their
fubjects.

" I leave to the wifdom of my executors the
care of extending the benefits of this bequeft to
the other parts of the world ; and if, by this
means, they fhould hope to fucceed in extin-
guifhing, throughout the world, the abfurd and
barbarous rage of war, I willingly confent that
they appropriate for this purpofe the further
fum of one hundred thoufand millions. I
wifh that fix thoufand millions may be offered to
his

his Majesty, the King of France ; namely, a
thousand millions to supersede the necessity of
lotteries, a sort of tax imposed upon wicked
men, which infallibly renders them a great deal
more wicked ; a thousand millions to buy in all
useless offices, which are attended with the sad
inconvenience, of persuading many persons that
it is a sufficient discharge of their duty to their
country to occupy an office without function,
and that an honour may be derived from bear-
ing a senseless title ; a thousand millions to buy
in offices, which, on the contrary, are too important to be left exposed to the danger of ve-
nality ; a thousand millions to purchase a do-
main for his Majesty, worthy of his Crown, and
sufficient for the expences of his Court, so that
the nation may clearly perceive, that the taxes
imposed upon them are applicable only to the
expenditures of the State.   The remaining two
thousand millions shall form a fund, whose annual produce shall be employed by his Majesty
in pensions and gratuities.   By these means, if,
sometimes, those favours should be conferred upon intriguing and undeserving persons, the nation will have no cause to complain of the im-
                                         proper

proper ufe of money, drawn from taxes and the labours of the hufbandman.

" I appoint a thoufand millions towards adding a thoufand livres to the fettled income of all the clergy in the kingdom, and fix hundred livres to that of their vicars, upon condition that they no longer demand fees for faying maffes. I had alfo fome thoughts of propofing to them the fuppreffion of fees for baptifms, marriages and burials ; but I have confidered thofe functions to be of a civil as well as religious nature, and that, on this account, the clergy may, without impropriety, be allowed to receive a pay, which is, in fact, more moderate than would be required by any other public officers in their places. Befides, this pay perhaps renders the fervice more exact, more fpeedy on their part, and lefs irkfome to the delicacy of fome of thofe who receive it.

" I appoint two thoufand millions towards forming an income of ten livres a month to all the children which fhall be born in the kingdom, till they are three years of age ; and I defire

fire this legacy to be increafed to thirty livres a
month to thofe children who fhall be nurfed
by their own mothers. I do not except even the
children of the rich ; on the contrary, I invite
rich parents to accept this donation without re-
luctance, as an honorary prize awarded to pa-
ternity and the cares of maternal love. They
may, if they pleafe, apply it to acts of charity
and benevolence.

" I appoint four thoufand millions towards
purchafing the wafte lands of the kingdom.
Thefe fhall be divided into five hundred thoufand little farms or tenements, of four or five
acres each, on which fhall be erected as many
commodious cottages. Thefe five hundred thoufand farms fhall be given as freeholds to an equal
number of married peafants, chofen in each parifh by a veftry compofed of ten of the moft
aged inhabitants. The poffeffors of thefe freeholds fhall be obliged to make them their
only refidence, to cultivate them with their own
hands and thofe of their families, and to report
every year the improvements of them which
they have made. Thefe freeholds fhall be hereditary.

reditary, but only upon condition that they fhall neither be divided, nor any two of them engrof-fed by one perfon. When a freeholder dies, without leaving behind him either wife, children, brothers, fifters, nephews, or nieces, who have lived and laboured with him for three years prior to his deceafe, the freehold fhall be declared vacant, and given anew, by the veftry of the parifh, to that peafant who fhall appear to deferve it beft.

" I defire that two thoufand millions be laid out in purchafing all the manors of which there fhall be fellers, and that the vaffals thereon be for ever afterwards exempted from all fervitude and fealty.

" Six thoufand millions fhall be employed in founding houfes of education in all the country parifhes, agreeable to the plan of the author of a work, entitled Patriotic Views refpecting the Education of the People. If, in executing this plan of a man of genius, and an excellent citizen, it fhould appear to want fome little amendments and alterations, I direct that they fhall be adopted.

" I

" I appoint twenty thoufand millions towards erecting in the kingdom forty thoufand houfes of labour, or public workhoufes ; to each of which fhall be appropriated from ten thoufand to fifty thoufand livres annual income. Every man and woman fhall have a right to offer themfelves at any time to be maintained and employed in them. I choofe to fay nothing of any other particulars in the government and management of thefe houfes, hoping that the ideas which begin to be formed concerning eftablifhments of this kind, will be perfected before the period fixed for thefe fhall arrive ; and that it will at length be univerfally acknowledged, that though it is dangerous and foolifh to give alms in money to a ftrong beggar, yet that fociety has no right to deprive him of his liberty, and inflict punifhments upon him, while it does not hold out to him any other means of fubfiftence, or at leaft point out to him a method of difcovering what means he is capable of ufing.

" I entreat the managers of thefe public workhoufes, to give the greateft encouragement to fuch trades as can be performed by women.
This

This fex, fo dear to all fenfible minds, has been neglected or oppreffed by all our inftitutions. Seductions of all kinds feem to confpire againft their virtue. Neceffity precipitates them involuntarily into an abyfs of infamy and mifery. The low price which is fet upon the labour of women, is out of all proportion to the inferiority of their bodily ftrength. Let the public work-houfes fet the example of paying them better.

" There are in France many houfes of correction, where the mifconduct of women is feverely punifhed, but where, in reality, it is only fufpended, mere confinement having no tendency to eradicate vice. Why fhould there not be one eftablifhment, where a young woman, conquered by temptation, and on the brink of defpair, might prefent herfelf, and fay, " Vice offers me " gold; I only afk for labour and bread. In " compaffion to my remorfe, affift and ftrengthen " me. Open an afylum for me, where I may " weep without being feen, expiate thofe faults " which purfue and overwhelm me, and recover " a fhadow of peace." Such an inftitution exifts

ifts no where. I appoint, therefore, a thoufand millions towards eftablifhing one.

" The fnares which are laid by vice for wo-men without fortunes, would make fewer vic-tims if more affiftance was given them. We have an infinity of eftablifhments for perfons in the higher ranks of life, which do honour to the generofity of our forefathers. Why have we none for this purpofe ? I defire, therefore, that two thoufand millions be employed in eftablifhing in the kingdom a hundred hofpitals, which fhall be called Hofpitals of Angels. There fhall be ad-mitted into each a hundred females, of the age of feven or eight years, and of the moft enga-ging forms. They fhall receive the moft per-fect education in regard to morals, ufeful know-ledge, and agreeable accomplifhments. At the age of eighteen they may quit the hofpital, in order to be married, at which period they fhall each be paid a portion of forty thoufand livres. I mention this moderate fum, becaufe it is my wifh that they be neither reproached for want of fortune, nor efpoufed from intereft. An an-nual income of two thoufand livres fhall be gi-ven

ven alfo to their parents, * * * *. Except once
in the year, at a folemn and fplendid proceffion,
they fhall rarely appear in public, but fhall be
conftantly employed in their afylum, in learning
all that can render them one day excellent wives
and mothers.

   " In order to fit them, in particular, for domeftic œconomy, I defire, that after they have
been taught the moft accurate ideas of expences
of all kinds, queftions be propofed to them from
time to time, to which they fhall be obliged to
give anfwers by word of mouth, and alfo in writing ; as for example : " If you had fuch and
" fuch an income, under fuch and fuch circum-
" ftances, how much would you appropriate to
" your table, your houfe-rent, your maintenance,
" and the education of your children ? How
" many fervants would you keep ? How much
" would you referve for ficknefs and unforefeen
" expences ? How much would you confecrate
" to the relief of the unfortunate and the public
" good ? . If your income depended either en-
" tirely or in part upon a tranfient advantage,
" or a place which was not affured to you, How
                          " much

" much would you expend annually? What
" fum would you referve for forming a capital?"
&c. &c. Prizes publicly given to the beft anfwers to queftions of this kind, would conftitute,
in my opinion, an exercife equally engaging,
and more ufeful, than the little comedies and
novels with which young perfons in the higher
ftations are generally entertained.

" The honours conferred upon great men have
always appeared to me the moft effectual means
of producing great men. I appoint, therefore, a
thoufand millions towards ftriking medals, and
placing in the halls of all towns, or in any other
convenient places, ftatues and bufts in honour of
fuch great men as fhall hereafter rife up. I defire further, that thefe honours be not paid them
till ten years after their deceafe, and that they
be decreed and proportioned by a tribunal, compofed of fuch upright, enlightened, and worthy
citizens, as fhall be moft likely not to be dazzled
by falfe virtues. It has been once reckoned,
that founding hofpitals for the fick is one of the
beft public fervices. For fome years, a conviction has been gaining ground, that breathing the
peftilential

peftilential air of hofpitals doubles the danger of difeafes, and that on this, and other accounts, they probably deftroy more lives than they fave. I defire, therefore, that ten thoufand millions be employed in eftablifhing in each parifh of the kingdom Houfes of Health, in which fhall be maintained a phyfician, a furgeon, and a convenient number of fifters of charity and nurfes. Thefe houfes fhall fupply the fick gratis, in their own houfes, with every affiftance in food and medicine, and none fhall be taken to the Houfe of Health excepting thofe whom it fhall be impoffible to affift at home.

" I have hitherto only directed the employment of about two hundred thoufand millions. There remain ftill near four millions of millions, the appropriation of which I leave to the difcretion of my executors. I wifh them to purchafe and pull down all fuch houfes as incommode the public way in all towns ; to multiply fquares, quays, fountains, gardens, &c. in order to give falubrity to the air of towns ; to empty ponds ; to clear heaths ; to deepen the beds of rivers, fo as to render them navigable, and to unite them

by

by means of canals. In a word, I wifh them to
co-operate in every poffible method with nature,
which feems to have defigned France to be the
moft delightful country under heaven.

" I hope that all good citizens will affift my
executors in the choice of fuch ufeful eftablifhments as fhall yet remain to be formed. I call
upon them to publifh the ideas with which patriotic zeal may infpire them, fince now they are
encouraged by the confoling certainty, that
funds for executing them cannot be wanting.

" I name for executors my deareft and beft
friends M. M. - - - - - - - - - -
(Here the teftator names fix executors, who do
not think proper at prefent to reveal themfelves,
and then goes on as follows :)

" I beg of them to meet as often as the affairs
of my executorfhip fhall require. In cafe of an
equal divifion of opinions, the oldeft fhall have
the cafting vote. When one of them dies, I defire the furvivors to fill the vacancy, as foon as
may be, with the moft honeft, zealous, and dif-
interefted

interefted citizen of their acquaintance, and to proceed in this manner for ever. I hope that during the firft years of their executorſhip, when the operations of the fund will be eaſy, they will tranſaƈt in this buſineſs out of regard to me and to the public. I foreſee, that in proceſs of time the ſums to be laid out will become ſo immenſe-ly great, as to render neceſſary voyages and other conſiderable expences, which will be pro-duƈtive of no profit. For this reaſon, I have left one hundred and twenty-five thouſand livres of the ſecond ſum, unappropriated; of the third, ſe-ven hundred and eleven thouſand ; and of the fourth, thirty-two millions. Theſe ſums I re-queſt them to accept, as a compenſation for their expences and trouble. I charge them always, as far as they can, without hazarding the ſecu-rity of the fund, to prefer thoſe ways of laying out the accumulating ſums which ſhall be moſt ſerviceable to individuals and the public.

" If a reduƈtion in the rate of intereſt, or any unforeſeen loſſes, ſhould injure the fund, ſo as to retard its increaſe, the execution of my deſires need only be poſtponed, in proportion to the in-terruption that ſhall happen.

" May

" May the fuccefs of thefe eftablifhments caufe one day a few tears to be fhed on my grave ! But, above all, may the example of an obfcure individual kindle the emulation of patriots, princes, and public bodies ; and engage them to give attention to this new, but powerful and infallible means, of ferving pofterity, and contributing to the future improvement and happinefs of the world !' "

REMARK BY THE TRANSLATOR.

IT is to be obferved, that if M. RICARD had directed the intereft of the money to be laid out every three months, it would have wonderfully increafed the fums with the difpofal of which his executors are intrufted.

One hundred livres will amount, if improved at 5 per cent. intereft,

	Paid yearly. Livres.	Half-yearly. Livres.
In 100 years, to	131,501	139,560
In 500 years, to	3,932,400,000,000	5,296,100,000,000

Paid

Paid quarterly.

In 100 years, to   143,890 livres.

In 500 years, to   6,166,000,000,000 livres.

If, therefore, the laſt 100 livres had been improved at 5 per cent. quarterly intereſt, his executors would have had an additional ſum of 2,234,000,000,000 livres, (nearly equal to a hundred thouſand millions Sterling), which is a ſum more than ſufficient to encompaſs the earth with a belt of guineas, all cloſe, and five feet broad.

No. VI.

No. VI. (Page 268).

EXTRACT of the Preamble to Cap. LXXI. of
the 42d of the King.

" WHEREAS the public burdens may at this
period be greatly alleviated, and the reduction
of the national debt at the fame time accelerated, by confolidating the public debt, and the
whole of the faid debt will thereby be redeemed
within forty-five years."

CLAUSE V. OF THE SAID ACT.

" And be it further enacted, That all monies
whatever which fhall be placed from time to
time to the account of the faid Commiffioners,
by virtue of either of the faid recited acts, (except fo far as the fame are hereby repealed), or
by virtue of this act, fhall, and are hereby appropriated to, and fhall accumulate in manner directed

rected by the faid acts, for the reduction of the
national debt of Great Britain, and fhall be from
time to time applied by the faid Commiffioners,
purfuant to the directions, and under and according to the reftrictions and provifions of the
faid recited acts, either in payment for the redemption, or in the purchafe of the feveral redeemable public annuities of Great Britain, un-
til the whole of the perpetual redeemable annuities, now charged upon the public funds of
Great Britain, including fuch charge as has ari-
fen, or may arife, on any loan made in Great Britain, before the paffing of this act, and alfo fuch
charge as fhall arife by any annuities, interefts,
and dividends, payable in confequence of any
loans made chargeable on the confolidated fund,
by an act paffed in this feffion of Parliament,
entitled, *An Act for repealing the Duties on
Income ; for the effectual Collection of Arrears
of the faid Duties, and accounting for the fame,
and for charging the.annuities fpecifically charged thereon upon the Confolidated Fund of Great
Britain,* fhall have been completely redeemed
or purchafed, fo as that the whole of the feveral redeemable public annuities now charged
upon

upon the public funds of Great Britain, including fuch refpective charges as aforefaid, *fhall
be paid off within forty-five years* from the refpective periods of the creation of fuch refpective
charges and public annuities as aforefaid."

No. VII.

No. VII.   (Page 269).

Statement, showing the Sum that must of necessity be abstracted from Expenditure, and converted into Capital, every half-year, by an annual Income of L. 5,585,572, accumulated half-yearly, at 3 per cent. for forty-five years.

Years.		Years.	
½	2,792,786.	3½	20,451,555.66
	2,834,677.79		3,099,559.334
1	5,627,463.79	4	23,551,114.994
	2,877,197.956		3,146,052.724
1½	8,504,661.746	4½	26,697,167.718
	2,920,355.926		3,193,243.515
2	11,425,017.672	5	29,890,411.233
	2,964,161.265		3,241,142.168
2½	14,389,178.937	5½	33,131,553.401
	3,008,623.684		3,289,759.301
3	17,397,802.621	6	36,421,312.702
	3,053,753.039		3,339,105.690
	20,451,555.66	6½	39,760,418.392

Years.		Years.	
	39,760,418.392		83,959,591.434
	3,389,192.275		4,052,179.871
7	43,149,610.667	13	88,011,771.305
	3,440,030.160		4,112,962.569
7½	46,589,640.827	13½	92,124,733.874
	3,491,630.612		4,174,657.008
8	50,081,271.439	14	96,299,390.882
	3,544,005.071		4,237,276.863
8½	53,625,276.510	14½	100,536,667.745
	3,597,165.147		4,300,836.016
9	57,222,441.657	15	104,837,501.761
	3,651,122.624		4,365,348.526
9½	60,873,564.281	15½	109,202,850.287
	3,705,889.464		4,430,828.754
10	64,579,453.745	16	113,633,679.041
	3,761,477.806		4,497,291.185
10½	68,340,931.551	16½	118,130,970.226
	3,817,899.973		4,564,750.553
11	72,158,831.524	17	122,695,720.779
	3,875,168.472		4,633,221.811
11½	76,033,999.996	17½	127,328,942.590
	3,933,295.999		4,702,720.138
12	79,967,295.995	18	132,031,662.728
	3,992,295.439		4,773,260.940
12½	83,959,591.434	18½	136,804,923.668

Years.		Years.	
	136,804,923.668		199,987,765.383
	4,844,859.855		5,792,602.480
19	141,649,783.523	25	205,780,367.863
	4,917,532.752		5,879,491.517
19½	146,567,316.275	25½	211,659,859.380
	4,991,295.744		5,967,683.890
20	151,558,612.019	26	217,627,543.270
	5,066,165.180		6,057,199.149
20½	156,624,777.199	26½	223,684,742.419
	5,142,157.657		6,148,057.136
21	161,766,934.856	27	229,832,799.555
	5,219,290.022		6,240,277.993
21½	166,986,224.878	27½	236,073,077.548
	5,297,579.373		6,333,882.163
22	172,283,804.251	28	242,406,959.711
	5,377,043.063		6,428,890.395
22½	177,660,847.314	28½	248,835,850.106
	5,457,698.709		6,525,323.751
23	183,118,546.023	29	255,361,173.857
	5,539,564.190		6,623,203.607
23½	188,658,110.213	29½	261,984,377.464
	5,622,657.653		6,722,551.661
24	194,280,767.866	30	268,706,929.125
	5,706,997.517		6,823,389.936
24½	199,987,765.383	30½	275,530,319.061

Years.		Years.	
	275,530,319.061		365,850,368.958
	6,925,740.785		8,280,541.534
31	282,456,059.846	37	374,130,910.492
	7,029,626.897		8,404,749.657
31½	289,485,686.743	37½	382,535,660.149
	7,135,071.301		8,530,820.902
32	296,620,758.044	38	391,066,481.051
	7,242,097.370		8,658,783.215
32½	303,862,855.414	38½	399,725,264.266
	7,350,728.831		8,788,664.963
33	311,213,584.245	39	408,513,929.229
	7,460,989.763		8,920,494.938
33½	318,674,574.008	39½	417,434,424.167
	7,572,904.610		9,054,302.362
34	326,247,478.618	40	426,488,726.529
	7,686,498.179		9,190,116.897
34½	333,933,976.797	40½	435,678,843.426
	7,801,795.651		9,327,968.651
35	341,735,772.448	41	445,006,812.077
	7,918,822.586		9,467,888.181
35½	349,654,595.034	41½	454,474,700.258
	8,037,604.925		9,609,906.503
36	357,692,199.959	42	464,084,606.761
	8,158,168.999		9,754,055.101
36½	365,850,368.958	42½	473,838,661.862

Years.		Years.	
	473,838,661.862		503,987,503.693
	9,900,365.927		10,352,598.555
43	483,739,027.789	44½	514,340,102.248
	10,048,871.416		10,507,887.533
43½	493,787,899.205	45	* 524,847,989.781
	10,199,604.488		
44	503,987,503.693		

No. VIII.

* In APPENDIX, No. VIII. the annual fum of L. 5,585,572 per annum, is ftated as amounting in forty-five years, when accumulated at 3 per cent., to L. 528,395,000. This difference is fuppofed to arife from the calculation delivered into the Houfe of Commons proceeding on the fuppofition of a quarterly accumulation.

No. VIII.   (Page 269).

THE following is the Statement of the Redemption of the National Debt, prefented to the
Houfe of Commons, 7th April 1802.

Amount of Stock purchafed in forty-five and forty-fix
Years, at the feveral rates of Intereft 3, $3\frac{1}{4}$, $3\frac{1}{2}$, $3\frac{3}{4}$,
and 4 per cent. by a Sinking Fund of L. 5,585,572
per annum.

	In 45 years.	In 46 years.
	£.	£.
At par, the confolidated finking fund purchafes, -	528,395,000	550,059,000
Confolidated debt, 7th April 1802, - -	488,987,656	488,987,656
Surplus, - - -	39,407,344	61,071,344
At $3\frac{1}{4}$ per cent. is purchafed,	612,737,000	639,020,000
Confolidated debt, 7th April 1802, - - -	488,987,656	488,987,656
Surplus, - -	123,749,844	150,032,344

In

	In 45 years.	In 46 years.
	£.	£.
At 3½ per cent. is purchafed, -	707,220,000	738,720,000
Confolidated debt, 7th April 1802, - -	488,987,656	488,987,656
Surplus, - -	218,232,344	249,732,344
At 3¾ per cent. is purchafed, -	812,395,000	850,370,000
Confolidated debt, 7th April 1802, - -	488,987,656	488,987,656
Surplus, - -	323,407,344	361,382,344
At 4 per cent. is purchafed, -	930,096,000	975,430,000
Confolidated debt, 7th April 1802, - - -	488,987,656	488,987,656
Surplus, - -	441,108,344	486,442,344

No. IX.   (Page 284).

Ετι δ̀ κỳ ἒ τѕ́των μόνον ἕνεκα τῶν εἰρημβ́ων εὐ-
φραίνἡ τὰ πεμπόμβα παρὰ βασιλέως, ἀλλὰ τῷ
ὄντι κỳ ἡδονῇ πολὺ διαφέρει τὰ ἀπὸ τῆς βασιλέως
τραπέζης. Καὶ τѕ̃το μέντοι οὕτως ἔχειν οὐδέν τι
θαυμαϛόν· ὥσπερ γ̀ δ̀ κỳ ἄλλαι τέχναι διαφερόντως

τως ἐν ταῖς μεγάλαις πόλεσιν ἐξειργασμέναι εἰσὶ,
κατὰ τὸν αὐτὸν τρόπον καὶ τὰ παρὰ βασιλᾶ σῖτα
πολὺ Διαφερόντως ἐκπεπόνηται. Ἐν μὲν γὸ ταῖς
μικραῖς πόλεσιν οἱ αὐτοὶ ποιᾶσι κλίνω, θύραν, ἄρο-
τρον, τράπεζαν· (πολλάκις δ' ὁ αὐτὸς ἔτ῭ καὶ οἰ-
κοδομᾶ, ᵏ ἀγαπᾶ ἱὼ ᵏ ἔτως ἱκανὲς αὐτὸν τρέφειν
ἐργοδότας λαμβάνῃ· ἀδώαλον ἔν πολλὰ τεχνώμε-
νον ἄνθρωπον πάντα καλῶς ποιεῖν)· ἐν ὃ ταῖς μεγάλαις πόλεσι, διὰ τὸ πολλὲς ἑκάσε σἷαϖ, ἀρκᾶ ᵏ
μία ἑκάσω τέχνη εἰς τὸ τρέφεαϖ· πολλάκις ὃ οὐδ'
ὅλη μία, ἀλλ' ὑποδήματα ποιεῖ ὁ μὲν ἀνδρεῖα, ὁ ὃ γυ-
ναικεῖα. Ἐςι ὃ ἔνθα ᵏ ὑποδήματα ὁ μὲν νευρορραφῶν
μόνον, τρέφεϛ, ὁ δὲ, χίζων· ὁ ὃ χιτῶνας μόνον ϛυν-
τέμνων, ὁ δέ γε, τὲτων ᵘδὲν ποιῶν, ἀλλὰ σωτιθὲς
ταῦτα. Ἀνάγκη ἔν, ᵗ ἐν βραχυτάτῳ Διατρίβον-
τα ἔργῳ, τᵘτον ᐸ ἄρισα διηναγκάϛ τᵘτο ποιεῖν.
Τὸ αὐτὸ ὃ τᵘτο πέπονθε ᵏ τὰ ἀμφὶ τὼ δίαιταν·
ᾧ μὲν γὰρ ὁ αὐτὸς κλίνην ϛώννυϛι, τράπεζαν κοσ-
μᾶ, μάτἷ, ὄψα ἄλλοτε ἀλλοῖα ποιεῖ, ἀνάγκη, οἶμαι, τᵘτῳ ὡς ἂν ἕκαςον προχωρῇ, ἔτως ἔχϫν· ὅπᵘ
ὃ ἱκανὸν ἔργον ἑνὶ ἕψειν κρέα, ἄλλῳ ὀπτᾶν, ἄλλῳ
δὲ ἰχθὺὼ ἕψϫν, ἄλλῳ ὀπτᾶν· ἄλλῳ ἄρτᵘς ποιεῖν,
ᵏ μηδὲ τᵘτες παντοδαπὲς, ἀλλὰ ἀρκᾶ ἂν ἐν εἶδος
ᐷδοκιμᵘν παράχῃ· ἀνάγκη, οἶμαι, ῗαῦτα ἔτω ποιᵘ-
μϫνα, πολὺ Διαφερόντως ἐξεργάϛαι ἕκαςον.

Xenophon de Cyri Inft. p. 576. Edit. Hutch.
in 4to.

No. X.

No. X.   (Page 288).

" Nous infifterons particulièrement fur les ref-
fources des méchaniques Angloifes, parce que
cette nation doit, en grande partie, la fupériorité de fa main-d'œuvre à l'ufage de fes méchaniques, dans toutes les opérations où elles ont
femblé praticables. En Angleterre, un courant
d'eau fait, par fon impulfion, agir en même
temps des machines à décarder, à dégroffir, et à
réduire par degré le coton à la ténuité néceffaire
pour l'adapter à la filature, dont l'opération fe
fait par d'autres machines que le même courant
d'eau fait mouvoir. Nous avons appris avec
plaifir, que dans la collection des méchaniques
faites à Paris, par ordre du Confeil, il en exifte
une très-parfaite en ce genre ; mais il eft très-
preffant de les multiplier et de les mettre en
ufage. Cette tentative difpendieufe vient d'être
entreprife à Louviers, avec affez de fuccés pour
ne pas faire regretter les avances qui y ont été
faites ; mais quoique cette utile entreprife foit
fuivie

Translation.

" We fhall infift principally on the refources the Englifh nation derives from machinery, becaufe that nation owes in a great meafure the fuperiority of its manufactures to the ufe of machinery in performing every operation in which it can be employed. In England, a fmall rivulet fets agoing machines which at once clean, card, and reduce the cotton into a ftate adapted for fpinning; which operation is alfo performed by other machines, put into motion by the fame current of water. We have learnt with pleafure, that in the collection of the machines made at Paris, by order of Council, there is one admirably calculated for executing thefe operations; and it is of the greateft importance, that a number fhould be made and introduced into ufe. This very expenfive undertaking has been juft attempted at Louvier, with fufficient fuccefs to leave no room for regretting the expenditure it occafioned. But although, in this inftance, this

very

fuivie par des négociants et des manufacturiers riches et éclairés, il devient très-important que le Gouvernement François daigne encourager fpécialement les premiers efforts de cette induftrie, et fe prêter aux difpofitions néceffaires pour en affurer le fuccès.

" Nous nous réuniffons fur cet objet, au vœu du mémoire que les intéreffés ont donné à M. le Contrôleur-Général ; il préfente les demandes les mieux motivées, l'inftruction la plus fatisfaifante fur cette entreprife, à laquelle ces meffieurs ont donné leur temps, leur zele et des fonds affez confidérables.

" Nous ne nous diffimulons pas que nous devons répondre aux objections qu'on pourroit faire, d'après l'opinion qui a long temps régné en France, que plus nos manufactures occupoient d'ouvriers, plus elles étoient utiles ; que l'on ne devoit pas trop chercher à fimplifier les différentes

very ufeful undertaking has been gone into by fome rich and enlightened manufacturers, to introduce it generally, it becomes very important that the French Government fhould fpecially encourage the firft efforts of this fort of induftry, and that it fhould make the neceffary arrangements for infuring its fuccefs.

" On this fubject we muft join in enforcing the views contained in a memorial prefented by thofe who are interefted in the undertaking, to the Comptroller-General: the requefts it contains are perfectly well grounded; and it affords the moft fatisfactory information on this undertaking, to the conduct of which thefe gentlemen have given up their time, and in which their zeal has made them embark a very confiderable part of their funds.

" We do not hide from ourfelves, that it may be thought that we ought to anfwer to the objection ufually ftarted on this fubject, that it has been an opinion long entertained in France, that the more workmen our manufactories occupied, the more they were ufeful; that it is an

error

tes opérations des fabriques ; qu'il ne convenoit
pas de faire faire à un feul ce qui pouvoit en
faire fubfifter vingt.   Nous ne nous étonnons
pas, d'après ce principe, fi on a moins cherché
en France qu'en Angleterre à encourager les arts
qui pouvoient diminuer le nombre des ouvriers
employés à chaque opération ; fi même on a
cherché à les éloigner.

" Les Anglois ont vu la même chofe d'une
maniere abfolument oppofée : ils ont penfé que
dans une nation riche et d'une grande agriculture, la main-d'œuvre devoit être chere ; que
fans une induftrie particuliere, leurs manufactures ne pourroient lutter avec celles des pays
où l'argent n'eft pas fi abondant ; qu'ils n'avoient
d'autre moyen de conferver l'avantage de leur
côté, qu'en faifant faire à un feul les opérations
qui en occupoient plufieurs ; qu'ils craindroient
mal-à-propos qu'une partie de leurs ouvriers re-
                                                ftât

error to endeavour to fimplify too much the different operations in the conduct of a manufactory, infomuch as it is a public lofs to do by the
hand of one an operation in performing which
twenty may acquire their livelihood. We are
not aftonifhed, confidering the prevalence of this
opinion, that in France there has been lefs anxiety than in England to encourage thofe de-
vices which tend to diminifh the number of
workmen employed in the conduct of each operation ; nay, we are not furprifed that there have
even been attempts made to difcourage fuch
contrivances.

" The Englifh nation have taken quite a different view of this fubject : they have thought,
in a rich and flourifhing agricultural country,
where the wages of labour muft be dear, that without particular contrivances, their manufactures
could not come into competition with thofe of a
poorer country ; that they had, therefore, no
other means of preferving a fuperiority, than by
contriving to execute the fame thing by one
hand that ufed to occupy many ; that it was a
foolifh ground of apprehenfion to dread that a
part

ſtât ſans travail, que s'ils pouvoient, en ſimplifi-
ant leurs opérations, baiſſer le prix de leurs étoffes, ils en augmenteroient infiniment les dé-
bouchés et la conſommation ; qu'enfin le pro-
duit de leurs manufaċtures ſe conſommeroit dans
l'étranger, ou dans leur propre pays ; que dans
le premier cas, ils n'auroient la préférence qu'au-
tant qu'ils vendroient à meilleur marché ; que
dans le ſecond, ce feroit une injuſtice de ne pas
employer tous les moyens qui pourroient les
mettre à portée d'établir, par leur propre indu-
ſtrie, et ſans avoir recours à l'étranger, au prix
le plus moderé poſſible, les choſes agréables,
utiles ou néceſſaires à leurs concitoyens."—Obſervations de la Chambre du Commerce de Normandie, ſur le Traité de Commerce entre la
France et l'Angleterre, p. 21.

" Il ſuffit de connoître la nature des établiſſè-
mens de commerce dans ce pays, (Angleterre),
pour ſentir tous les avantages qu'ꞮꞮ doivent
avoir ſur ceux de France, même à cir onſtances
égales ; que ſera ce avec tous ceux que leur donnent leur conſtitution, la qualité de leurs productions,

part of their workmen would remain without employment; for that by fimplifying the procefs of manufacturing, they lowered the prices of their ftuffs, and by that means augmented greatly the demand for them, and the confumption of them. Finally, as the produce of their manufactures could only be confumed abroad, or at home; that, in the firft cafe, they could alone command a preference in the market, by felling at a lower price; and that, in the fecond, in juftice they owed to themfelves to employ every means that could be fuggefted, of eftablifhing by their own induftry, without having recourfe to foreigners, the manufacture at the cheapeft poffible rate, of all thofe things which are either ufeful or agreeable to their fellow-citizens."—Obfervations of the Chamber of Commerce of Normandy on the Commercial Treaty with England, p. 21.

" It is fufficient to be acquainted with the nature of commercial and manufacturing eftablifhments in England, to be convinced of all the advantages which that country muft have over France, even without thofe advantages which they muft derive from their Government

and

ductions, la perfection à laquelle ils ont pouffé leurs inventions pour améliorer leurs étoffes et diminuer le prix de la main-d'œuvre, et enfin l'abondance de leurs capitaux, et le bas prix de l'intérêt de l'argent.

" On fentira que tous ces avantages les mettent en état de fournir leurs marchandifes à bien meilleur marché, et de gagner où il n'y auroit que de la perte pour ceux qui n'en jouiffent pas, fans que le Gouvernement s'en mêle et faffe des facrifices. C'eft fur quoi on entrera dans quelques détails.

" Les établiffemens de tous genres d'induftrie en Angleterre font très-confiderables, et font foutenus par de très-gros fonds, parce que leurs entrepreneurs les fuivent de père en fils fans changer d'état, et que les fonds s'y accumulent, ainfi que les moyens et les talens, &c. ; ce qui les met en état de travailler en grand, de fe pourvoir à l'avance abondamment et au meilleur marché,

des

and Conftitution, the quality of their productions, the perfection to which they have pufhed
inventions for ameliorating their manufactures,
and diminifhing the coft of manufacturing ; and
finally, the abundance of their capitals, and the
low rate of the intereft of money.

" It is plain, that all thefe advantages enable
England to furnifh its merchandife much cheaper than France, and to gain by felling things at
a price that would occafion a lofs to a country
which did not enjoy the fame advantages; fo that
unlefs the Government of France lends affiftance, and makes facrifices, there could be no
competition.   On this fubject it is neceffary to
enter into fome detail.

" The eftablifhments for the conduct of all
forts of manufactures in England are on a great
fcale. They are fupported by very large capitals.
The manufacturers, from father to fon, follow
the fame profeffion ; by which means, their
funds accumulating, they can carry on very extended operations, provide for themfelves the
raw materials at the cheapeft rates, undertake
                                                the

des matures premieres, de faire les plus grandes entreprifes, et de fournir facilement et promptement aux demandes les plus fortes."—Seconde Partie du Recueil de divers Mémoires relatifs un Traité du Commerce avec l'Angleterre, p. 17.

No. XI.

the moſt extended commiſſions, and execute
with eaſe at a moment the largeſt orders."—
The Second Part of the Collection of Memorials relative to the Treaty with England,
p. 17.

No. XI.

No. XI.   (Page 289).

" It feemed a paradox, nay, almoft a miracle,
to all the world, that you loft a whole continent,
containing fome millions of conftant cuftomers,
and yet that you did not experience any confiderable diftrefs ! Suppofing the colonies purchafed from England to the amount of three
millions per annum ; Manchefter may reafonably be fuppofed to have furnifhed at leaft one-
tenth part of this fum ; and one would think a
demand to the amount of three hundred thoufand pounds a-year could not be loft, without
being very fenfibly felt in that place and neighbourhood. The machines for carding, roving,
and fpinning cotton, thofe ingenious machines
that, in a fit of madnefs, your people have lately
deftroyed, can alone unfold the myftery. Thefe
machines, which ingenuity had long been labouring to produce, and which, about this time,
were happily brought to a confiderable degree
of

of perfection, enabled you to make your goods better and cheaper than ufual ; which produced new and extraordinary demands from the continent of Europe, and faved your work-people and manufactories from diftrefs and ruin."—Letters on the Utility and Policy of employing Machines to fhorten Labour, p. 9. Publifhed in 1780.

" For the relief of the woollen manufactories, the remedy muft, I think, be obvious. Let fimilar machines to thofe invented in Lancafhire, but particularly adapted to carding and fpinning of wool, be put into the hands of the wool and jerfey fpinners, &c. ; the confequence of which will be, that the fpinners will get three times as much money as they have hitherto been accuftomed to do ; that they will make much more yarn, much better and much cheaper, and confequently that the manufactures will be fo improved, and brought to market to fo much greater advantage than ufual, that the demand will probably increafe, even under all our prefent difficulties and obftructions ; and if peace fhould foon be happily eftablifhed, and the way to foreign markets be made more open and eafy,

the

the profpect of improvements, and of the extenfion of our woollen trade, would become great,
and even boundlefs.

" We muft change our methods of proceeding
with the ftate of things, which are always chan-
ging ; or we muft keep within our own ifland,
and refolutely cut off all communication with
the reft of the world. We cannot make cheap
goods in dear times, and under high taxes, and
expenfive habits of life, without extraordinary
affiftance. The competition of Europe is now
become rather a conteft in fkill and ingenuity
than in natural ftrength."—Hints for the Improvement of the Woollen Manufacture, p. 30.
Publifhed in 1780.

" THE aid that has been given to labour in the
cotton-manufacture by machinery, is not likely
to be applied to the linen manufacture in any
great degree. The fly-fhuttle and the flax-mill
are the principal aids lately acquired by the latter. The ingenuity of Mr ARKWRIGHT and
others has done much for manufactures ; but the
nature of flax makes it difficult to apply to it
the

the cotton-machinery, even to the degree that has been introduced into the woollen manufacture within three or four years, efpecially in fpinning and fcribbling."—Obfervations on the Manufactures and Trade of Ireland, by Lord SHEFFIELD, p. 65.

" The furprifing advances of chemiftry, and the effects of its application to manufactures; the wonderful combinations of chemiftry and mechanics, for the reduction of labour,—thefe are the happy means by which bankruptcy has been hitherto averted. The fecurity of property, and the fpirit of liberty diffufed through the nation, have called forth the talents of our people. Britain has grown profperous in fpite of the wretched politics of her rulers. The genius of WATT, WEDGWOOD, and ARKWRIGHT, has counteracted the expence and folly of the American war."—Letters Commercial and Political, by JASPER WILSON, p. 7.

" THE following brief ftatement will ferve to exhibit the rapid progrefs of the cotton manufacture,

facture, as well as its prefent importance to the interefts of the Britifh Empire :—

" In the year 1765, cotton, as an article of commerce, was fcarcely known in this country.

" A few years afterwards, Mr ARKWRIGHT obtained his patent for working cotton by machinery.

" In 1782, the whole produce of the cotton manufacture did not exceed two millions Sterling.

" In 1801, the import of cotton wool into Britain was forty-two millions of lbs. ; and the eftimated value of the cotton manufacture fifteen millions Sterling : fuch was the rapid increafe of this trade to the end of the year 1801.

" From the documents procured, it appears, that the import of this article in 1802 has not been lefs than fifty-four millions of lbs. ; and the particulars of the trade are as follow :

" The

" The raw material, when delivered on board the merchant fhips, now cofts about four millions Sterling. Upwards of thirty thoufand tons of fhipping, and about two thoufand feamen, are conftantly employed in bringing the cotton-wool to this country, and in exporting the goods manufactured from it. To work the wool into thread, requires a capital in building and machinery, to the amount of nine millions two hundred and twenty-five thoufand pounds ; and thofe buildings and machinery are chiefly compofed of bricks, flates, glafs, timber, lead, iron, copper, tin, and leather ; from moft of which, in one fhape or other, a confiderable duty is collected for the fupport of the State.

" This trade gives employment or fupport to upwards of eight hundred thoufand individuals, and the annual return of the manufacture is nearly as follows :

" Coft of cotton in the countries where it grows, infurance, freight, other fhipping charges and merchant's profit,   -   -   L. 4,725,000

Carried forward,   L. 4,725,000

Brought forward, L. 4,725,000

" The intereſt, at 5 per cent., upon
the capital of L. 9,225,000, ſunk
in building and machinery, with
10 per cent. for wear and tear of
ditto,   -   -   -   -   1,383,750

" Wages of ſpinning, value of materials conſumed in the proceſs of
ſpinning the cotton into thread,
and ſpinner's profit,   -   -   5,100,000

" Value of materials conſumed in
ſubſequent manufactures, manufacturing wages, intereſt of capital and profit,   -   -   -   9,000,000
                                    ————
                        L. 20,208,750

Of which ſum, at leaſt thirteen millions Sterling
are paid in wages to the natives of Great Britain."—Obſervations on the Cotton Trade of
Great Britain, printed at Glaſgow.

" Should it be ſuppoſed that we have little to
fear from foreign competition, it may be juſtly
aſked, what is to become of the produce of the
cotton-mills now eſtabliſhed in France, Pruſſia,
                                          Saxony,

Saxony, and other places upon the continent, where it can eafily be proved, this manufacture is now in a more perfect ftate than it was in this country twenty years ago? It is alfo well known, that fome of thefe powers are holding out the moft flattering inducements to many of our fellow-fubjects, whom they imagine competent to the tafk, to go and put thefe eftablifhments upon an equal footing with the beft in Britain ; and out of fo great a number now in the knowledge of this manufacture, it cannot be doubted that many individuals will be tempted by thefe offers."—*Ibid.*

No. XII.

No. XII.   (Page 324).

STATEMENT of the population which a farm of
504 acres of fertile land will maintain, when
under a judicious mode of cultivation, the inhabitants living entirely on vegetable food ;
and the numbers which can be fupported on
animal food by the produce of a like farm
when in pafture.

" WITH a view to afcertain this point with as
much precifion as the nature of the calculation
will admit of, I called at the families of feveral
labourers and mechanics in this place, who live
entirely on vegetable food, to learn if poffible
the exact amount of their confumption, which I
knew, that, out of policy, they are always at
pains to exaggerate.   In the firft houfe I entered, I luckily found the kettle full of potatoes,
juft ready to be put upon the fire, to be boiled
for dinner : the family confifted of one man, his

wife,

wife, and one child, a remarkable ſtout boy of
eleven years of age. I was informed, they regu-
larly dined and ſupped upon them every day,
and that the quantity in the kettle ſerved them
for both the meals. I immediately weighed the
potatoes in the kettle, and found that they
amounted to nine pounds avoirdupois, and was
informed that eight pounds of oatmeal ſerved
them for breakfaſt, in pottage, a week. The ſecond
family I entered was compoſed of three men,
one woman, and ſix healthy children, three of
whom were born at one birth : this family alſo
dined and ſupped upon potatoes ; the quantity
they had prepared to dreſs for dinner weighed
thirteen pounds, and I was informed it required
near four pounds oatmeal each day for their
breakfaſt. After examining the conſumption of
ſeveral families that had two meals of potatoes
per day, I found, to my aſtoniſhment, that about
$2\frac{2}{3}$ lbs. avoirdupois raw potatoes, and $5\frac{1}{3}$ ozs.
good oatmeal, when made into pottage, did ac-
tually maintain, for one day, in good health and
condition for labour, on an average, each individual of a family, compoſed of two parents and
three children, as long as their ſtock of potatoes
laſted.   Having thus aſcertained the length
which

which potatoes and oatmeal will go as food, when a vegetable diet only is ufed, I fhall proceed to calculate the quantum of population that the farm of 504 Englifh ftatute acres, fertile land, well cultivated, will maintain, under the following mode of cropping :

PRODUCE AFTER DEDUCTING SEED.

No.   *lbs. potatoes,*

I. 84 acres of potatoes, average produce of Lancafhire 250 bufhels per acre, at 90 lbs., deducting 18 bufhels for feed,   -   1,753,920

II. 84 acres wheat, at 30 bufhels per acre, at 58 lbs. per bufhel, deducting 3 lbs. per bufhel rough bran, product 2520 bufhels of *lbs. meal.* meal, at 55 lbs. per bufhel,   -   138,600

III. 84 acres peafe and beans, at 24 bufhels, 2016 bufhels, one half eaten by the horfes on the farm; one-half, 1008 bufhels, at 40 lbs. meal per bufhel,   40,320

252 *acres.*   178,920

No.   *lbs. meal.*

    252 *acres,*   178,920

IV. 84 acres barley, at 36 bu-
      fhels, 3024, at 46 lbs.
      meal per bufhel, -   139,104
                         ——— *lbs. bread.*

           Pounds meal, 318,024 or 397,530

V. 84 acres clover confumed by cattle.

VI. 84 acres oats, at 60 bufhels, 5040 bufhels'
      13,440 pecks of oatmeal, at 8 lbs. per
      peck.

    504 *acres,* ⌈ 1,753,920 lbs. po-
                 tatoes, at $1\frac{1}{3}$ lbs.
                 per meal to each *Meals.*
                 individual, -   1,312,940
arden   26 *   397,530lbs. bread,
ind.   ———   at $\frac{3}{4}$ lb. per
    530 *acres,*| meal to ditto, - 530,040
                13,440 pecks oat-
                meal, at 24 meals
               ⌊ per peck to do. 322,560

365 days, at 3 meals per day, 1095)2,165,540(1977

                                      In

" In this manner, 504 acres of fertile land, the garden ground not included, will maintain, when well cultivated, 1977 people old and young ; and if the population of Great Britain amounts to nine millions, it would require only 2,412,746 fertile acres, well cultivated, to maintain them when living on the fame portions of vegetable food as the common people do in Scotland.

" I fhall next proceed to inquire into the number of people which the fame farm of 504 acres, in pafture, would maintain when living entirely on animal food.

" This branch of rural œconomy, of determining the quantity of animal food which land will produce, although of confiderable importance, has never been properly attended to. Mr YOUNG, indeed, has begun the invefigation ; but as yet it has been confined to afcertain the fattening quality of different animals and vegetables. Upon confulting feveral intelligent farmers, it feemed to be their opinion, that an acre of good grafs might, in the feafon, increafe the weight of the animals fed upon it twelve ftone,

ftone, at 14 lbs. to the ftone ; which, at 5 s. per
ftone, would afford a good rent, and leave a
handfome allowance for management and profit
on the capital employed. Fixing, therefore,
upon twelve ftone as the quantum of animal food
which an acre of our farm will produce ; upon
this data, the 504 acres will give 6048 ftones, or
84,672 lbs. I have not been able to learn what
proportion of weight the bones in the carcafe of
an ox bears to the flefh ; but allowing three
quarters of a pound of bones and flefh, on an average, to a meal for each individual, at 3 meals
per day, 84,672 lbs. will fupport an individual
37,632 days ; or, in other words, the produce of
the farm will fupport a population of 103 individuals throughout the year ; dividing thefe into
20 families, and allowing one-fourth of an acre
of garden ground to each family, it amounts in
all to 509 acres. Upon calculating from thefe
data, it will be found, that it would require
44,475,728 fertile acres, to maintain the population of Great Britain, each individual, upon
an average, confuming $2\frac{1}{4}$ lbs. of butcher-meat
per day ; but the fame number of acres would
fupport a population of 165,921,725 individuals

of

of all ages, if the inhabitants lived on the fame
portions of vegetable food which at prefent fubfift the common labourers in Scotland."—*See
Mr Mackie's fecond Letter to the Editor of Di-
rom's Inquiry into the Corn Laws, printed as a
Supplement to that Work*, p. 241.

On the fame fubject, there is much information to be found, Chapter II. of Mr Arthur
Young's Effay on the converfion of Grafs Lands
into Tillage, printed in the third volume of
Communications to the Board of Agriculture.
That the number of the inhabitants of Great
Britain nourifhed on animal food has greatly increafed is notorious. The proportions
therefore of land requifite to furnifh a man with
animal food and with vegetable food, becomes
a queftion of the greateft importance, and well
deferves the further confideration of our writers
on agriculture ; for the folution of it will give
the beft, perhaps the only poffible explanation
of the extraordinary fact, (ftated by the Lords
Commiffioners of the Council, in their report on the Corn Laws and Corn Trade, 1790),
that this country, which from the year 1746

to

to the year 1765, exported on an average fix
hundred and fifty-one thoufand pounds worth of
grain per annum,—has not for many years,
notwithftanding its great agricultural improvements, been able to raife a fufficiency for its own
inhabitants.

No. XIII.

———

No. XIII.   (Page 338).

Draperies.

" Les fabricans François de Louviers, Abbeville et Sedan, ne craignent point la concurrence
de ceux Anglois : ils font même perfuadés que
fi ceux-ci trouvoient de la confommation en
France, ils en feroient dédommagés par celles
qu'ils trouveroient en Angleterre.   Ce feroit de
part et d'autre l'effet du caprice des gens riches
des deux nations ; ainfi rien à craindre ni à gagner fur l'objet des draps fins de la concurrence
réciproque.

" Les draps communs et les petites draperies
donnent lieu à des obfervations dont les refultats
font bien différens."—*Obfervations fur le Replique de M. Eden à M. de Rayneval.   Recueil
de divers Mémoires, relatifs au Traité de Commerce avec l'Angleterre*, p. 137.

" L'Angleterre

———

TRANSLATION.

WOOLLEN CLOTHS.

" THE French manufacturers at Louviers, Abbeville, and Sedan, are not afraid of a competition with thofe of England : they are even perfuaded, that if the latter fhould find a demand
for their goods in France, the French manufacturers would be indemnified by a demand for
theirs in England. In both cafes, this would
depend on the caprice of opulent perfons in the
two countries ; fo there would be nothing either
to fear or to gain from a reciprocal competition
refpecting fuperfine cloths.

" The common and coarfe cloths furnifh obfervations of which the refult is very different."
—Obfervations, &c. p. 137.

" IN

" L'Angleterre a les moyens d'établir, dans
tous les marchés étrangers, leurs draps ordinaires,
et une grande quantité de petites étoffes de
laines à des prix beaucoup au-deſſous de celles
de France. C'eſt ce que l'on a vu conſtamment en Eſpagne, où les femmes du peuple
ſont habillées généralement d'étoffes Angloiſes ;
c'eſt ce que confirment tous les mémoires qu'ont
fourni en dernier lieu les Conſuls de ce pays ; et
ceux qu'ont fourni ceux d'Italie, preſentent ex-
actement les mêmes détailes, ſans que les fabriques de France puiſſent entrer en concurrence
avec les Anglois ſur la plupart de ces étoffes."—
Ibid. p. 141.

" Les Anglois ſont forcés de rendre juſtice à
la beauté des draps de Louviers, ainſi qu'à ceux
d'Abbeville et de Sedan : ils ne peuvent ſi diffi-
mulés qu'ils ſont plus doux que les leurs ; et que
les couleurs en ſont plus vives et plus ſédui-
ſantes."—*Obſervations de la Chambre du Commerce de Normandie ſur le Traité de Commerce
entre la France et l'Angleterre,* p. 37.

" Nous eſtimons que, dans les draps ordinaires
de cinq quarts de large, et du prix de 15 à 16
liv.

" In all the foreign markets, England poffeffes the means of eftablifhing its common cloths, and a great quantity of coarfe woollen ftuffs, at much lower prices than thofe of France. This may be conftantly feen in Spain, where the women of the lower orders are generally dreffed in Englifh ftuffs; which is confirmed by the lateft memorials from the Confuls of that country : and fuch as have been furnifhed by thofe of Italy exhibit precifely the fame details; the manufactures of France being unable to fuftain a competition with thofe of England refpecting the greateft part of thofe ftuffs."—Ibid. p. 141.

" The Englifh are under the neceffity of doing juftice to the beauty of the broad cloths of Louviers, as well as thofe of Abbeville and Sedan ; they muft confefs that they are fofter, and of a more vivid and captivating colour than thofe of England."—Obfervations, &c. p. 37.

" We reckon, that as to common cloths, five quarters broad, and of the price of from 15 to

16

liv. l'aune, les fabriques d'Elbeuf ne pourront foutenir la concurrence des draps de Leeds, appellés draps de Briftol, qui, dans le même laize, ne coûtent pas 11 liv. Tournois l'aune. Les fabricants d'Elbeuf ont plus de confiance dans leurs draperies plus fines."—*Ibid.* p. 41.

" Ce font donc les draps de Wiltz et de Glocefter qui fe débitent à Londres, qui pourront entrer en concurrence avec ceux de Louviers; et nous ne doutons pas que le Gouvernement Anglois ne fe foit déjà occupé des moyens propres à encourager les fabricants de ces draps, à combattre non feulement en Angleterre, mais jufqu' en France même, la préférence à laquelle les draps d'Abbeville, de Sedan, et particulierement ceux de Louviers, peuvent prétendre aujourd'-hui."—*Ibid.* p. 59.

" Les draps de Leeds, dits Refoulés et à Double Broche, obtiendront en général la préférence fur ceux de Vire. Déjà depuis la paix, ces derniers ont perdu leur crédit chez les Americains; et il eft certain qu'à mefure que la fineffe de nos

tiffus

16 livres a-yard, the manufactures of Elbeuf
cannot vie with the cloth manufactured at
Leeds, that go by the name of Briftol cloths,
which, though of the fame breadth, do not coft
11 livres a-yard. The Elbeuf manufacturers
have greater confidence in their cloths of a finer
quality."—Ibid. p. 41.

" The cloths of Wiltfhire and Gloucefterfhire,
which are brought to the London market, are
thofe which will enter into competition with
the cloths of Louviers ; and we have no doubt
that the Englifh Government have already taken the proper fteps for encouraging the manufactures of thofe cloths, in order to do away, not
only in England, but even in France, the preference to which the cloths of Abbeville, Sedan,
and efpecially of Louviers, have at prefent pre-
tenfions."—Ibid. p. 59.

" The cloths of Leeds, which they call Double
Tweeled and Drab, will, in general, be preferred to thofe of Vire.   Already, fince the peace,
thefe laft have loft their credit with the Ame-
ricans ; and it is certain, that in proportion as
                                        our

tiffus diminue, ou que nos draperies approchent des qualités communes, les draperies d'Angleterre ont un avantage fenfible fur les nôtres." —*Ibid.* p. 61.

Soieries.

" Celles de France l'emportent beaucoup fur celles d'Angleterre, pour le goût ; ce qui, joint au bon marché, doit donner l'efpoir bien fondé d'en importer beaucoup, fi les droits font fur un pied modéré."—*Recueil de Mémoires,* &c. p. 86.

M. de Rayneval a demandé, de la part de la France, qu'on fixât les droits, 1. Sur les vins, eaux-de-vie et vinaigres ; 2. Sur les foieries et modes ; 3. Sur la batifte, linons et autres toiles ; 4. Sur les glaces.

" Quant au premier, M. Eden efpére qu'il a donné une réponfe fatisfaifante, pour ce qui eft

du

our ftuffs diminifh in finenefs, or our cloths approach the common qualities, thofe of England
have an obvious advantage over ours."—Ibid.
p. 61.

Silks.

" Those of France have a decided advantage
over thofe of England in point of tafte ; a circumftance which, joined to their cheapnefs, furnifhes well-grounded hopes of a large quantity
of that article being imported into England, if
the duties are fixed on a moderate footing."—
Collection of Memoirs, &c. p. 86.

" M. de Rayneval has demanded, on the
part of France, that the duties fhould be fixed ;
1. Upon wines, brandy and vinegar; 2. Upon
filks and millinery goods ; 3. Upon cambric,
lawns, and other linen cloths ; 4. Upon glafs.

" As to the firft, Mr Eden hopes he has given
a fatisfactory anfwer. With refpect to the fecond,

du deuxième ; comme la prohibition en Angleterre fur les foieries venant de l'étranger eft générale, excepté pour les crêpes de foie, et une
efpéce de foie appellée tiffanie, des manufactures
d'Italie, qui peuvent y être introduites en payant un droit affez confidérable, cette prohibition
ne peut pas être abolie pour des raifons affez
connues, quoiqu'il y ait plufieurs articles dans la
foierie où l'Angleterre auroit grandement l'avantage fur la France, nommément dans les rubans,
peut-être auffi dans les bas de foie, les gazes, et
prefque toutes les étoffes mêlées de foie."—*Re-*
plique de M. Eden *à M.* de Rayneval. *Ibid,*
p. 150.

Toileries.

" Celles de Saint Quentin font les feules de
France que l'Angleterre foit dans le cas de con-
fommer ; elle tire toutes fes autres toiles d'Ir-
lande, de la Suiffe, de la Frandre et de l'Alle-
magne.

" Il s'eft établi en Ecoffe des fabriques de
toiles de même genre que celles de Saint Quentin ;

cond ; as in England the prohibition of foreign filks is general, except filken crapes, and a kind of filk called *tiffany*, both Italian manufactures, which may be introduced on paying a confiderable duty ; that prohibition cannot be abolifhed for reafons fufficiently known, although there are many articles in the filk manufacture wherein England would have greatly the advantage over France ; in ribbons, for inftance, perhaps alfo in filk ftockings, gauzes, and in almoft all ftuffs mixed with filk."—Reply, &c. p. 150.

LINENS.

" THOSE of St Quintin are the only French linens that find confumption in England ; all the reft of her linens are drawn from Ireland, Switzerland, Flanders and Germany.

" Linen manufactures of the fame kind with thofe of St Quintin have been eftablifhed in Scotland ;

tin ; mais, malgré tous les encouragemens qu'elles reçoivent, elles font encore fort au-deffous de celles-ci."—*Obfervations délivrées à M.* DE CALONNE, *fur la Note fournie par le Miniftre de France. Recueil de Mémoires*, p. 84.

" M. DE RAYNEVAL a demandé, de la part de la France, qu'on fixât les droits, 3°, fur la batifte, linons et autres toiles."—*Replique Confidentielle, remife par M.* EDEN *à M.* DE RAYNEVAL. *Recueil de Mémoires*, p. 150.

" QUANT aux troifième, c'eft-a-dire fes batiftes, linons et les autres toiles, M. EDEN a déjà répondu à ce qui concerne les toiles, et il croit à la fatisfaction des Miniftres de fa Majefté Très-Chretienne.

" Sa Majefté fera prête d'entrer en negociation pour lever les prohibitions fur les batiftes et linons importées de France, et de reduire les droits à environ 12 ou 15 per cent. ou 6 fh. pour demi pièce, à l'entrée du Royaume aux batiftes et linons de France, principalement aux plus fines,

Scotland ; but notwithftanding every encouragement given them, they are ftill far inferior to
the manufactures of St Quintin."—Obfervations, &c. p. 80.

" M. DE RAYNEVAL has demanded, on the
part of France, that the duties fhould be fixed,
3dly, on cambric, lawns, and other linens."—
Confidential Reply, &c. p. 150.

" As to the third article, to wit, cambrics, lawns,
and other linens, Mr EDEN has already anfwer-
ed as far as concerns linens, and, he believes, to
the fatisfaction of the Minifters of his Moft
Chriftian Majefty.

" His Majefty will be ready to enter into a
negotiation for taking off the prohibition on
cambrics and lawns imported from France, and
to reduce the duty nearly to 12 or 15 per cent.,
or 6 s. for the half piece, upon the entrance of
French cambrics and lawns into the kingdom,
                                        efpecially

fines, dans lefquelles les François excellent principalement."—*Ibid.* p. 154.

MODES.

" LE goût qui s'eft introduit à Londres pour
les modes Françoifes, eft fufceptible de la plus
grande augmentation ; il eft donc très-interef-
fant d'obtenir à l'admiffion de celles de France,
les conditions les plus amples et les plus favo-
rables."—*Obfervations délivrées à M. DE CA-
LONNE, fur la Note fournie par le Miniftre de
France. Recueil de Mémoires*, p. 86.

" A l'égard de l'article des modes, que M. DE
RAYNEVAL range avec celui des foieries, on
penfe qu'il eft à propos de laiffer cet article dans
la claffe de cette multitude d'objets qui feront
compris dans la règle générale dont leurs Ma-
jeftés font convenues."—*Replique Confidentielle,
remife par M. EDEN à M. DE RAYNEVAL. Recueil de Mémoires*, p. 152.

" LA France a demandé l'entrée de fes modes ;
M. EDEN renvoie cet article dans la claffe des
objets

efpecially on the fineft forts, in which the French
chiefly excel."—Ibid. p. 154.

Millinery.

" The tafte that has been introduced in London
for French millinery is fufceptible of the greateft augmentation ; it is, therefore, of very great
confequence to obtain for the admiffion of articles of this nature, made in France, the moft
ample and favourable terms."—Obfervations delivered to M. de Calonne, &c.   Coll. Mem.
p. 86.

" With regard to the article of millinery,
which M. de Rayneval ranks with that of filks,
it is thought it would be fitteft to leave that article to be arranged along with that multitude
of objects to be comprifed in the general rule on
which their Majefties are agreed."—Confidential Reply of Mr Eden, &c. p. 152.

" France demanded the liberty to import into England millinery goods ; Mr Eden wifhes

to

objets généraux, renvoyés à être traités comme
la nation la plus favorifée ; tournure plus que
fufpecte, ne pôuvant ignorer que les modes font
un genre de commerce qui eft particulier à la
France.''—*Supplément aux Obfervations, &c.*
p. 43.

" Le commerce des modes, qui eft une
branche intereffante de celui de la France, et
dans laquelle elle réuffit fi bien par le goût de
fes artiftes, fembloit devoir être une efpece de
compenfation et de dédommagement pour la
France ; mais l'Angleterre l'a rendu prefque il-
lufoire par les defenfes et les reftrictions qu'elle
met à leur admiffion.''—*Septieme Mémoire.
Commerce que la France fait en Angleterre, en
confequence du Traité. Recueil,* p. 62.

" Malgre' le dédain du patriotifme Anglois
pour nos modes et nos ufages, l'élégance de nos
parures eût infenfiblement triumphé de la réfift-
ance nationale, fi le Gouvernment Anglois n'en
eût

to refer that article to the clafs of general objects; a ftyle of anfwer more than fufpicious, as
he cannot be ignorant that millinery is a fort of
manufacture peculiar to France."—Supplement
to the Obfervations, &c. p. 43.

" MILLINERY, which is an interefting branch
of the commerce of France, and in which the
tafte of her artifts enables her to be fo fuccefsful,
feems to be an article which ought to afford a
kind of compenfation and indemnification for
France ; but England has rendered that advantage almoft nugatory, by the prohibitions and reftrictions fhe impofes upon its admiffion."—Se-
venth Mem. &c. Coll. p. 62.

" In fpite of the contempt expreffed by Englifh patriotifm for our millinery and articles of
fafhion, the elegance of our dreffes would have
triumphed over the refiftance the nation made
to receive them, if the Englifh Government had
not forefeen the advantage we were likely to derive

eût pas prévu l'afcendant."—*Obfervations de la Chambre du Commerce de Normandie*, p. 65.

GLACES.

" LES droits établis fur celles de France équivalent à une prohibition.   Il feroit, fans doute, fort intereffant d'obtenir une modération qui pût donner lieu à une introduction plus forte."—*Obfervations délivrées à M. DE CALONNE, fur la Note fournie par le Miniftre de France.   Recueil de Mémoires*, p. 87.

" M. DE RAYNENAL a demandé, de la part de la France, qu'on fixât les droits. 4°, fur les glaces."—*Replique Confidentielle, remife par M. EDEN à M. DE RAYNEVAL. Recueil de Mémoires*, p. 150.

" QUANT au quatrieme, pour ce qui concerne les glaces, les Miniftres d'Angleterre penfent qu'il eft queftion tant des glaces pour les miroirs, que d'autres efpeces de verres plats ; et ils font à même de prendre des informations pour conftater s'il eft poffible de fixer un certain droit fur lequel

rive from it."—Obfervations of the Chamber of
Commerce of Normandy, p. 65.

GLASS.

" THE duties impofed on thofe of France are
equivalent to a prohibition; it would no doubt be
of very great confequence to obtain a diminution, which would give a profpect of a greater
quantity being introduced into England."—Obfervations delivered to M. CALONNE, &c. p. 87.

" M. DE RAYNEVAL has demanded, on the
part of France, that the duties on importation
in England fhould be fixed, 4thly, on glafs."
—Confidential Reply delivered by Mr EDEN,
p. 150.

" As to the fourth demand, which concerns
glafs, the Englifh Miniftry thinks that it is neceffary to take under confideration not only glafs
in the fhape of mirrors, but all other forts of flat.
glafs; and they are at prefent occupying themfelves to get information, that will enable them

to

lequel cette marchandife peut être impofée dans
l'un et l'autre royaume."—*Ibid.* p. 156.

" Pour ce qui regarde les glaces, attendu que
les etabliffemens de France font bornés, et ne
font pas fufceptibles d'une grande augmentation,
par rapport à la difette des bois, qui deviennent
tous les jours plus rares.   Mais il n'en feroit
peut-être pas de même vis-à-vis de l'Angleterre,
pour les criftaux, qu'elle feroit dans le cas de
fournir à la France, vu la grande fuperiorité
qu'elle a dans ce genre d'induftrie."—*Obferva-*
tions fur le Replique, &c. p. 157.

Porcelaine.

" M. Eden ajoutera ici, que les Miniftres de
fa Majefté Très-Chretienne fouhaitent peut-
être que la meilleure porcelaine François foit
admife en Angleterre, fur un droit raifonable :
Les Miniftres d'Angleterre fouhaitent auffi,
qu'il foit fait quelque changement fur les droits
que la fayence et la poterie devroient payer à
                                                    la

to afcertain whether it is poffible to fix certain rates of duties, under which this fort of merchandife may be admitted into the one and the other kingdom."—Ibid. p. 156.

" As to what regards glafs, it muft be obferved, that the eftablifhments in France are limited, and are not fufceptible of great augmentation, upon account of the deficiency of fuel, which becomes every day more fcarce. But this, perhaps, would not be the cafe with England, in relation to articles of cryftal, with which fhe would certainly furnifh France, confidering the great fuperiority fhe enjoys in this fort of manufacture."—Obfervations on the Reply, &c. p. 157.

CHINA.

" Mr EDEN muft here add, that as the Minifters of his Moft Chriftian Majefty may perhaps wifh that the fine French china fhould be admitted into England, on paying a moderate duty ; fo the Englifh Minifters wifh that there fhould be fome change made on the duties which ftone-ware and coarfer forts of pottery are

la conclufion de ce Traité, en vertu du premier
article des deux déclarations."—*Replique de M.*
Eden, p. 156.

" Cette derniere infinuation de M. Eden fur
la porcelaine, fur la fayence et poterie, donne
lieu à quelques réflexions.

" La porcelaine de France peut être recherchée
en Angleterre. On doute cependant que cet
objet d'induftrie qui eft très-cher, et par confequent ne peut être qu'à la portée des gens très-
riches, pût donner lieu à une exportation im-
portante.

" Mais la poterie et la fayence ne font pas
dans ce cas là : les Anglois ont fur ces deux objets
une fupériorité décidée fur les François."—
Suite des Obfervations fur le Replique de M.
Eden, p. 158.

Orfevrerie, Bejouterie, Quincaillerie.

" On eft perfuadé que la France a l'avantage
fur

are to pay at the conclusion of this Treaty, in a manner consistent with the spirit of the first article of the two declarations."—Reply of Mr EDEN, &c. p. 156.

" THIS last insinuation of Mr EDEN, on the subject of china, stoneware and pottery, gives rise to some serious reflections.

" The china of France may be in high esteem in England. It is a matter of doubt, however, whether this article of manufacture, which is very high priced, and which of course can only be sought after by men of great fortune, can be exported to any great extent.

" But the pottery and stoneware of England are not in the same situation, and the English have on these two articles a most decided superiority over the French."—Sequel of the Observations on the Reply to Mr EDEN, p. 158.

GOLDSMITHS WARE, JEWELLERY AND HARD-
WARE.

" THERE is a general conviction that France
has

fur les articles d'orfévrerie et de bejouterie fur
l'Angleterre, par le goût et le talent de fes artiftes.   Il eft queftion de favoir s'ils font fujets,
en Angleterre, aux mêmes droits et aux mêmes
loix qu'en France : parce que fi les droits en
France étoient plus forts, et les loix plus gênan-
tes, il faudroit mettre les François de niveau,
par une prime proportionnée à la fortie et par
des modifications fur les loix."—*Obfervations
délivrées à M.* DE CALONNE, p. 88.

" POUR fervir de compenfation à ces avantages, qui certainement font très-importans, on
attend que la France fe prêtera de fon côté à des
arrangemens dont la Grande Bretagne puiffe
profiter à fon tour.   On efpère donc que la
quincaillerie, en y comprenant tous les ouvrages
d'acier et de fer, fera admife mutuellement en
payant des droits modérés."—*Replique de M.*
EDEN, p. 132.

" L'ENTREE des quincailleries d'Angleterre
eft

has the advantage over England in articles of goldfmiths ware and jewellery, in confequence of the tafte and talents of her artifts. It becomes, therefore, an interefting circumftance, to learn whether thefe articles, on exportation, are fubject to the fame rates and regulations in England as in France ; becaufe, if in France the duties are greater, and the regulations throw more difficulty in the way of exportation, it would be neceffary to put the French artifts upon an equality, by moderating the reftraints of the law, and giving a proportional bounty on exportation."—Obfervations delivered to M. DE CALONNE, p. 88.

" To ferve as a compenfation for thefe advantages, which certainly are very important, it is expected that France, on her fide, will adopt arrangements by which Great Britain may acquire fimilar advantages. For this purpofe, it is expected that the hardware, comprehending all works in fteel and iron, may be mutually admitted by the two countries at a moderate rate of duty."—Reply of Mr EDEN, p. 132.

" THE exportation of the hardware of England

eſt défendue en France ; elles entrent en contrebande. L'Angleterre a, ſur cet objet d'indu-
ſtrie, un avantage infini ſur la France, dont les
établiſſemens dans ce genre ſont ſi inferieurs à
tous égards, qu'ils ne peuvent entrer en compa-
raiſon."—*Obſervations*, &c. p. 133.

" L'ANGLETERRE poſſede abſolument l'objet
de quincaillerie ; et eſt depuis long temps en poſ-
ſeſſion d'en approviſionner, en contrebande, la
France, qui eſt ſi arriérée dans ce genre d'indu-
ſtrie, qu'à peine eſt elle en état de ſe ſuffire pour
les objets les plus groſſiers."—*Recherches ſur ce
qui eſt relatif aux étoffes de Cotton, aux Quincaillerie, &c. Quatrieme Mémoire relatif au Traité
de Commerce*, p. 37.

No. XIV.

land is prohibited in France. Great quantities of it, however, are fmuggled into that country. England has, in the manufacture of thofe articles, an infinite advantage over France, whofe manufactories of thefe goods are fo far inferior in every refpect, that they cannot ftand a comparifon."—Obfervations on the Reply of Mr EDEN, p. 133.

" ENGLAND poffeffes a complete fuperiority in the manufacture of hardware. For a long time fhe has been accuftomed, by means of fmuggling, to fupply France with thofe articles, who is fo far behind hand in this manufacture, that fhe is fcarcely in a condition to fupply herfelf even with the moft common and coarfe articles."—Refearch into what relates to the manufactures of Cotton and Hardware. 4th Memoir on the Effects of the Commercial Treaty, p. 37.

No. XIV.

No. XIV.   (Page 269).

EXTRAIT d'une Lettre de Me. la Marquiſe de
* * AM. *.   Du 17. Août 1767.

" J'AI fait une route ſuperbe juſqu'à Poitiers,
par Orléans, Blois, Tours, et Poitiers, ou pour
mieux dire, juſqu'aux Ormes de M. d'ARGEN-
SON ; car des Ormes à Poitiers, il y a beaucoup
de terrein qui ne rapporte rien, et depuis Poitiers juſque chez moi, il y a vingt-cinq mille
arpens de terrein qui ne ſont que de la brande
et des joncs marins ; les Payſans y vivent de
ſeigle, dont on n'ôte pas le ſon qui eſt noir et
lourd comme du plomb ; dans le Poitou et ici,
on ne laboure que l'épiderme de la terre avec
une petite vilaine charrue ſans roues, dont je ne
puis vous faire la deſcription, qui oblige l'hom-
me d'être preſque couché comme une bête à
                                                    quatre

Translation.

Extract of a Letter from the Marchionefs of —— AM. Dated 17th Auguſt 1767.

" I travelled through a fine country to Poitiers, by Orleans, Blois and Tours, to Poitiers,
or rather, I may fay, till I reached the elms of
M. Argenson ; for from thefe elms to Poitiers
there is a great deal of ground that carries nothing, and from Poitiers to my houfe there are
twenty-five thoufand acres that carry nothing
but brufhwood and fea-rufhes. The peafantry
live on bread made of rye, from which the bran
is not abftracted, which is black, and as heavy
as lead. In Poitou as well as here, they only
fcratch the mere furface of the earth with a
little nafty plough without wheels, which I can
hardly defcribe to you ; it obliges the man to be
almoſt

quatre pattes, cela fait pleurer à voir. Chez moi
cette affligeante charrue va avec deux bœufs
très-doucement, en Poitou elle va avec deux
ânes.   Depuis Poitiers jufqu'à Montmorillon,
il y a neuf lieues qui en valent feize de Paris,
et je vous jure que je n'ai vu que quatre hommes,
et trois de Montmorillon chez moi, où il y a
quatre lieues, encore les avons nous apperçus de
loin, car nous n'en avons pas trouvé un feul fur
le chemin.   Vous n'en ferez pas étonné dans un
tel pays, je le fuis fort que ces pauvres Métayers
ne fuient pas tant de malheurs et de mifere, et
les Propriétaires font bien heureux qu'un fentiment pour le Pays natal, ou pour mieux dire
l'amour conjugal et paternel les empêche de dé-
ferter, et de finir une vie fi dure et fi miférable :
on a foin de les marier d'auffi bonne heure que
les Grands Seigneurs, le pays n'en eft pas plus
peuplé, car prefque tous les enfans meurent ; les
femmes n'y ont prefque pas de lait, les enfans
d'un an mangent de ce pain dont je vous ai
parlé ; auffi une fille de quatre ans a le ventre
gros comme une femme enceinte.   Si ces bonnes
gens devenoient donc éclairés, les Propriétaires
fe trouveroient avec beaucoup de terrein ré-
duits

almoſt on all fours when he is working it ; the
ſight of it makes one miſerable.　With us this
ſorry plough is worked with two oxen, and in
Poitou with two aſſes.　From Poitiers to Montmorillon they count nine leagues, which are
equal to ſixteen Paris leagues, and I ſwear to
you, that in all that country I only ſaw four
men ; and from Montmorillon to my houſe,
which is four leagues, only three, and thoſe we
only ſaw afar off, for we did not meet one perſon on the road.　I do not know whether you
are aſtoniſhed, I am ſure I am very much, that
in ſuch a country the poor tenantry do not run
away from ſuch a ſtate of miſery and misfor-
tune.　The proprietors are very happy that a prejudice in favour of their native ſoil, or rather
the love of their wives and families, prevents
them from deſerting, or from putting an end to
a life of ſuch hardſhip and miſery.　They mar-
ry as early as their landlords ; but the country is
not better peopled on that account; for almoſt all
the children die ; the women have hardly any
milk ; the children at one year old eat that black
bread of rye I have mentioned ; and a girl of four
years old has a belly as big as a woman with
child.

duits à mourir de faim, et il ne feroit plus queftion des impôts qui écrafent ces malheureux.
Les feigles ont été gêlés cette année le jour de
Paques, il y a peu de froment. De douze mé-
taïries qu'a ma mere, il y en a peut-être dans
quatre. Il n'a pas plu depuis Paques, peu de
foin, point de pâturage, aucun légumes, point
de fruit : voilà l'état du pauvre Payfan, par
confequent point d'engrais de beftiaux : la
Taille eft ici beaucoup plus forte à proportion
qu'en Champagne. Tout le monde dit du bien
de M. T * * *, mais on fais qu'il n'eft pas le
maitre de faire tout le bien qu'il defire ; ma
mere qui avoit toujours plufieurs de fes grêniers
pleins, n'y a pas un grain de bled, parceque depuis deux ans elle nourrit tous ces Métayers et
les Pauvres, car elle fuit la morale de votre doctrine, elle donne à manger à ceux qui ont faim,
à boire à ceux qui ont foif, panfe les bleffés,
confole les affligés, et même une vie plus douce
que les plus grandes Dames de la Cour."—*Ephémerides du Citoyen*, 1767, *Tome Neuvieme*,
p. 146.

" J'AI

child. If thefe poor people became more enlightened, the proprietors would find themfelves
poffefling great extent of territory, and reduced
to die of hunger; and taxes, which reduce thefe
people to abfolute mifery, would be out of the
queftion. The rye was froft-bit this year at Eafter, and they have very little wheat. Out of
twelve farms which my mother has, there is, perhaps, a little in four of them. It has not rained
fince Eafter; there is no hay, no pafture, no vegetables, no fruit; of courfe the animals cannot be
fattened. Such is the ftate of the poor peafantry. The poll-tax is higher here than in Cham-
paign. All the world fpeak well of M. Turgot, but they know he has it not in his power
to do all the good he would wifh. My mother,
who had always feveral granaries full, has now
not a fingle grain of corn; for during two years fhe
has fed the tenantry and the poor. She, poor woman! follows the old maxim, of giving meat to
thofe who are hungry, and drink to thofe who
are thirfty; fhe takes care of the wounded, comforts the afflicted, and leads a life of greater fatisfaction than that of the fineft ladies of the
Court."—Ephémerides du Citoyen, 1767, vol. ix.
p. 146.

                                   EXTRACT

" J'ai parcouru une grande partie des Provinces de Touraine, de Poitou, du Limofin, de la
Marche, du Berry, de la Xaintonge, de l'Angoumois ; j'ai arpenté plufieurs Domains, j'ai tiré
des Mémoires des autres Provinces, j'ai pris les
produits et le prix de plufieurs années ; on en
verra les réfultats dans les articles fuivants, et on
fera fans doute étonné que dans toutes les terres
de petite culture, il n'y ait prefque aucun *pro-
duit net*, que le Roi foit, mais fort à fon défavan-
tage, le feul propriétaire de plus de la moitié
des terres de fon Royaume.   La moiffon de ces
terres fuffit à peine pour la fubfiftance des Cultivateurs ; en forte que ne contribuant point ou
très peu à la nourriture des autres claffes d'hommes de la Nation, les mauvaifes années font fort
redoubtables en France par la difette, qui s'étend
jufqu'aux Colons mêmes reduits à cette petite
.... s'en fuit, que par rapport à l'état,

                                                    on

Extract from the Apology made for the diftinction betwixt the Great and the Little Mode
of Cultivation, by M. Butre', of the Societies
of Agriculture of Paris and Orleans.

" I have gone over a great part of the provinces of Touraine, Poitou, Limofin, Marche,
Berry, Xantonge, Angoumois. I have meafured
moft of the eftates in thofe countries ; I have
drawn up memorials from the different provinces; I made accounts of the produce and the
price for feveral years, and the refult will appear
from the following articles. It will no doubt
appear extraordinary, that all thofe eftates
which are cultivated by poor tenantry, without
capital, there is almoft no fum to be carried to
account after paying the expences and taxes ;
that the King, very much to his difadvantage,
is thus the fole proprietor of half the lands in his
kingdom. The produce of thefe lands being
fcarcely fufficient to nourifh thofe who cultivate
them, can in a manner contribute nothing to the
nourifhment of the other claffes in the kingdom.
A bad feafon muft of courfe afflict France with

a

on peut regarder les terres qui y font employées
à peu pres comme en non valeur ; ainſi nous pou-
vons en ce ſens faire remarquer, qu'il y a dans le
Royaume beaucoup plus de terres en friches que
l'on ne penſe."—*Ibid.* p. 9.

CARSE

famine that extend itself to all those who are employed in conducting this forry fpecies of cultivation ; from which it follows, that with refpect to the State at large, thefe lands are in a manner of no value, which authorifes us to remark, that there is much more wafte land in the kingdom than people think of."—Ibid. p. 9.

CARSE.

———————

CARSE OF GOWRIE.

" THE Vale or Carfe of Gowrie, fo much celebrated for its fertility, merits a particular and
feparate defcription, which, however, fhall be
made as concife as poffible.

" This valuable tract is fituated in the eaft cor-
ner of the county of Perth, and is every where
fkirted by high hills, except on the fouth, where
it is bounded by the frith and river of Tay, both
of which have been long and juftly famed for
the great numbers of falmon with which they
abound.

" The Carfe of Gowrie, including the floping
lands on the northern boundary, contains about
thirty thoufand Englifh ftatute acres. The rent
of thofe farms which have been let within thefe
eight or ten years, may be reckoned at rather
above 35 s. the Englifh acre.

" The

" The foil in the vale or plain is a deep rich clay ; on the fides of the hills a hazle-coloured loam moft generally prevails. In ftating the grofs annual produce of the foil, (which, it is believed, is equal in quantity and value to any other diftrict of fimilar extent in Britain, the vicinity of large cities or manufacturing towns only excepted), it may be proper to obferve, that the mode of cropping generally approved of, and now for the moft part adopted, is, 1. Fallow ; 2. Wheat ; 3. Peafe or beans ; 4. Barley with red clover, and a fmall quantity of ryegrafs ; 5. Grafs ; and, 6. Oats ; and as all the crops are cultivated in equal proportions, the following table will fhow, not only the average returns, but alfo the prices at which they have been fold for a number of years bypaft ; and may at the fame time be depended upon, as being more correct in regard to data than tables of this kind generally are.

" A

―――

" A Table, exhibiting the Extent and Value of the annual
Grofs Produce of the Carfe of Gowrie, fuppofing it to
contain 30,000 Englifh Acres, and to be all cultivated
agreeable to the Rotation above mentioned.

Rotation and number of Acres.	Average produce per acre in Bufhels.	Total produce in Winchefter quarters.	Average prices per quarter.		Total crop of hay, in ftones of 22 lb. Amfterdam.	Average price of hay per ftone.	Value in Money.		
			s.	d.			L.	s.	d.
5000 fallow,									
5000 wheat,	27	16,875	43		—	—	36,281	5	0
5000 peafe or beans, -	23	14,375	27	4	—	—	19,645	16	8
5000 barley,	38	3,750	21	10	—	—	25,927	1	8
5000 grafs, which may average 140 ftone of hay per acre, -	—	—	—		700,000	7 d.	21,416	13	4
5000 oats, -	46½	29,062½	20	4	—	—	29,546	17	0
Produce of orchards, -	—	—	—		—	—	1000	0	0
30,000 acres		84 062½			700,000		132,817	13	8

" By

" By this table, it appears, that the annual grofs produce of grain in this diftrict may be eftimated at upwards of eighty-four thoufand Winchefter quarters. But as on many farms rotations of cropping are adopted, whereby more than one-fixth part is every year under wheat, it is probable that the value of the crops is rather above than below what is ftated.

" In no part of the ifland are more luxuriant crops of red clover to be feen than in the Carfe of Gowrie. The fecond crop is frequently made into hay, and the third is often mown, for the purpofe of feeding the horfes in the ftable, and the cattle in the ftraw-yards.

" As the inhabitants of the diftrict do not exceed eight thoufand, it is evident that the exports of grain muft be very great indeed. Glafgow is the principal market, though large quantities are alfo fent to London, Leith, and other places on the fouth-eaft coaft.

" The

" The fize of the farms are in general from one to three hundred acres; but the greateft proportion is occupied by farmers who poffefs upwards of two hundred acres."

STATE